ADVANCE PRAISE

"A compelling read, the lovely, often funny narrative of *Raising Gentle Men* both draws you in and breaks your heart."
  – Jane Gerety, RSM, Ph.D.
    President, Salve Regina University

"*Raising Gentle Men* is a well written, easily read book –warm, sometimes poignant and sometimes funny. It's a wonderful book."
  – Dr. Alec Peck Ph.D.
    Chair, Dept. of Teacher Education, Special Education, and Curriculum & Instruction, Boston College

"*Raising Gentle Men* is not full of dramatic, life-altering events. And yet, the story is perfect. The power of Jay's story is in the small details: a bed-time story, a brief moment holding hands. And isn't that the lesson for us all when searching how to serve others? We shouldn't underestimate God's power to work in small ways."
  – *America Magazine*

"A beautifully written and inspiring story."
  – Nell Minow – *The Movie Mom Blog* – Belief Net.com.

"When Jay Sullivan ventured into a section of Kingston closed to tourists, he brought a caring heart to the boys of Alpha—a heart that served as a magnet for their dreams of a better life."
  – Camille D'Arienzo, RSM
    A Past President of the Leadership Conference of Women Religious

RAISING GENTLE MEN:
LIVES AT THE ORPHANAGE EDGE

Jay Sullivan

Apprentice House
Loyola University Maryland
Baltimore, Maryland

First Edition
Printed in the United States of America
ISBN: 978-1-934074-81-7

Design by Chelsea McGuckin
Cover photo by Jay Sullivan

Published by Apprentice House

Apprentice House
Loyola University Maryland
4501 N. Charles Street
Baltimore, MD 21210
410.617.5265 • 410.617.2198 (fax)
www.apprenticehouse.com
info@ApprenticeHouse.com

All of the incidents in this story are true, although they are not presented in exactly the order in which they happened. The nuns are all real people, as are Desmond Plunkett, Q, O'Brien, Richard, Irene and Mr. Sullivan. All of the other characters are composites of the many boys who lived at Alpha Boys School from 1984 -1986. The Boston College teachers are also composite characters of more than 20 BC alumni who lived and worked in Kingston during those years.

The letters from Sister Magdalen are actual passages from her letters.

Chapter 2 appeared in an earlier form in the Winter 1995 edition of Boston College Magazine.

For Mary

ACKNOWLEDGEMENTS

None of us accomplishes anything on our own. This story would remain a jumbled collection of distant memories without the help of my early readers. Irene Thompson, Marilyn Johnson, Joe Wallace, Sharon AvRutick, and Kate Howe, thank you for your guidance and encouragement over the last few years.

Wendy Fried – from those early meetings in your office, when you found something nice to say no matter what, to the questions you asked that helped me find my own way to tell the story, you were amazing. Thank you for bringing conflict into my life.

Desmond, thank you for letting me tell your story. It is a testament to the brave and honest and honorable man you are, that you are willing to be so open.

All of Maggie's friends – Aine, Erin, Maria – thanks for always asking about the book. I finished it just so I could stop hearing, "Mr. Sullivan, aren't you done with that yet?" and, "Wow. Are you still working on that?"

Chelsea McGuckin of Apprentice House, thank you for your diligence, your patience, and your insights. You made it easy for a first time author.

Thank you to the Sisters of Mercy and Jesuits of Jamaica. The examples of your lives are an inspiration to everyone you touch.

John, Sam, Teresa and Maggie, thanks for your patience as I talked about this project for most of your conscious childhood.

Mary, thank you for your complete partnership in life, and in this project. Your constant support and honest feedback have been more valuable than you will ever know. I look forward to having our evenings together again, now that this is done. Thanks for everything.

Sept. 21, 1988

My dear Jay,

Just a few hurried lines, but I know you will be anxious to hear our news after the pompous visit of hurricane Gilbert. You just missed it boy!

Thank God we all came out of it without a scratch. When we heard the warning, my brother Louis spent all the evening & part of the night – nailing doors & windows & barring everywhere – which was quite a good thing. The boys & all of us stayed at Junior Home Dormitory. It's only meant to sleep 96 and we had all 250 boys there! Louis & I and a couple of boys stayed on the verandah watching everything, until the Junior Home Hall's roof came flying by with terrific speed & screeching. Then we ran into the dormitory. It was awful.

When we came out after the storm, it was desolation everywhere you look. We lost the roofs on part of the Senior Home Dormitory, the tailor shop, and Father's house. The convent – the part facing the entrance – lost all the roof & part of the verandahs. Most of the sisters had to abandon their rooms – as everything – clothes, bed, etc., was soaking wet. Now they are scattered all over putting beds in some dry corners. What is very hard is the damage done to the electricity. Just to fix the lights outside on the compound it is going to cost us $40,800, and then all the wiring inside has to be changed.

Most of the mango trees were destroyed.

We were lucky to have a water pipe at the back still working.

We just heard on the news that another storm has started in Africa & by Sunday we will know its course. Louis says it must be Sullivan – if it comes we will have Gilbert & Sullivan. I prefer Jay! Joking apart, I do not think that we could take another one so soon. I know God will spare us.

I must stop now, as I want to write to Irene. I would go on writing pages – but no time to do it.

The storm was bad, but it didn't scare me as much as the fire did. After the last incident, I've become quite afraid of fire.

Our Sister Provincial has come down from Cincinnati for four days & is leaving tomorrow – so she offered to mail our letters for us, that is how you got this letter. Do please give my love to your Mom & all at home. You know you have mine always.

God bless you dear.

Sr. Magdalen.

1
FIRE & AIR

Morris Mathers wasn't afraid of fire. He wasn't afraid of getting caught, or catching a beating, or going hungry for a while. At ten years old, he understood how to live on the street. He took care of himself, mostly by reading other people. He knew that everyone acted only in his or her own best interest, and that constant gave him structure and security.

The woman at the food stall at the intersection of Vineyard and South Camp roads squatted on a small wooden stool in front of a fire burning inside a wheel rim. The fire occasionally flared up through the metal grate that lay across the opening, lending an eerie glow to the darkening sky. The woman's ample behind hung off each side of the stool, which was completely hidden under her long skirt, making her seem planted in the spot. Her shoulders swayed gently in rhythm with the tune she was humming. On the grate, five scrawny chicken legs sizzled in a frying pan. The smoke, infused with thyme and hot peppers, didn't waft gently upward as much as it smacked you in the face as you drew close to the stall.

"Here now! What you want?" the woman said to Morris as he stood a few feet away from the stall, clutching a blue plastic bag and staring at the woman.

"Me beg you some chicken," he nodded at the woman.

1

"Me *sell* you some," she offered.

"Me not have any money," he replied indignantly, slapping the torn pockets of his shorts.

"Den not tonight now boy. Me got me own ti feed." She nodded toward the side of the shack where two young girls sat in the dirt playing. "Git along now, boy."

Morris started to move by the stall. Just as he was passing in front of the fire, one of the young girls smacked her sister, who screamed and started to cry. The woman turned her head and shifted her body toward them. Morris stuck his hand into the hot smoky pan, grabbed a chicken leg and ran.

The woman couldn't do much more than yell after him. In the time it would take her to hoist herself from the stool, Morris would be too far away to catch.

Morris couldn't juggle the hot chicken leg while running, so he dropped it into the plastic bag with the orange he had stolen earlier that evening. He sprinted around the corner, and, knowing he wasn't being pursued, slowed to a walk as soon as he was out of sight. Fifty yards further on, he sat down in a narrow grassy area between the busy street and the deep concrete gully that carried water from the city during the deluges of the rainy season. A low wall ran the length of the gully to keep goats and people from falling in. With his back against the wall, Morris could keep an eye out for any threats, and no one could approach him from behind. He scraped what meat he could from the chicken leg and then peeled the orange, tossing the rind on the ground. The evening breeze was picking up, and when he let go of the thin plastic bag it floated up in the air and over the gully. Morris headed south to the central market. There was more food there, and more people, and at night, there was safety in numbers.

* * *

"Plunkett!"

Desmond Plunkett was afraid of everything. He was afraid he would go hungry. He was afraid he wouldn't have a safe place to sleep. He was afraid of another beating. He was afraid of Sister Ignatius and that she wouldn't be happy with him as an "office boy." But mostly, he was afraid he would be separated from Wayne. His younger brother was only ten, and was his only connection to his life before the orphanage, and he needed that tie to his past, and to his former and true self.

"Plunkett!" Sister Ignatius called again from the porch railing of the convent.

"Yes, sista! Right 'ere, sista!" Plunkett dashed from his bench on the verandah below the convent porch to where Sister Ignatius could see him, and craned his neck up to the porch above. "What can I do for...?"

Before he could finish his sentence, Ignatius started, "Bring these keys to Mr. Guardman at the gate. He will need them to lock up properly tonight." She tossed him the keys.

"Yes, sista. Right away, sista." Plunkett darted off to the main gate, about thirty yards down the driveway from the convent and office.

Plunkett had arrived at Alpha Boys School more than two years earlier. For many months he had kept track of how long it had been since his last beating, his last split lip, his last kick in the back. But on his 14th birthday last month, he realized he had stopped keeping track. He wanted to put behind him those dark days before Alpha. That he had lost track of the time frame told him he would eventually let go of his former life. Now, keeping Sister Ignatius happy was, he thought, the best way to make that separation permanent.

The tall open-mesh fence that surrounded Alpha had only one gate to the street, manned until midnight by Mr. Guardman during the week, and one of the older boys on the weekend. The driveway off the street led over a short narrow bridge that crossed the gully. The gully acted as a moat between the school and the street, keeping intruders out, and the boys in. Plunkett handed the keys to Mr. Guardman; he looked out at the light traffic on South Camp Road. In between the buses, the cabs, and the occasional private car, he could see a smaller boy, about Wayne's age, scamper quickly down the road, in the direction of Kingston's central market. He knew that many kids lived by their wits on the street, and he knew he and Wayne wouldn't last long if they tried. As Desmond walked back to the office, he was conscious of how the night breeze cooled the thin layer of sweat on his forehead, the first comfortable moment of the day. As he looked up into the sky to say a quick prayer to God for keeping him safe tonight, he spotted a lone plastic bag flying over Alpha's fence, landing in the vegetable garden by Junior Home.

* * *

In the morning, Q walked barefoot down the row of banana trees, just a step behind Richard, and a step in front of O'Brien. The three boys were part of a line of ten from the Junior Home, each balancing a gallon canister of water on his head. Q liked the feel of the cool ground on his feet in the morning and the drops of dew that would brush off on his arms as he walked between the towering plants. It took half an hour for the boys to water the rows of scallions and yams in their section of the Junior Home gardens. While their cans were full, they kept their heads straight and their eyes on the shoulder of the boy in front of them. After they emptied their cans, they would scan the ground around them for any treasure that might have landed in the garden overnight. The evening breezes often picked up bits of trash from across the gully and a torn piece of cardboard, or length of string could prove an invaluable play-thing. It was September and the stronger fall breezes would start soon. The ninety-six boys in Junior Home needed to gather supplies to build their kites, and Q and Richard and O'Brien, the smallest boys in the place, did not want to be left out of the fun.

Q spotted a blue bit of something on the ground poking out from under the wide fallen frond of a banana tree a few yards away. Probably a strip of plastic from a shopping bag, he thought, maybe long enough to be a panel on the kite he, Richard and O'Brien were building. His eyes darted side to side to see if anyone else had noticed it yet. He bent over as if to scratch his leg, and when the rest of the boys in line passed him, he dashed to the side and pulled it from under the frond. An entire bag, intact! A tremendous find! O'Brien saw him break ranks and Q turned to show him the bag, holding it as high as he could. They both beamed. Just then, an older boy stepped up behind Q and grabbed at the bag. Q quickly stuffed it in the pocket of his shorts, "It mine! G'way!" he flicked his wrist at him.

The older boy smacked Q sharply in the head, then looked around quickly, "Mi a git you yet, Q. Sista cannot always be watching."

Q hissed at him, rubbing his head as the older boy walked off.

Just then, Samuel, the Senior Home boy in charge that morning, came over shouting, "You dere! What you doing?" as he whacked at some branches with the thin dowel he always carried. Q, only eight, had been at Alpha for four years already, and knew that Samuel wouldn't strike him. Although Q had suffered his lumps from some other boys, he had never been beaten by a staff member. He knew the threat of violence kept most of the boys in line, and he liked, and needed, that. He just wished Samuel had arrived a few moments earlier, which would have saved him being hassled by the other boy. Q ran back into place and got in line to refill his can.

By the end of morning chores, O'Brien had found a few lengths of string, but Richard hadn't found any scraps to contribute to the boys' project. Richard always feared losing his place with his friends if he couldn't produce, but Q and O'Brien didn't care – they liked Richard. Besides, they needed him. The three stuck together to defend themselves from the older boys at Junior Home. As soon as afternoon playtime began, Richard snuck off to the alley between the boys' dormitory and the gully on the edge of South Camp Road. Although he didn't find any trash, he collected as many sticks as he could, so they could start building the kite's frame. When he heard Samuel approaching him and calling his name, he panicked. Unlike Q, Richard remembered all too well the feel of a beating. He dashed away, bursting around the other end of the dormitory, and ran to find his two friends.

Later that afternoon, after the sun passed over the open plaza in front of Junior Home, the boys sat cross-legged in shorts and t-shirts in the shade on the floor of the verandah, flattening their bare legs out sideways to take advantage of the coolness of the tile. They added the sticks Richard found that morning to a stash they had already collected, and spread the pile in front of them, arranging them in a web, and tying the joints together with small bits of string. Q worked quietly, his nimble fingers carefully forming knots. O'Brien and Richard kept moving the sticks around, suggesting different patterns, trying to make the kite frame as large as possible. When the three boys finished, they stood the frame on end. Q's intricate pattern of small triangles and squares supported the larger spaces Richard and O'Brien had crafted. The whole work was taller than Q himself, not a difficult feat, but a cause of pride and laughter for the boys. They carefully laid the frame on the verandah and Q ran into the dormitory. He pulled back the thin mattress on his bed and quickly gathered the plastic bags they had collected. He pulled from his pocket the prize he found that morning, and using a sharp rock, split the bag along the seam. Once splayed out flat, it covered almost a quarter of the kite. The boys added a few more twigs for support, and their work was complete. They stood proudly by it.

"Let's fly it now!" O'Brien said.

Richard readily agreed.

Q shook his head. "We can't."

"Yes we can," O'Brien insisted. "There's still time before da bell rings for supper." Again, Richard was on board.

"No," Q said. "We used all the string to tie the sticks together. We don't have any left to fly de kite." It would take them weeks to gather enough string to get the kite airborne. O'Brien kicked at the ground with disgust. Richard followed his lead. Q, however, was already thinking about where he could get more string. He could think of three sources: Sister Magdalen, Mr. Solomon and Miss Irene.

2
BEDTIME

"And now it's time for bed." I closed the battered brown volume of children's stories and scanned the young faces before me. On the tile floor surrounding the old Adirondack chair with its peeling paint and splintered arms sat twenty-five boys between the ages of seven and twelve.

"De train story next, Mr. Solomon! De train story!"

"No, Waldemar. No more stories tonight. It's getting late. Some of the other boys are trying to sleep. Please put this away for me." I handed him the book, and his three-foot self became very important as he hugged the large volume to his chest and walked to the glass-enclosed bookcase.

As Waldemar placed the book back on its shelf, the boys started to get up. Their soft thank-you's drifted back over their shoulders as their calloused feet carried them down dark rows of cots, past already-sleeping brothers. Each would pull back his thin mattress and check his cache of worldly possessions: string, buttons or bottle-caps, a picture from a magazine, a prayer card given him by one of the nuns. Under their mattress was their only private space where they could keep their valuables safe from each other. In the morning, most of their trinkets would get stuffed in their pockets and carried with them all day. The youngest boys and the bed-wetters slept on tarps stretched across empty bed frames. Inevitably some boy's tarp would tear and he would spend the night curled up on the hard floor.

The last to bed was Anthony, a waif of a seven-year-old who acted more like he was four. Anthony looked over each shoulder cautiously, to make sure no one was standing close by. He had a very important question that he didn't want anyone else to hear. Anthony had an important question every night.

"Mr. Solomon," he started, "tomorrow in de game room, mi can get de puzzle wit de kittens on it?" Anthony's Jamaican patois had a country lilt to it that made him stand out from the boys from Kingston.

"Anthony, you know you can always get a puzzle if you come to the game room."

"And you build it wit me, Mr. Solomon?"

"Sure, Anthony. We'll build it together. Anything else?"

"No, Mr. Solomon." He stood still in front of my chair.

"All right, Anthony. Come on." I pulled myself up from my chair, tucked him under my arm like a football and charged the length of the dormitory before plopping him on his bed, with him laughing and shrieking the entire way. I loved his laugh, and didn't hear it enough before Anthony left Alpha, only to be replaced by Morris Mathers, who was only to be replaced by someone else.

The Junior Home dorm was one large room housing ninety-six boys in eight rows of twelve cots. Dented metal louvers on the windows let in a slight breeze and, on weekends, the pulsating beat of reggae from a bar down the street. The air flow made sleeping easier, unless it blew from the direction of the outdoor bathroom. The dorm itself had cinderblock walls, concrete pillars and a low poured-concrete roof. It was much sturdier than the wood-frame Senior Home dorm, which had a peaked roof of tin sheaths. Many years earlier the original Junior Home building had been destroyed in a hurricane that killed two boys and seriously injured one nun. The sisters rebuilt Junior Home as the storm shelter, and during subsequent storms, the Senior Home boys were shepherded up to the Junior Home for safety.

The walls were painted a faded orange to about four feet high and a brighter yellow above that. The whole place was sorely in need of a paint job. A lone bulb over my chair was the only light left on at night.

As the boys shuffled off to bed, I turned on the tape deck. Tonight, some baroque piano solos – Christmas music, even though it was late September.

As I read to them in the evenings, I realized that the boys carried with them to bed all of the fears and anxieties of the day. Bedtime is sacred. It's the hour when we reflect on our day and amplify the hurts and the victories; it's when we dream big or stew in our anger. When I noticed Sister Magdalen's tape deck in the corner one evening, it reminded me of my own bedtime as a child. My mother would come into the room I shared with my much younger brother, sit on the side of his bed, and sing to him "Lovely Lady Dressed in Blue," her favorite lullaby. She would then kiss us goodnight, say, "Sweet dreams," and leave the bedroom door ajar so the light from the hall would keep us from complete darkness.

When I began visiting Alpha, before I moved in, I had struggled to find something substantive to do for the boys. My salary as a teacher at a local Kingston high school didn't provide me the means to buy them anything that would make a difference. I couldn't give the boys their mothers' love. I couldn't wrap them in the total sense of security and protection my parents had provided me. I couldn't change their reality, but I hoped to at least affect their mood. I hoped I could literally give them sweet dreams. And I hoped those dreams would help them grow into confident men, and their lives would flow as smoothly as the gentle breeze through the dormitory on those early fall nights. I hoped a lot in those days.

While the piano music played softly in one corner of the room, I slowly made my way up the rows, stopping beside each boy who was still awake.

"Mr. Solomon," Jomo whispered, extending an arm and flexing his thumb, challenging me to a thumb-wrestling match. Picking scallions and calaloo, a spinach-like green, gave the boys hands of manual laborers – large and tougher than mine. Jomo and I hooked fingers, thumbs pointed to the ceiling. On the count of three, our thumbs bobbed and flexed until one pinned the other.

While our hands were locked in combat, Jomo boasted, "Sista say I can try out for the band this year, Mr. Solomon."

"That's great, Jomo. Do you know what instrument you want to play?"

"Yes sir. The drums, sir."

If the boys each had their way, Alpha's band would have fifteen drummers and no one else. As each boy prepared to move from the Junior Home to the Senior Home, just across the play field, he was assigned to a trade, depending on his abilities and interest. The boys might work in the carpentry shop, the print shop, the tailor shop or the band. The band was the school's pride and joy and its best fund-raising tool. It played at school events, and was often asked to perform for official government receptions. More significantly, the musicians were often sought out by the Jamaican army band – an enormous relief to the older boys, whose greatest worry was where they would go after they left Alpha.

As I reached the end of the first row, the music from the tape deck grew faint. Its luxury seemed incongruous in such spare surroundings. The boys were fed, but not enough. (Growing boys can never be fed enough.) They were clothed, but modestly. And like all children without a home, they were starved for attention. They had, by the standards I grew up with, nothing. And yet on those nights, the breeze through the dormitory carried the richest music ever composed: Tchaikovsky, Vivaldi, Mozart. The boys' lives were haphazard. The music was immortal.

I had visited Alpha frequently during the 1984-85 school year, my first year in Kingston, reading to the boys three or four nights each week. The boys soon became accustomed to the story hour and thumb wrestling. But now that I had moved in, it was different. They expected me to read to them every night, and so far, I was o.k. with that.

As I walked up and down the rows, from each bed an arm would raise, sometimes thrust in challenge, sometimes meekly proffered, searching only to be held. What I thought of at the time as gentleness on their part,

I later recognized as desperation, their longing for the only chance that day for a soothing touch, for the kind of physical contact with a parent that most kids take for granted.

As I drew close to Francis, he unwrapped himself from his tattered gray sheet and held it up to me. "Mr. Solomon, tomorrow can I please get the book you gave Waldemar? Please?" The big Richard Scarry picture dictionary was the most popular piece of literature in the place and any boy lucky enough to secure it for an afternoon or an evening could easily trade it, attention spans being what they are, for a few measures of kite string or some rubber bands.

"Yes, Francis. Remind me tomorrow," I assured him, taking the sheet from him. He fidgeted, settled into a fetal position with his thumb in his mouth, and closed his eyes extra tight. I laid the sheet over him and tucked it in around the edges as he squirmed and giggled and settled again. At ten, Francis had the mind and body of a younger boy. He had been undernourished before coming to Alpha and was now in a class with other slow learners.

The breeze picked up the strains of Pachelbel's Canon, and I crossed the aisle to see Silent Malcolm. Nine or ten years old, Malcolm was one of the gentlest, and therefore, most vulnerable creatures I had ever met. In the two years I worked at Alpha, I never heard him speak. He was alert, and got into a line or out of the way appropriately. He smiled in response to a smile and frowned in response to a frown. He was present, but couldn't participate. He didn't seem to understand language at all. If you asked him to sit down, he would stand there and stare at you. If you gestured to the bench, he would sit. Occasionally in the afternoon, if I was standing on the verandah talking with someone, Malcolm would stand close by and gaze across the dusty field at the boys playing soccer. If I tried to interest him in even a simple game of patty-cake, his attention would drift back to the field. But at night he always wanted to thumb wrestle. He couldn't count to three to begin the match, and he didn't understand the game; but that didn't matter. He would stare into my eyes as his thumb moved randomly until I gave in and surrendered my thumb under his. He would lie back with a smile on his face. Even I, with an unlimited ability to believe that everything would turn out well, had limited hope that life would be anything but cruel to Malcolm.

The stroll up and down the rows took about half-an-hour. At the end, I turned the music lower and returned to my chair under the light. The chair was just outside the door to Sister Magdalen's office and bedroom. At the bedtime hour she was down at the convent with Sister Ignatius and Sister Marie Therese. She would come up to her room at Junior Home by nine o'clock for the night, every night. Sister Magdalen was the Gibraltar in the boys' lives.

Leaning back in the Adirondack, I was just high enough to gaze across the sea of beds before me. It was an odd life I had created for myself at the age of twenty-three. There are very few benefits to being the only man at the convent. I had no role models and no defined job, so I made up each day as it came. At times, that served me well, but at other times, it left me floundering. I had been lonely before, having moved from school to school as a child, and knew I would be lonely at times here too. But I could stave off the loneliness if I stayed busy. Busy is better than bored, and loneliness can be a sacrifice offered up to God. But how often can you tell yourself that before it sounds flat? I needed to feel productive. I needed a calling – a role of my own. Four years as an English major at Boston College had taught me that putting language around events and feelings would help me understand them, and quantify them, and use them to grow. I needed a name for who I was, and a title to define my purpose.

My contemplation was broken by Q's gentle whisper. His bed was closest to the chair, and he was leaning over the side of the metal frame waving, trying hard not to attract the attention of the other boys. "Mr. Solomon," he breathed loudly.

I leaned forward in the chair, "What is it, Q?"

"Mr. Solomon, O'Brien and Richard and I need string for de kite. Do you have any, please?" The sparkle in his eye and the smirk on his face told me he knew what a pushover I was.

"I'll find some for you tomorrow, Q," I smiled back.

"Tank you, sir," he said, as he rolled back onto his bed smiling broadly.

I sank back into my chair wondering if "Storyteller" and "Provider of String" were job titles with which I could be satisfied this year.

When the music stopped, I took the tape and said goodnight to Benjamin, the Senior Home boy who was assigned to watch the younger ones until Magdalen returned from the convent. The screen door squeaked as I swung it open, which caused Patches, the mangy orange-and-white watch dog, to lift her head. She slept in front of the door at one end of the dormitory, and Yappy, the younger black Labrador mix, slept at the other end. Between the two, they provided adequate alarm if any strangers should approach the dorm. Given the number of boys and the assorted adults who belonged there, I never understood how the dogs could recognize a stranger. But that was their calling, and they did it well. (They were lucky dogs in that regard.)

The path from the Junior Home to the Senior Home and the convent and my room changed without reason from paved path to gravel and back again numerous times. But whether you were walking on concrete or gravel, you couldn't walk twenty feet at Alpha without kicking up dust, even at night.

The chirping of the katydids in the bushes, the sound of the band practicing in the Senior Home refectory, the distant barking of a dog, the pulsing music from the bar down the street, the rumble of a bus heading up South Camp Road just over the fence and across the gully all blended together into the night symphony. Across the playing fields, the full moon sat just off the end of Long Mountain, the eastern boundary of the city. I could see the slope of the hill and pictured where it meets the Caribbean just outside Kingston Harbor. The navy blue sky, the deep green hill and the sparse brown playfield, even in the limited light of the moon, were each clearly defined. If only everything that year had been as clear as that evening sky. I had come to Jamaica for a quick adventure, a fun interlude between college and law school. I hadn't planned to stay a second year. Now, only a month into living at Alpha, my life didn't make practical sense. At times I had considered becoming a priest – but I never anticipated I would live in a convent. I had come from a loving and stable home – and now lived among orphans. I had grown up in a community where the one black family in town had almost celebrity status – and now I was the minority. And the ironies were only beginning.

Still, one thing was clear. I knew every night, as I walked back to my room at the convent, that I was being given a gift by being here - the people I met, the stories I heard, the days, whether ordinary, absurd, or terrifying – all were gifts, to be held and cherished. I didn't know then that gifts often come with a price. I didn't know that when you insert yourself into other people's lives you lose parts of your own.

* * *

That night, no one read stories to Morris Mathers. He heard no strains of classical music. Instead, Morris curled himself into the deep doorway of a storefront just off the central market square in Kingston. He had stolen and eaten enough food that night that he actually felt full, and the feeling made him sleepy. In his dream, he stood in front of a street higgler at her stall, eying the small piles of fruit stretched out on the tarp at her feet. She welcomed him to help himself and he reached for a large orange in the pile closest to him. But then someone grabbed his arm and twisted it behind him, causing him to drop the fruit.

He awoke abruptly to the heavy breath of rum in his face. A fat drunk man had Morris' arm pinned behind him. He forced the boy's head into the corner of the doorway, pinning his chin to the concrete slab, so he couldn't open his mouth to yell, and couldn't turn to bite his assailant. Morris kicked at the man as hard as he could, but he was a scrawny ten year old and no match for the weight on top of him. As the man pulled the boy's shorts off him, Morris knew the pain he was about to suffer, and he knew the humiliation he would feel afterward. He concentrated instead on the pain in his head every time the man's thrusts jammed his forehead into the wall. Morris hated to cry but could feel the tears on his face as the assault continued.

When the man was done and started to stand, Morris tried to kick at him, but he was too exhausted. He cursed instead, and the man kicked him sharply in the side as a warning not to follow him. Morris pulled his shorts back on, knowing he would have to either steal another pair or find a way to fix the new tears in these. He stumbled a few blocks away to where he knew a water pipe stood in an alley. He washed himself, trying to get rid of the man's stink. The cold water stung his skin, and the tears on his backside. Once he felt clean, and covered, he knew he needed to look for a new doorway. He picked up a broken brick at the base of the water pipe. He wanted to find the drunk and smash his head with the brick. Instead, Morris returned to the doorway where the attack had happened. He slammed the brick against the grill covering the storefront. He slammed it again and again, until the glass door behind the grill smashed. Then he went in search of a new doorway. He knew he wouldn't sleep this time, and he knew he wouldn't dream again.

3
COMPANIONSHIP

Irene DeGroot squirmed her way out of the tightly packed minibus on South Camp Road, just past Alpha's main gate. As the bus pulled away, the conductor, hanging from the side of the open van door, didn't hide his interest as he ran his eyes up and down her body. "Pretty lady. Call me now. Ya hear?" Irene rolled her eyes as she shook her head. She pulled her knapsack up on her shoulder as she walked back toward Alpha's main entrance, A large truck rumbled past, belching black diesel exhaust, which Irene waved away from her face. The boy manning the entrance had seen her step off the bus and was already pulling open the large metal gate to let her in. She thanked him and headed left, up the driveway toward Junior Home. At least a half-dozen boys swarmed to greet her. As usual, Richard and O'Brien reached her first. She slipped her umbrella into her bag and pulled the strap up higher on her shoulder so she could extend hands to both boys. After exchanging pleasantries with Nurse, she borrowed the key to the cabinet in the game room and set out the puzzles and games and decks of cards.

Irene had arrived in the country two months earlier. Each year, the Boston College International Volunteer Program sent recent graduates like Irene and me to Jamaica and other countries to teach at Catholic schools and help run the schools' ministry programs. When I wasn't working with the boys at Alpha, I taught English at St. George's College, a Jesuit high school a few blocks away. Irene taught Math at Immaculate Conception, a girls' school run by Dominican Sisters in the foothills of the

Blue Mountains, on the edge of Kingston. The Jesuits and Dominicans strive to create "men and women for others," so even poor students in developing nations who attend Catholic high schools are required to participate in outreach programs to learn to serve other people. Part of the BC teachers' roles in Kingston was to help run those programs. Irene was considering having girls from Immaculate volunteer at Alpha. Involving herself with Junior Home was a big commitment; Alpha was more than an hours' bus ride from Immaculate.

As I approached the gameroom, O'Brien ran to greet me.

"Miss Irene here already, Mr. Solomon!" he blurted. But I had already heard her laughter from across the Junior Home courtyard, and had quickened my pace. In the game room, the Junior Home refectory, which we commandeered each afternoon to play cards and board games, Irene was sitting with Richard and O'Brien playing checkers.

"You can't move there!" she laughed. Almost everything she said to the boys rang with delight, as if she were constantly amazed by them. Richard smiled as broadly as he could, knowing that his triple jump didn't really count. His face always lit up when he saw Irene, and he loved it when he could make her laugh, which was often. Irene had wavy shoulder-length blond hair, pale skin and delicate features. She carried herself with an air of confidence and had a matter-of-fact approach to just about everything. Like the other BC teachers, she complained at first about the heat and the cockroaches and the smell of urine in the streets. But after a few weeks, she already seemed unfazed by Kingston.

Irene was leaning back on the bench watching Richard try to make another illegal move on the checker board, when I walked up behind her a put a hand on her shoulder. "Well hello Mr. Sullivan," she laughed, and quickly turned her attention back to the boys. "Richard! You know you can't do that."

"Richard is winning, Mr. Solomon!" O'Brien shouted, snapping his fingers together with a quick flick of the wrist.

"His name is 'Sullivan', not 'Solomon'" Irene insisted. The boys at

Alpha either couldn't hear or couldn't pronounce the "v" in "Sullivan." So to them, I was "Mr. Solomon." Father Quinn at my parish back in Pleasantville, New York, had always preached that as Catholics, we should view Jews as our wise elders, our older brothers, the tribe from whom we inherit our faith. Now, in this place of ambiguous ties - an orphanage run by Catholic nuns, populated with children of unclear affiliation, in a country of many faiths - I had gained a Jewish name. I would hear Father Quinn's voice often that year, asking me if I heard the wisdom of my elders.

There were about twenty boys in the room today and almost every table was occupied. I was glad the boys found the game room an attractive option in their afternoon. But the crowd made it impossible to spend any length of time with any one of them.

"Mr. Solomon, play cards with me, Mr. Solomon, please," O'Brien pleaded.

"Why don't you set up a game of Concentration, O'Brien."

"Yes, Mr. Solomon. Right away." O'Brien went to the first table, "Move now boys. You heard Mr. Solomon! Move away."

"O'Brien, don't make them move. There's an empty table right over there."

"Yes, Mr. Solomon," he said with a huge grin, and he hustled over to the empty table.

I walked over and stood behind Irene, leaning over the game. "How was school today?" I asked more quietly than I had spoken to the boys.

As Irene looked up, Richard stuttered, "Fine," as he continued staring at the checker board, trying to figure out his next move.

Irene raised her eyebrows at Richard, "Mine too," she laughed. "And yours, Mr. Solomon?"

"Good actually. The craziness at George's wasn't too bad today. All the other teachers showed up. The boys behaved. I'm pretty sure some learning actually took place." I sat down across from her, and helped Richard figure out his next checker move.

"I keep telling you, those Jesuits need to learn from the Dominican sisters," Irene said. "Discipline is never an issue at Immaculate. Sister Mary Katherine runs a tight ship. Those girls are scared to death of her. It's great." In fact, both Sister Mary Katherine at Immaculate and Sister Bernadette at Alpha Academy, the girls' high school at the other end of the Alpha compound, were known throughout Jamaica at tough-as-nails nuns who ran exemplary schools and believed in strict discipline.

"Well, boys are more difficult than girls," I offered.

Richard lifted his eyes from the checker board, and flashed a sly smile.

"Yes, they are," Irene said, throwing an arm around his shoulders and pulling him closer to her. "And we love them for it." If Irene had kissed him on the head, which would have seemed completely natural, Richard would have exploded on the spot. As it was, his grin stretched as far as the scars around his mouth would allow. Richard's mother had been brutal. The surgery the sisters arranged after he was brought to Alpha repaired his torn lips, but the scar tissue narrowed his ability to smile. The emotional scar tissue would surface much later in his life. But that afternoon, in the game room, with Irene's arm around him, Richard was happy.

"But, don't underestimate the ability of teenage girls to act up. Sister Mary Katherine just knows how to help them control themselves."

"Yeah, except I hear from the George's boys that the Immaculate girls are the wildest of all the girls in town when they aren't at school."

"I'm sorry," she said indignantly. "Are you telling me that high school boys are talking about how easy some high school girls are? I'm shocked!"

"Are you mocking me, Miss Irene?" I smiled.

"Not at all, Mr. Solomon."

O'Brien had taken over one of the long tables, spreading the cards out face down in neat rows. While he waited for me, he straightened each card carefully, a nice attempt at order that we would undermine the minute we started to play. "Mi ready when you are, Mr. Solomon."

When I first opened the game room a year earlier, some of the staff were concerned that the card games would encourage the boys to gamble. In Kingston, it seemed every neighborhood had not only its own church, but its own faith, and many of those faiths were adamantly opposed to a wide array of vices. There were billboards all around Kingston with praying hands and the line, "Please, God, keep gambling from our shores." I had to show Nurse and Cook that the games we would play did not involve gambling and instead involved memory, counting and simple arithmetic. Young boys soak up knowledge and skills. All we had to do was lay it all in front of them.

"So, what's everyone doing this weekend?" I asked Irene, referring to the other BC teachers she lived with.

"Mr. Solomon, the game is ready sir," O'Brien interrupted.

"Just a minute O'Brien."

"Yes, sir. The cards are ready when you are, sir. Did you want to go first, sir? I went first last time we played."

"He's not going to stop talking until you go over there," Irene said smiling.

"You win, O'Brien," I said, moving to his table. "And you can go first." While we were playing, I became aware that Q was standing silently by my side.

As soon as I felt his presence, he leaned over to me and whispered, "You 'member the string, sir?" His eyes were darting back and forth, watching for interlopers.

I looked at him askance and winked, as I pulled a coil of twine from my pocket, slipping it into his hand with far more discretion than was warranted.

"Tank you, sir," he said softly, as he shoved the string in his pocket.

O'Brien and I were well into our game when I remembered something. "O'Brien, where's Anthony today? He made me promise last night that I would build a puzzle with him today."

"Gone to 'im mudda, sir," O'Brien said staring at the cards, trying to find a match for the Jack of Hearts he had turned over.

"Anthony's gone! I had no idea he was going home." I was stunned that he could leave and disappointed I wouldn't get to say goodbye, a completely selfish concern.

"Him not know either, sir. 'im mudda show up and take him. 'im so excited to see her!" O'Brien had stopped concentrating on the game, and now seemed intent on reading my reaction. Children are students of human behavior. By watching adults they learn to react appropriately, understand how to express sadness, to share joy, to show remorse. Children who grow up neglected, or in orphanages, don't have the opportunity to learn those fundamental behaviors. "Him mudda got a job in Spanishtown, and she wanted Anthony back so she came and took 'im."

"Well you certainly know all the details, don't you, O'Brien."

"Yes sir," he bragged. "Sista gave them a *heap* of food, and then walked them out to the road to catch de bus."

I was sad at the thought of never hearing Anthony's laugh again in the evening, or the silly questions he would ask about the stories, or the "very important question" he had to ask me every night so that he would get a short chance to speak privately with an adult, a chance to be special for a moment. Because I was happy at Alpha, I often forgot that the boys were not. No matter how well they were treated, no matter how much we could take the edge off the loneliness, every boy only wanted his own home.

"Well, I'm glad for Anthony, but I wish I'd had a chance to say goodbye."

"Sista says some new boys are coming in tomorrow, so you won't miss Anthony for too long, sir."

O'Brien wasn't being mean – just honest.

Sitting off by himself on the floor in the corner, another boy, Garfield worked methodically and intently, trying to cram one piece after another into a small puzzle. I left him on his own, knowing that previous offers of help had been silently rebuffed. In the whole time I worked at Alpha, Garfield spoke to me only once, when another boy had taken something from him and he wanted my help to get it back. Even then, the conversation was terse and focused. I didn't know at the time what rage he suppressed. He got in the occasional fight once he moved to the Senior Home, but nothing serious. It wasn't until years after he left Alpha that his anger spilled out. One night in a bar, an equally troubled soul smiled too strongly at the woman Garfield was with. Most men who get into bar fights have friends who pull them back after a few punches. Garfield had no one to protect him from himself. He didn't stop even after the other man was on the floor and bloodied. He didn't stop until there was nothing left to fight.

The trial didn't last long. At the sentencing, the dead man's family forgave Garfield, and asked the court to show mercy. Nevertheless, the court sentenced Garfield to life at the General Penitentiary, a fierce battleground of a prison down by the waterfront. It was the antithesis of Alpha, a black hole swallowing all hope and goodness. Today in the game room, my distraction with the other boys and inattention to Garfield was just another missed opportunity.

For the next hour, the gameroom buzzed as boys wandered in and out, asking for a deck of cards or a puzzle or a board game. The sound of the pop-um in the center of the Trouble game was a constant part of the background noise.

Eventually, Cook came in to say dinner would arrive soon. The boys went off to wash up. Irene and I wrapped up the games, and headed to my room. I was the only one in the BC program who didn't live "in community" with other BC teachers, so I was always the last to know any gossip and news of any weekend plans. Irene was my link to that community.

Back in my room, I pulled two Cokes from the fridge, as Irene sat at my small kitchen table with her feet up on a chair. Her blue and white skirt draped over her legs, almost reaching the floor. She tilted her head back to drink the soda. The beads of condensation on the cold bottle matched the beads of sweat on her neck.

"Richard did the sweetest thing today in the game-room," she said, wiping her brow after her first swallow. "He brought me a flower he drew in class."

"Did he say anything?"

"Yeah, he said, 'Here.'" She made of shoving motion with her hands, laughing.

"I guess he hasn't learned the finer points of impressing a woman," I said. "Want a bite to eat before you head back?"

"Sure. What've you got?"

I hesitated. "Actually, nothing, now that I think of it. Unless you want a thick slab of Hard-Do bread and some peanut butter." Hard-Do Bread is a Jamaican staple, and its name says it all. Imagine an entire loaf of bread the consistency of a bagel. Each loaf weighs about two pounds and comes unsliced. With Hard-Do, you get your morning workout just slicing your toast.

"I'll pass. Thanks."

"So, how was school today?" I asked.

"It was fine, but I think the honeymoon is over. I can feel the girls testing me already," Irene said. "But my aunt back home is a teacher and gave me some helpful pointers. How was George's today?"

In the privacy of my room we could have a more substantive discussion than in front of the boys. "I'm finding this year very different from last," I said. I felt that as a returning, second-year teacher, I should mentor Irene and the new batch of teachers to give them perspective, and assure them that the job gets easier. I could offer her advice, but I could only long for the confidence she conveyed so effortlessly. "Last year, I struggled to have discipline in the classroom. The kids walked all over me. This year is much smoother."

"Why does Alpha seem so well run, with so few discipline issues?" she asked..

"It could be because it's a home first and a school second," I said. "Or because the nuns have the boys for 100% of the time and don't have any outside influences on the boys to contend with. You and I see the kids in the game room where we have something they want and where our only agenda is to have fun with them. I'm sure if we were trying to teach math to Mr. Estig's class we might have a different view. How are things at the house?"

"Fine," she shrugged. "I think Melissa is miserable though." Her roommate, Melissa had arrived on the island with Irene. She had been terribly homesick from the start and disgusted with the living conditions. She wasn't a whiner - just clearly unhappy. "I don't think she will last the year."

"What's her problem?"

"I'm not sure." She ran her fingers along her temples and pulled her hair up and away from the back of her neck to cool herself. "I think she came into this with different expectations."

I nodded, even though I wasn't sure what she meant.

"What were your expectations coming down here?" I asked.

She sat forward, picked up a folder from the table, and fanned herself. Her eyes trailed off to the ceiling.

"I had talked to some earlier volunteers. I had been on a Haiti trip during Spring Break my Junior year. I knew what the Caribbean was like, and Jamaica is so much better than Haiti, there's just no comparison. Jamaica at least has some hope. Haiti is going backwards. I need to know I'm doing more than putting a Band-Aid on a bleeding artery. I need to see progress. Here, I know I can make a difference." She took another drink. "I mean, don't get me wrong. I don't think I'm saving the world here. But I made some kid in a Third World orphanage smile this afternoon by playing checkers with him."

"And you got Richard to express a positive emotion."

"That too. What about you?"

"You want me to express a positive emotion?"

"No," she laughed. "What were your expectations coming down

here?"

"I don't recall thinking about coming down here until I was on the plane on the way."

"Literally? *You didn't think about it?*"

"Well, I'm sure I did. I must have. I had to fill out the application. Go on the interview. Clear it with my parents. So I must have *thought* about it. But I remember sitting on the plane – the flight attendants had just closed the door. The pilot announced, 'Prepare to take off.' And for the first time, I thought, 'What am I doing? How did this happen?' At the time, I didn't even know whether I would be living on a beach or in a slum, or in a slum on the beach."

"That doesn't make any sense."

"I was surprised myself when I finally realized what I had committed to. I really feel like it was the proverbial 'hand of God' leading me here." I hesitated. I didn't know Irene very well yet, and I was leery of sounding like a religious nut. But I felt safe with her and I didn't have any other peers to share my thoughts with.

"That's it? The 'hand of God?' That's the best you've got?" she said.

Now I was stuck. I had started the confession and I had to finish it. "Well, senior year at BC I applied to law school. I always knew I'd be a lawyer. I honestly believe that if I had truly reflected on coming here, I would have chickened out. And I think God knew I was too stupid to make the right decision so He didn't let me think about it until it was too late. I wish I could say I had 'bravely responded to a call,' or had some 'burning desire to serve the poor.' But I think I was just duped by God."

"So you just sat back," Irene leaned back in her chair, "and abdicated any responsibility for making a major decision in your life. That's some life strategy you've got going there, Mr. Solomon," she said smirking.

"It's working well so far," I said, gesturing at the humble surroundings of my room. "I have my plans," I lied. "I'll get to them eventually." I took a drink, wanting to change the topic. "Tell me about Immaculate."

She talked about her day, her own challenges with her students, and the tests she was planning for next week. "But in the meantime, we're all going to the Carib on Friday to see *Return of the Jedi* and then going to New Kingston for dinner." New Kingston, a small collection of office buildings, had developed in the last few years around the Pegasus Hotel, a pink behemoth that shared a parking lot with the Sheraton, the only other American-feeling hotel in Kingston. I would get details later in the week from the other BC teachers at St. George's.

While I listened to Irene, I thought about how easily our relationship had developed. We had started dating shortly after she arrived on the island. I certainly hadn't come to Alpha looking for romance, but here I was, enjoying a drink in my room with a woman who was smart, funny, beautiful, kind and clearly in love with life. Alpha provided an unusual and somewhat exotic, if not technically romantic setting. I had been too shy to date much in college, so I was surprised how easy it had been to grow close to someone here. But I also knew that our social network in Kingston was limited so far to the dozen or so BC teachers on the island, most of whom were women. My luck with women had improved more because there was a limited pool of choices for them than because of any increased skill or confidence on my part.

Our conversations in my room never lasted long. Irene had a half-hour bus ride home and roommates who would be holding dinner for her. As we walked by the office, the staff was locking up and the office boys were running their end-of-day errands.

"Hello Miss Irene." They all said nodding. "Hello Mr. Solomon," they said to me, with slight smirks on their faces. I rolled my eyes in response.

I walked Irene out to South Camp Road and waited with her until the bus pulled up.

Public transportation in Jamaica was a hodgepodge of bus routes served by both state operated buses and privately owned minivans. The minivans were almost always the more efficient option, since they ran more regularly, adapted their routes quickly based on the needs of the community, and treated most of the regulations as "suggestions." The minivans were mostly old Volkswagen twelve-passenger vans, with the sliding door tied open or simply removed. The buses were usually overcrowded. If you were lucky enough to get a seat, you could expect that a passenger getting on after you would hand you his briefcase, bag, chicken or child to hold while he or she stood, bent in half, leaning over other passengers.

The late day traffic had begun and the sound of gears grinding prevented any attempt at conversation. A red minibus with a white number "6" hand-painted on the front and side approached. The conductor, about nineteen years old, hung off the side of the bus as if he were windsurfing up the street, his feet perched precariously on the edge of the doorway and his fingertips tucked under the roof of the van. His open shirt flapped in the breeze; his black, pin-striped dress slacks were held up with a Jamaican green, yellow and black knitted belt, tied in a knot; the ends hung down almost to his knees. Like so many young men, he wore beat-up dress shoes, no laces or socks. I never understood how their shoes didn't fall off. A kerchief was tied around his neck. He spotted Irene waiting, and, as the bus approached at breakneck speed, he pounded on the roof to signal the driver, jumped off and shouted, "Crossroads! Crossroads!" as he jogged up to the bus stop. In his left hand he had a wad of bills folded length-wise, each denomination wrapped around a different finger.. Every conductor carried his bills the same way.

Irene's squinted into the packed van trying to figure out how to fit in. A man got out of the front seat and, nodding, squeezed his way into the back of the van. Irene thanked him and slid into his seat, wedging the woman already there up against the stick shift.

"See you Friday," she called.

The conductor jumped back onto his perch, hanging on with his right hand. With his left, he banged on the roof of the van and yelled, "Drive driver! Drive!" The minivan belched a black cloud as it pulled from the curb and drew Irene away from Alpha back into the heat and sweat of an early Kingston evening.

Rather than head back to my room, I walked up to the bar on the next corner. If I were living in a neighborhood in Boston, working at a regular job, living with regular roommates, I probably would have been a regular at the local bar, and the bartender and I would know each other's names. But I was in Kingston, and I lived behind a tall fence, over a wide gully, with a bunch of nuns and kids. The neighbors knew me because I was the only white man they saw walking in and out of Alpha and occasionally waiting at the bus stop. But that was the extent of my interaction with our neighbors. I didn't shop for groceries, run personal errands, or attend a local church. Alpha and St. George's were my communities, and those institutions provided structure and security, and all my basic needs. But we all need things beyond the basics.

As I reached the corner, a minivan pulled to a stop in front of *You Must Come In*, the local bar. As the conductor jumped off the bus and onto the sidewalk, he nodded to me, "Whitey. Come. We head downtown."

I shook my head and walked up the few steps to the porch of the bar. Even though it was only early evening, *No Woman, No Cry* by Bob Marley and the Wailers was blaring from the jukebox. I would still hear the music hours later when I read to the boys. A couple on the porch looked up and nodded hello as I parted the beads hanging in the doorway and stepped inside.

The large woman behind the counter wiped out a glass and threw her towel over her shoulder as I entered. "Good night," she greeted me, and flashed a smile that included two gold caps. "What can mi get fi you?"

I ordered two Red Stripes and asked her not to open them. I would save them for after dinner. As she fumbled around in the cooler searching for cold bottles, I looked around the bar. It was early and I was the only patron inside. A young girl, about ten, slowly swept the floor. She could easily be the sister of one of the boys at Alpha or at George's. She wore boys' sneakers too big for her feet. Only one shoe had a lace, and it was undone and trailed on the floor. One hand gripped the broom handle tightly, while the other held the top of the loose broom-head together. Despite her effort, she lost strands of straw from the broom every time she stopped to pull the strap of her loose fitting dress back up on her shoulder. It was a broom barely held together by a girl barely held together. I wondered what Kingston was like for young girls in the same position as the boys at Alpha. There must have been orphanages for the girls. Were they as well run? Girls are so much more vulnerable than boys. I knew it must have been much tougher to keep them safe.

I didn't know if it was considered more offensive to say hello or to ignore someone, but I smiled at the young girl anyway. She stopped sweeping and stared back at me. Her stare made me uncomfortable, as if she and I both knew I was out of place. I settled up with the woman behind the counter as she handed me a plastic bag with the two Red Stripes, said a quick thank you, and left.

The couple on the porch was too involved with each other now to nod a goodbye. The jukebox blared *Get Up, Stand Up* as I headed home. Whatever my calling would be this year, I knew I was more likely to find it within Alpha's walls than outside.

Feb. 4, 1987

My very dear Jay,

I wanted to write to you ever since you left, but never got the chance. No need to tell you how thrilled we all were with your unexpected visit. You should see how lovely your bathroom looks now – wall all tiled! The kitchen & washing machine room is almost ready. I love that washing machine. I do not have to carry the laundry down to the other convent & sometimes wait for days till I find a machine not in use.

The boys enjoyed the candy you brought. We gave it to them as a treat after we show them movies on Friday night.

Irene had some troubles with her tonsils. I took her to the doctor & got her the pills, which were not good & the doctor had to change them & it worked better this time & she is all right again. She also brought the boys gifts - candy, books & pencils, etc. I hope you will soon hear from the boys. They are too lazy to write. My wretched boys - all they like doing is eating. They can eat all day long!

I hope my letter is not keeping you away from those huge tomes of law. Never mind, I'll soon stop. Sorry I'm scribbling so much – my thoughts go faster than my pen – a sign of intelligence!!! Even if I say so.

I heard on T.V. the awful bad weather you are getting over there. Sorry I cannot send you some of our sunshine. We have enough to spare. You have to be satisfied with the warmth I send you from my heart & if I add that of your boys here – I'm sure it will thaw out most of the snow you have!

Well, Jay, take good care of yourself – keep sweet, a big God bless you – Love Always,

Magda.

4
THE SOURCE

The physical, spiritual and emotional center of Alpha was the convent. A faded green, two story building with a peaked roof, it dominated the front of the grounds. The center of sustenance at Alpha was The Pipe, the main source of water, and in that regard, Alpha shared a heart and soul with every other neighborhood in Kingston.

Jamaicans speak of The Pipe with the same reverence and importance with which characters in the Bible speak of The Well. All cultures grow around a water source: the meeting of the Tigris and Euphrates, the headwaters of the Hudson, the deep waters of Kingston Harbor, or The Pipe. From Kingston's main reservoir at the base of the Blue Mountains, water was channeled across the city, ending in each neighborhood in a single pipe with a simple spigot at the end. Sometimes the pipes emerged in seemingly random locations. Eventually, someone would put a stone slab at its base so when people came to fill their jugs, they wouldn't have to place the jug in the mud. Families would build their shacks in clusters around the pipe, and over time, that slab of stone would become the rudimentary town square for the neighborhood. Most shacks in Jamaica were sheets of corrugated zinc fastened together to form walls and a roof. Floors were often formed by a board thrown over a number of shipping pallets stolen from the docks. Having plain dirt floors isn't practical when every rain storm puts a stream through your house. Each small "yard" of shacks developed an identity as the families that shared the pipe grew to rely on each other. And, as in other poor countries, each community aligned itself with a particular politician, whoever handed out the most cash, or in some neighborhoods, guns. If your party won power in the next election, your muddy yard might get paved, and your lean-to home might become your new cinderblock house. If your politician lost, your pipe might not get fixed the next time there was a problem, or your yard might be targeted for demolition. Because so much rode on the success of your political benefactor, the rivalry between communities led to bloodshed, which led to the need for places like Alpha, where orphans could find a home.

There were actually several pipes at Alpha. The one nearest the office poked from the ground near the base of the stairs leading up to the convent. It stood about three feet high and had a brass faucet on the end. A small oasis had formed around it. The sisters planted grape vines and built an arbor. Under the arbor, they even installed a small goldfish pond. Over time, large trees grew, providing shade to the convent and office. The same greening effect took place around each of the pipes on the grounds.

Jamaica's Ministry of Youth Services provided Alpha a stipend for each boy in its care. The payments arrived sporadically, and were never enough. So Alpha had, since its founding more than a hundred years ago, grown much of its own food. The nuns would make up many shortfalls in the boys' lives.

The water supply in Kingston was reliable only in its complete lack of reliability. The sisters knew they couldn't count on the public water that fed Alpha's Pipe to keep the garden growing and the boys fed, so decades ago, they dug a well. Years later, they installed a backup diesel generator, since electric power was even more sporadic than the water supply. The well and the generator gave the sisters security. For all their talk of "God will provide," the nuns' true motto seemed to be, "God will provide, but keep the generator in good repair."

The nuns efforts made one of the most unreliable provisions in Jamaica one of the most reliable at Alpha. The boys at Alpha might hunger for many things, but they would never thirst.

As I came down from the Junior Home dorm after an evening of reading, I spotted Wilbert, one of the Office Boys, getting a drink from the pipe. When he saw me walking along the verandah, he turned off the faucet and ran over, wearing his usual sly look. Wilbert always seemed to be up to something, and although he was a good kid, he stood just a little bit too close when he spoke to you, which always made me check for my wallet when he would step back.

"Sir, can we get the tape tonight?" He meant my radio and cassette player, which got better reception than the transistor radio the Office Boys listened to.

"Sure Wilbert, I'll get it now." We rounded the corner to where the other Office Boys sat. "Do you want to play cards or checkers tonight?" I asked.

"Checkers, Sir," said Plunkett, with his nervous, hopeful smile. He was the most reliable of the half-dozen Office Boys.

Outside the office were two benches where the Office Boys spent each evening, playing cards, or checkers or just talking. The Office Boys, mostly from the Senior Home, ran errands for the sisters and were given responsibility for little things. They enjoyed two luxuries the other boys at Alpha would not experience: they had variety in their days, and they had freedom. At times, they accompanied the sisters on errands, trips to the airport being the best because they would be off the grounds for hours on end. While the other boys stood in line for everything and had to ask permission to go to the bathroom, the Office Boys kept their own schedule, within limits. Only the most reliable boys were given the role, and the sisters often disagreed who among the boys could be trusted.

The convent building housed the office and chapel on the first floor, and the sisters' living quarters upstairs, reached by a flight of concrete steps on the side of the building. Three or four times an evening Sister Ignatius would come to the railing of the patio upstairs, lean over and call out, "Wilbert. Plunkett! Worldhead! Come," and one of the boys would yell, "Yes Sister" and run around the corner and up the stairs. "Bring these keys to Mr. Driver." "Fetch the prayer books from the refectory." Or "Put these clothes in the sewing room for Mrs. Laundry." It had taken me a while to get used to the names in Jamaica. The sisters called Wilbert by his first name, Plunkett by his last name, and Worldhead based on the fact that he had a head the size of the whole world. And many of the adult staff were referred to almost exclusively by their role.

I brought the tape out and we listened to a Simon & Garfunkel "greatest hits" collection. It was more my taste than theirs, but given their circumstances, I'm not sure how much they had developed their own taste in music yet.

"How was school today, boys?"

"Fine, sir." School was "fine" just about every time I asked.

"Nothing special went on today?" I asked. It was often hard to have much of a conversation with teenage boys. I didn't realize until much later, when I had my own kids, that the value was in the asking, not in the enlightening conversation.

"Well actually, sir," Desmond offered, "I 'eard dat teacher got very frustrated today wit' New Boy."

"Who is the new boy, Desmond?"

"Um, mi forget him name sir, but 'im the black one sir," he said definitively.

"He's the *black* one, Desmond? Could you maybe be a little bit more specific? You're all black to me." I had long since gotten past the delicacies of discussing race in a black country. Jamaicans, and, I learned, pretty much everyone other than Americans, speak much more openly about racial identity and skin color than I was used to.

"No sir!" he said, surprised. "I'm brown. Wilbert's light brown. The new boy is *black* like Worldhead," Desmond said, pointing at Worldhead sitting next to him. Worldhead waved in acknowledgement without looking up from the checkers. Worldhead was about as black as you can be. In the daylight, when his face showed a thin film of sweat, he took on an almost purple hue. At night, his face completely absorbed the little light available.

"Why was Mr. Estig angry at New Boy?" The new boy would continue to be known as "New Boy" until a newer boy arrived. If he stayed around for at least two weeks, the other boys would bother to remember his name.

"Mr. Estig always gets mad at the new kids, 'cause they don't know how to act. He had to 'tump 'im on the head a few times to get him to stay in line. But New Boy got it after a while and he behaved." Although there were half a dozen teachers at the school, all of the younger new boys started in Mr. Estig's class for slow learners, under the assumption that they would need help. Mr. Estig was in his late sixties. He was rail-thin, with skin the color of sandalwood, a voice that spoke of a gentle authority, and perfect posture. He had taught at Alpha for more than thirty years. He taught a small class of the younger boys during the morning and early afternoon. By mid-afternoon he was perched on a small metal chair under the shade of a scraggly tree on the edge of the Junior Home playfield, keeping an eye on the hordes to make sure no one wandered off. He carried a thin wooden classroom pointer at all times, and wielded it like a baton when on the playground to motion to boys in the distance to stay in sight. At other times, it was more like the right hand of an angry God, swinging out at an unruly child. By the time I knew Mr. Estig, his arthritis prevented him from moving too quickly, and the boys always ducked the rod. Years of experience had taught him that the threat of discipline was enough to ensure order. Decades earlier, there had been flocks of sisters in long habits keeping the boys busy, extending the school day, monitoring the gardens, roaming the grounds. Now there were three sisters plus Cook, Nurse and Mr. Estig, who filled in for each other as necessary. Not better or worse than a dozen sisters, just different. There were only two sisters in the novitiate now, and hadn't been many for years. Eventually there would be no sisters at all. But the sisters' well and their generator would endure. Whether their spirit would continue remained to be seen.

In Kingston in October, the nights are still warm. Plunkett and Worldhead sat on two steps of the verandah playing checkers. Wilbert listened to the music and asked occasional questions about the lyrics. "Who is Mrs. Robinson?" "Where is this Scarborough Fair? Do they have rides there?" Wilbert and I took turns playing chess with Michael Winters. Michael was the oldest office boy at sixteen. He was a concern to the sisters. He suffered from sickle-cell anemia and his left leg was turned outward, causing him to limp. Although he took longer to run errands, he was one of the most articulate boys at Alpha, speaking with the same clear diction and deliberate intonation that Sister Ignatius used. The sisters had arranged for Michael to spend one weekend each month with Mrs. Samuelson, a widow, in another part of Kingston. Mrs. Samuelson was getting older and wanted someone to help her with errands and household chores. The goal was to get Michael and Mrs. Samuelson used to each other so that when Michael aged out of Alpha at 18, he could move in with her. He had been visiting her for about six months already and the relationship seemed to be working. However, the time he spent living in a real home had given him a taste for the "finer things" as he put it. At Alpha, he had started to comment on the food, compare his bench on the verandah with Mrs. Samuelson's plush sofa, or talk about the wonderful shows he watched on her color TV. It only took one shove and a threatened beating from the other boys to teach him not to put on airs. Although Michael's sickle cell caused him daily pain and discomfort, this year it would also provide him with an unexpected opportunity.

Where to place the boys when they left Alpha was a constant challenge. Since Sister Ignatius was in charge of the Senior Home, she was responsible for making sure the boys weren't just turned out on the street. The boys couldn't go home to family if "home" was unknown and "family" was an ambiguous term. Because the boys had grown up in an institution, Sister Ignatius did her best to get them placed into another

– the Jamaican military. But the army wasn't the right fit for everyone. Nevertheless, without exception, every boy was gone by his eighteenth birthday. Without the firm deadline, some of the boys would have hung on forever. Even though they wanted the security of the place, the older boys resisted the restrictions and tested the boundaries too much, as would be natural. They created an unsafe and unhealthy atmosphere for the younger ones. Their added comfort and security didn't justify their impact on the smooth running of the operation.

As Wilbert and I played checkers, Michael read The Daily Gleaner, Kingston's main newspaper. "What's the news today," I asked. The Gleaner covered not only local news, but always seemed to search the world's newspapers for the most arcane stories.

"My Lord, sir! This headline says, '80 Year Old Woman Carries Mummified Fetus for 60 years! Lord almighty!"

"Dat not possible!" Plunkett said. "Is dat possible, Mr. Solomon? Read da rest a da story," he said to Michael. After that headline, I couldn't image there was much left to tell, but Michael read on anyway. "It happened in Mexico," he started, and conveyed the entire one paragraph story, trying to emulate a reporter's detached tone, but betraying a young man's disgust. When he finished, he made the sign of the cross. I'm not sure if it was a short prayer for the baby, or to ward off its evil spirits.

"Dat's what happened to my mudda," Wilbert said, to no one in particular.

"You mudda carry a baby inside her for 60 years?" Worldhead asked.

When impatient, a Jamaican boy will "kiss his teeth," with a loud and juicy "tsk."

"No," Wilbert sneered, kissing his teeth and waving away the comment. "My brudda died inside her. When de doctors went to take him out, she died too."

My eyes widened at his story, not because of its content, but because of its delivery, a factual recounting of a family history, not a plea for pity or a measured mourning.

"I'm so sorry to hear that, Wilbert." I was surprised the other boys didn't express condolences as well, but they all carried their own sorrows, and didn't dwell on them, at least not publicly.

"I was only a little boy at the time," he continued. "I never really knew her. After a few years, my grandmudda couldn't care for me anymore, so she brought me 'ere.'"

"Here's another one," Michael jumped in, folding back another page of The Gleaner. "Man Gets New Nose from Pig's Ear." Dateline, Shanghai. None of the boys had a story about a family member getting a new nose, so after we heard the details, our conversations drifted back to the checkers and card games. All year, I would learn about the boys' lives in snippets. They shared facts, but since we were always in a group, the feelings behind the memories stayed private. The hurt and the loneliness, the sense of injustice and, perhaps, betrayal, had to be there, but were usually belied by the straightforward telling of the stories and the tone of voice that said, "That's just the way it is." And that's just the way it was at Alpha: no griping, no complaining, no self-pity. Just acceptance and perseverance.

When it was Wilbert's turn to play against Michael, I moved to another bench and corrected English papers from one of the classes I taught at St. George's. During my senior year at BC, when my friends and I applied to BC's International Volunteer Program, they sought to go to Central America. Since I didn't speak Spanish, I thought I would be more useful elsewhere. In 1984, Option B was Jamaica.

During my first year in Kingston, I lived with five other BC teachers in a small four-bedroom house in the Vinyardtown neighborhood, a two mile walk to St. George's. My roommates and I grew close as we learned to deal with the typical headaches experienced by first-year teachers and the typical heartaches of living away from the security and comfort of home.

That first year, I passed Alpha on the way to and from school. In the morning I saw the boys tending the garden, slowly walking single file through the rows of scallions and calaloo. In the afternoon, I heard their shouts from the soccer field. The Alpha compound was close to St. George's, and seemed like a convenient place for me to bring a group of George's boys for their ministry project. After introducing myself to the sisters and getting their permission, I started bringing St. George's boys to Alpha to teach the younger boys soccer or just read with them. The boys had a lot in common, but all of the boys at George's returned to their homes each night.

The George's boys volunteered at Alpha the entire first year I lived in Kingston, and while some of them enjoyed it, and some tolerated it, I fell in love with the place. With its vegetable gardens and open, albeit dusty, playfields, Alpha was a spacious and agrarian retreat in the middle of a bustling city. On the days when I didn't bring George's students in the afternoon, I visited in the evening to read bedtime stories. The story hour had become my favorite part of the day. I had held a job and lived with roommates before. Those elements of life were not new. But my role at Alpha was vague and undefined, and therefore, unique.

In May of 1985, as the school term ended, the other BC teachers made their plans for the following year. My roommates planned to move further away from downtown. If I had moved with them, my commute to St. George's would be difficult and reading to the boys in the evening impossible. But by the end of that first year, I needed the story hour to maintain my sanity. It was the antidote to the challenge of a day of teaching. It renewed my energy and replenished my spirit. I realized I could not be in Kingston without it. In order to keep teaching at St. George's, I had to move in at Alpha. I moved in without any plan, just with the knowledge that I liked being there and that it made my life more convenient. It took Sister Magdalen only a few days to get her Mother Superior to approve. "It'll be good for both of you," she said, when she gave me the news. I smiled, not quite sure what she meant at the time.

The other BC teachers from my year challenged me on whether it was the right move, pointing out that I would, in many ways, be living alone. But at the time, it seemed like the only logical choice. As a child, I attended five different grade schools, mostly as a result of widespread closing of Catholic parochial schools during the 1960s. I realized much later in life that my grade school transience had taught me to let go of people and relationships easily. I learned that year at Alpha that friends can come and go, but a child who disappears on your watch can haunt you forever.

When I was growing up in a large Irish-Italian family, most of the activity – the loud conversations, the storytelling, the laughter - took place in the kitchen. At Alpha, most of the activity took place on the verandah, where you had the best chance to catch even the slightest breeze. It was here I would get to know the boys and so many other people. And it was on the verandah that I would witness acts of kindness and cruelty, acts of mercy and forgiveness. The pipe was the source of water, which brought life. The verandah was the source of community, which gave that life meaning.

After a month living at Alpha, I was beginning to interpret the sounds of the community. The minivan buses versus the full-size vehicles; whether the dog's bark was coming from Junior Home, or from across the street; the footsteps of the various Office Boys; the occasional gunshot, usually from the TV upstairs in the convent, but occasionally from the neighborhood across South Camp Road; Sister Ignatius' footsteps - all were becoming the background noise of the evening.

From our perches on the verandah, the boys and I heard the door of the convent open, and the familiar sound of Sister Ignatius' heels on the porch above our heads. Plunkett and Michael stopped and looked up, waiting to be called. Wilbert and Worldhead kept their concentration on their games. But Sister Ignatius just walked around the corner of the porch to the top of the stairs and placed what sounded like a large plastic bag near the gate and returned inside the convent.

Sister Ignatius was tall and exceedingly thin. She was a perfectionist who spoke slowly in a high-end tone, the Jamaican patois version of the Queen's English. She rarely showed any emotion in her voice except, occasionally, disgust when things did not move smoothly. She enunciated every syllable, a trait she learned when attending Immaculate Conception High School in another part of Kingston, where Irene now taught. Apparently, the Dominican nuns who ran that school were disappointed when Ignatius decided to join the Sisters of Mercy instead of their order. (I think the Dominicans would have preferred she just leave the Church altogether rather than join a different order.)

Upstairs, Ignatius walked down the short hall in the convent, passing two small bedrooms on the left and one on the right. Each bedroom door had an open lattice-work transom above it to allow breezes to flow. Sisters Ignatius and Marie Therese slept in the two rooms on the left. Since Magdalen slept up at Junior Home each evening, Marie Therese had turned the third bedroom into a small office.

The hall led to an open living space where the three sisters, all in their sixties, relaxed in the evening. There were four metal chairs and a Formica table trimmed in aluminum. High above, suspended from the peaked ceiling, a wide-blade fan rotated slowly. A countertop with a stove and sink ran along the back wall. Thin curtains hung on the windows by the table. Pictures of Pope John Paul II and Mother MacCauley, the founder of the Sisters of Mercy in Jamaica, hung on the wall in the hall. The whole setting was simple and functional.

The sisters did not cook for themselves. Because they were busy tending to the boys until late in the evening, dinner was always sent up from the main convent at the other end of the compound, down by the girls' high school, where another dozen sisters lived. After eating, Magdalen, the youngest and spryest of the three, would clean the dishes and talk about the boys. Magdalen was considerably shorter than Ignatius, and although not stocky, more solidly built. She also moved quickly and occasionally at a frenetic pace, a dramatic counterpoint to Ignatius' slow and steady gait.

Ignatius sat down in a large cushioned chair off to the side, put her feet up on a small foot stool, opened <u>The Gleaner</u>, and pretended to listen to Magdalen's stories while she read, starting with the horoscopes. Marie Therese, the oldest of the three and the official head of Alpha Boys School, sat at the table with a long ledger in front of her going over some numbers. The light over the table wasn't very strong, and she squinted to see the numbers correctly, rubbing her eyes often.

"Magdalen, did you see the letter from your brother, Louis, today?" Marie Therese asked as she thumbed through the day's mail.

"No, did he write?" Magdalen quickly dried her hands and walked to the table. "I always tell him in my letters that he needs to write more often," she said, holding the envelope carefully. "I love the stamps from Malta. That's Valetta in the picture," she said to no one in particular. She put the envelope down on the table without opening it, and returned to finish the dishes. "The refrigerator in the kitchen is still having problems, Ignatius," she said over her shoulder, referring to the large walk-in cooler that held most of the food for the boys.

"I will call the repairman in the morning," Ignatius said from behind her paper.

Marie Therese flipped to the next page in her ledger and privately worried where she would get the money for a new refrigerator. As in any household, the sisters each had their roles. In my own family, my father would have been lying on his back on the kitchen floor, whistling as he fixed the pipe under the sink, while my mother fretted over the check book, wondering how much the plumber would charge to fix whatever additional damage my father was causing.

"The bread delivery was short again today," Magdalen added from the sink. "I have to watch that delivery man like a hawk. He always tries to cheat me."

"I am going to visit family this weekend, Magdalen," Ignatius said. "I will be gone on Saturday afternoon."

Many people struggle for balance between their work and their personal life. The sisters seemed to accomplish this naturally, even though "work" lived downstairs.

When Magdalen finished the dishes, she and Ignatius joined Marie Therese at the table and the three sisters said their evening prayers. Marie Therese said goodnight and retired to her small room. Ignatius returned to her chair, "Why don't we see what is on the television this evening," she said, as if she hadn't just seen her favorite police drama in the TV listing in The Gleaner. Magdalen turned on the TV and sat in one of the chairs at the table, putting her feet up on another chair. Ignatius loved police dramas and westerns. Magdalen would watch anything Ignatius had on, and in exchange, Ignatius would listen to Magdalen's stream of consciousness about how silly or violent or absurd or beautiful a particular scene or character or line or plot seemed to her.

Downstairs, we didn't have a television, so when I finished correcting papers, I helped Plunkett build his puzzle for a while and then played the most recent winner at chess. Our evenings on the verandah were the quietest part of my day. It's not normal to live with a few hundred people. But our small group on the verandah, under the convent porch, felt like a family. In 1985, my younger brother back home was fifteen, the same age as Wilbert, and a year younger than Michael. In the company of these boys, I played older brother. I gave them access to games and music, and they gave me the comfort of home.

As I listened to the boys' stories during our many nights on the verandah, I knew I would never really know their world, could never experience their lives without the safety and resources of my own. I would never truly be a part of the orphanage; I would exist only on its periphery. They, for their part, would never be able to escape having grown up there. The relationships they built, with each other and with those of us on the outside, would keep them from being alone in life, but would always be filtered through the prism of life in an institution. We were all on the edge of the orphanage, some looking in, and some out.

At nine o'clock, we heard Ignatius' footsteps again. This time, the boys scrambled to pack up their games. Ignatius stepped back out onto the porch overhead, leaned over the railing and called down to the boys.

"All right boys. You may turn in now. Come where I can see you to say goodnight."

Since we were sitting on the verandah below her, each boy dashed out a few feet from the steps and looked up at her. "Yes, Sister," they each replied. They liked that she wanted to personally see them every night. They didn't realize she was checking to make sure none had wandered off or gone to bed early.

"Plunkett, come to the top of the stairs. I have a bag for you to carry up to Junior Home for Sister Magdalen. The rest of you can go back to your dormitories." As Plunkett raced up the stairs, the other boys said their goodnights and finished packing up their games.

"Is that you down there as well, Mr. Jay?"

"Yes, Sister," I replied, stepping out into view.

"It is very beautiful music on the tape, Mr. Jay. We can hear it upstairs."

I couldn't tell if her compliment was really a rebuke for playing the music so loudly that it disturbed their evening. I looked up at her leaning over the railing of the convent porch. Ignatius wore the same uniform every day – a cream-colored tunic that reached almost to her ankles, a black shoulder-length habit and black shoes with a slight heel, like Marie Therese. Since the upstairs verandah was technically part of the convent, Ignatius had taken off her habit. Her close-cropped gray hair was matted from a day under wraps in a hot Caribbean sun, and she looked younger, more comfortable and more accessible than when she wore the habit.

"Mr. Jay," she continued. "Tomorrow, we will have other guests staying in the visitor flat over the Senior home. Will you be around tomorrow?"

"Yes, Sister, I don't have any plans."

"Good. We will probably have a special dinner then tomorrow evening."

"I look forward to it, Sister." A *special dinner* meant we would be ordering takeout Chinese food, Ignatius' favorite. She loved her General

Tso's chicken. We ordered the same Chinese takeout every time there was a visitor at Alpha.

I packed up my papers and grading book. Wilbert and Michael went around the corner to the Senior Home dormitory. Worldhead reached through the open window of the office turned out the single light bulb over the benches. Then he joined Plunkett and Magdalen at the base of the stairs and the three of them headed up the path to Junior Home. They all knew their part in this school play, and the choreography was the same every night.

My room was just inside the verandah, in the library, just off the main office area. Calling the space a library was a stretch. It was a large open space used for an occasional gathering, like the special dinner we would have the following evening. Low bookcases lined the walls, under the windows. My room was sectioned off from the main hall with plywood walls and a flat dropped-ceiling within the high peaked roof of the library. This inner roof helped muffle the overwhelming rattle when a heavy rain would pound the high zinc roof. It also kept the boys from getting into my room during the day and stealing things.

In addition to my bed with its mosquito netting, I had a wardrobe for my clothes, a small kitchen table and two chairs, a propane tank and cook-top to make breakfast, a refrigerator, and a small shelf for food. It was more space than I had had in my dorm at BC, but still Spartan by any standard. I had my own bathroom, with a small sink, barely big enough to shave in, a toilet, and a stall shower. The shower seemed odd, with only one knob in the middle – for cold water. In the house where some of my fellow BC volunteers lived, the shower had a knob for hot water as well. There wasn't actually any hot water – the builder simply installed the plumbing should the owner of the house ever be able to afford a water heater. Even so, just having the extra knob to turn made you feel better. You could pretend the water was actually warming up, even if your body was simply adjusting to the water temperature. I had only the one knob, so there wasn't any pretending for me.

I sat at my table in my boxer shorts and read the latest edition of <u>Time</u> magazine that I had on hand, already two months old, while I listened to the BBC evening report, the main radio news in Jamaica. It always made me feel like I was somewhere exotic to hear the BBC broadcast, but I found the sign-off disconcerting, if not downright inaccurate, since the newscaster paused in the wrong place. Each evening, instead of saying, "And that's the end...of the world news," he would say, "And that's the end-of-the-world...news." A bit pessimistic, I thought. But I was only a second year English teacher. Who was I to argue with the BBC?

Late evenings could be lonely and it was hard not to worry about the boys. But too much reflection can be unhealthy. I realized early on that I needed a distraction. I decided to read the Bible – even outline it, to *really* learn it. Using a spiral notebook, I began, of course, with Genesis. I jotted down the chapter and verse, and one line about the content. I lost interest before Noah finished the ark.

Then I decided to say the rosary each evening. That lasted a week. Instead of killing time, it just made me feel more alone. It also felt forced. My prayer life was then limited to shorter bursts of gratitude, or pleas for strength, or searches for wisdom, depending on the need at the moment. But, then I found the Prayer of St. Francis, and something about its powerful challenge stuck with me. I made that my nightly ritual, though I struggled to get through even that short prayer uninterrupted.

Lord, make me a channel of your peace.

Where there is hatred, let me sow love.

These boys aren't hated. Hatred takes energy. Indifference is the bigger threat to love in these boys' lives.

Where there is injury, pardon,

Where there is doubt, faith.

Where there is despair, hope.

Malcolm doesn't feel despair. I feel it for him. God, what hope is there for him?

Where there is darkness, light.

Where there is sadness, joy.

*Joy. How do these kids smile? Even once? They have nothing. Maybe
ignorance is bliss.*

Oh divine Master,

Let me not seek so much to be consoled, as to console.

To be understood, as to understand.

To be loved, as to love.

Love is easy. But love is fleeting. It's loving <u>consistently</u> that's hard.

For it is in giving that we receive,

It is in pardoning that we are pardoned,

And it is in dying that we are born into eternal life.

Clearly, whatever calling I would find at Alpha would not be as a
contemplative monk. Contemplation requires concentration, and I had
the attention span of a gnat.

I stared up through the mosquito netting at the shadows on the
ceiling, cast by the light of the streetlamp just outside my window. I
wondered how I had had the good fortune to end up as part of this
community, for however long I would be here.

I was about to doze off when a slight breeze came through the window,
causing a shimmer across the mosquito netting, and I remembered my
final ritual for the evening. I slid out of bed, out from under the netting
and went in the bathroom for a handful of toilet paper. I climbed back
onto the bed and stood up in the center of the mosquito netting, where
it fanned out from a center ring which hung from the ceiling. I used the
toilet paper to carefully wipe the small spiders out of the peak of the net.
Now I could sleep.

* * *

Plunkett's end-of-day ritual followed its own pattern. He arrived
back at Junior Home with Sister Magdalen, who always had one or two
small chores left for the day. As they walked into the dormitory, she

sent Benjamin, the Senior Home boy on duty, back to his dorm. A few children who were still awake peeked up from their beds said a quick, "Good night, sista."

She whispered a quick, "Hush now! Go to sleep," and waved them away.

"Plunkett, put that bag here in my office," she instructed him in hushed tones, since many of the boys were already asleep. "Lock the screen door and turn out the bathroom light when you are finished. Good night."

"Yes, sista." Good night, sista."

"Oh, and say your prayers."

"Yes, sista," he nodded.

Magdalen walked up and down each aisle, seeing who was already asleep and who needed to be covered. Once she was sure everyone was safely in bed, she quietly closed her door.

Plunkett locked the two eye-hooks on the screen door, which constituted the security for Junior Home. After finishing in the bathroom, he turned off the bathroom light, walked the perimeter of the dormitory so he could check on his brother, Wayne, and went to bed. The main lights in the dormitory were already out for the evening, so it was too dark for him to read a book. Instead, he lay in bed and stared at the ceiling. He recited the Lord's Prayer in barely a whisper. Then, a soft melody would seep into his head; when Desmond and Wayne were small, their mother would sing them Jamaican spirituals based on her favorite part of the Bible, the Book of Psalms. She especially loved Psalm 91.

> *Whoever dwells in the shelter of the Most High*
> *will rest in the shadow of the Almighty.*
> *I will say of the Lord, "he is my refuge and my fortress,*
> *My God, in whom I trust.*

The sound of her voice was seared into his memory.

> *Surely he will save you*

from the fowler's snare
and from the deadly pestilence.
He will cover you with his feathers,
and under his wings you will find refuge.
His faithfulness will be your shield and rampart.

Also seared into his consciousness was the painful, confusing moment when he and Wayne arrived home from school one day and she was gone.

Desmond Plunkett grew up in Annotto Bay, in St. Mary's Parish on the east coast of Jamaica. His father and mother were together, and apart, for more than twenty years, during which time, they had eight children together. Desmond and Wayne were the youngest. The family moved from one small house to another, the moves coinciding with times when money was tightest. Desmond longed for just one place to call home. Desmond and Wayne shared a bedroom with their sixteen-year-old brother, Trevor, the crowded conditions only exacerbating the stifling heat of the small room. In the mornings, their mother would ready them all for school, preparing a small bowl of oatmeal, served with a tired smile before she sent them out the door. Even as a small boy, Desmond could feel the sadness in his mother's heart, although he didn't know its source. Their father was never with them at breakfast, having left already for his job at the St. Mary Parish Council.

Desmond was responsible for walking Wayne, the two miles to and from school, protecting him from bigger boys who would prey on them for fun. Although he learned a good defensive posture, it didn't keep him from taking the occasional beating.

A month before Christmas, when Plunkett was nine years old, he and Wayne walked home from school with their mostly-empty book bags on their shoulders. They were surprised to see their father sitting in the doorway of their house. He had never been home early before.

"Your mother's gone," he said. "She won't be coming back. She doesn't love you anymore." Their questions were met with angry commands to be quiet. Desmond thought those first few days would be the worst, as they adjusted to their new routine. Their father woke them the each morning and made an effort to fix breakfast. But by the next week, he needed to leave early for work, and Trevor was at the helm. Trevor did his best, but was barely able to manage himself, let alone his siblings. On his own, their father couldn't hold the family together. Desmond's sisters soon went to live with relatives, and other brothers moved in with neighbors. Desmond and Wayne were sent to Homestead, a children's home in Stony Hill, St. Andrew Parish, and then shortly thereafter, to Alpha. Desmond did his best to protect Wayne during the moves and the uncertainty.

And now, Sister Magdalen had mentioned to him that he would soon move again, this time from Junior Home to Senior Home, with the other boys his age. Plunkett wasn't just concerned about being in a different dorm than Wayne, and spending less of his time with his brother. Rather, he was more frightened by the prospect of being around older boys. A number of them looked the same size as Trevor, and he knew that some were very comfortable beating on the weaker boys. Plunkett didn't realize that he had grown quite a bit physically since coming to Alpha, and that the relative size difference between him and the older boys was not the same as it was with Trevor three years ago.

Desmond's bed was just beneath one of the windows that looked out onto the verandah. At night, the lamppost outside the dormitory that lit the way from Junior Home to Senior Home shone through the metal louvers, casting shadows on the support column near Desmond's bed. Every night for more than two years, Desmond lay in bed counting the louvers by staring at their shadows – always the same eight louvers, the same eight lines of shadow on the wall. But tonight, Desmond noticed something new. Because of the vertical bars supporting the louvers, the shadow was actually a series of crosses. Eight louvers, two support bars, causing what looked like dozens of crosses on the column near his bed. He thought of the Jamaican spirituals. He thought of the cross Christ bore. He thought of Christ's suffering, and the suffering him own mother must have felt at leaving her family, and the suffering her leaving caused her children. He thought of his mother's Psalm.

You will not fear the terror of night,
nor the arrow that flies by day.

He started that night to associate each cross on the wall with a different cross in his own life. Then, when he looked around the room, he noticed the same pattern of crosses on each column near each window. The Junior Home dorm was awash in crosses to be borne.

5
THE TENSION TREE

The central market is the alarm clock for any town. As the market starts to buzz, the community comes to life. In Kingston, the first sounds of morning were the clanking of the bells on the goats, as they began their daily forage among the litter strewn in the central square. They could always find something in the pile under the large wooden sign advertising the renovation project that would turn the square into a dazzling showcase of urban renewal. The sign had been erected by the Ministry of Development years earlier, and was the only part of the project ever completed.

Mr. Shipman stretched his arms wide as he lay on his back on a thick pad on the ground beneath his cart. He slept under the cart in the market all week, returning to his outer-Kingston neighborhood only on the weekends. He rolled slowly onto the sidewalk, and pulled himself upright, wincing as he arched his back. He was nearing forty and pushing a cart around town all day was taking its toll on his back and legs.

He untied the ropes that held the tarp down over his wide wooden cart and checked his inventory of coconuts; their smooth green husks held his livelihood and, while they were plentiful in the market and therefore, unlikely to be stolen, he counted them anyway, as any good businessman would.

Mr. Shipman had only twenty coconuts left from yesterday. His cart could easily hold two hundred. He rolled up his pad, tied it in a bundle along with his blanket, and secured it under the long handles of the cart.

Then, Mr. Shipman headed toward the market to join a half-dozen other coconut vendors in line at the large truck that had just pulled into the square. Along the way, he passed a small boy stirring awake in a doorway. Mr. Shipman had four children of his own at home, the youngest about this one's age. He stopped, slid a long stalk of sugar cane from the edge of the cart, along the side of the coconuts, cut off a foot-long section and handed it to the boy. Morris took the cane warily, and, keeping one eye on Mr. Shipman, immediately tore off a piece with his teeth. As Mr. Shipman stepped back and resumed his walk to the market, Morris chewed the stalk to a pulp, and spit the first clump onto the sidewalk.

It was Thursday morning. If he filled his cart today, Mr. Shipman would have enough coconuts to last through the weekend. Today, he would make his way through town, sleeping tonight in another part of Kingston, closer to home. But he would make sure to be on North Street by mid-afternoon. Business there had picked up, especially since the new American teachers had come to St. George's.

* * *

Father David F.X. Doyle stepped out of the red-brick Spanish-style Jesuit residence at St. George's College, a boys' high school. His 6'4" frame was weighed down not only by his ample weight, but by a pile of books and papers under one arm, and a large boom-box in the other. He walked past the cars parked just outside the door, beneath the large tree in the center of the parking area. The tree was actually a collection of trees, but over the years the trunks had all melded into one, not unlike the population of Jamaica. In fact, it was unclear whether some of the thin trunks surrounding the thick inner core were trunks running up, or vines running down. It had become impossible to tell which trunk constituted support, and which was burden. Doyle had made the tree, at the center of the school's campus, the subject of many essays for his students; ruminations on the struggle to grow while being held back, on the inherent tensions in life, on the need to band together to survive. Doyle knew how to take something immediate, something staring you in the face every day, and turn it into the profound, into something that made you think. The tree, for its part, shaded the cars beneath it, and, through Doyle's essay assignments, sharpened the minds around it. Like the watchdogs at Alpha, even the plants here had a calling to fulfill. Father Doyle headed to the Third Form block of classrooms.

St. George's was founded by the Jesuits in the 1800s, and had educated the sons of the country's elite for generations. Years later, when the city had spread further north, the Jesuits opened Campion College, and when Campion went coed, some of the more affluent Jamaicans saw it as a better option than heading all the way into downtown Kingston for St. George's. St. George's was still a popular choice and was thriving, but the students were now drawn from all social strata. Some St. George's boys arrived in private cars with private drivers. Others walked from bus stops up to two miles away, saving the fare to add to their meager lunch money.

Each grade, or "form" at St. George's had its own "block," a row of classrooms on a raised concrete platform. Each classroom opened onto a verandah. As Father Doyle arrived at the Third Form block, he interrupted a dozen boys playing cards on the lower verandah. The boys gathered their cards and stood up quietly. Doyle nodded hello, and the boys nodded back. He handed one boy the tape deck and grabbed the stair rail to help himself up to the second floor. The boys followed in silence. Father Doyle was in his late fifties, and had been teaching at St. George's for more than twenty years. His lightweight pale blue shirt hung loose on his shoulders but taut across his considerable middle. By noon he would perspire through both his undershirt and the light blue over-shirt. He was panting heavily by the time he reached the second floor, and handed another boy the key to the room. The boy hurried ahead and opened the door. Doyle had long ago commandeered a storage room, little more than a large closet, next to the classrooms on the second floor, which he had turned into a library and reading room. The walls were lined with fully-stocked shelves. Space was limited, so the boy who opened the door pulled a single school desk and chair out of the room onto the verandah. Father Doyle sat at the desk and plopped down his papers. The boy with the tape deck placed it by the side of the desk. Everyone knew his part in the routine.

In spite of his size, Doyle was a shy man. He carried on conversations easily if engaged and about an academic topic, but didn't seek them out, and he never started them. Like all Jesuits, he had studied for the better part of a decade, earning two Masters degrees and a doctorate, and participating in enough contemplative retreats to last a lifetime, and prepare for an eternity. He had dedicated his life to training boys' minds. So every school day, Doyle sat in his library from 7:00 a.m. until just before classes started, and any boy interested in finding a new book, sitting quietly and reading, was welcome to join him. The door was always open, and the word passed quickly among the boys not to make any noise on the upstairs verandah before classes started. Doyle never raised his voice, so the general quiet seemed a product of respect rather than fear.

From his seat on the verandah, Doyle angled the tape deck to face the library and played classical music softly, so that the boys could read without being distracted. Bach and Brahms were his favorites. The Jesuits at St. George's all came from the what the Jesuits called their "New England Province," and many had roots at BC or Weston Theological Seminary, or both. Doyle's reading room seemed like an attempt to bring a little bit of Boston to Kingston. His reading room was a labor of love, and a little bit of sanity for himself, a little bit of home.

* * *

My morning had its own routine. I had become very adept at making toast by frying two thick slices of HardDough in a pan on the cook top, and I had grown to enjoy the taste of guava jelly in lieu of the strawberry or grape of my childhood. My entire wardrobe for my two years of teaching at St. George's consisted of four pairs of khakis and an assortment of polo shirts. With my knapsack on my shoulder, I headed toward Alpha's main gate. On the way, I'd see the Junior Home boys already working in the garden, large cans of water on their head. From the pipe in the Junior Home garden they walked single file down the rows of banana trees, peas, tomatoes, peppers, onions and calaloo, that formed the buffer between the Junior Home building and the traffic on the street.

"Mr. Solomon, good morning."

"Mr. Solomon, can I have the picture book tonight?"

"Mr. Solomon, can I have a deck of cards at game room this afternoon?" We exchanged waves and I was on my way to my other identity. The boys would soon be having their own breakfast and starting their own school day. I headed left down South Camp Road, a busy artery that connected central Kingston to the waterfront, for my ten-minute walk to school. In the 1980's, almost half of Jamaica's population was under the age of 18. In the morning and late afternoon, the streets teemed with schoolchildren. Almost all of the boys, from six through fifteen, were dressed in khaki pants and matching shirts, only the patch on the shirt pocket identifying the school they attended. The older boys, if they were still in school, traded in their khaki shirts for crisp white shirts, starting to make the transition from school-boy to professional. The girls' uniforms varied in color by school, but were usually plaid jumpers over white shirts. Uniforms are a great equalizer, keeping the wealthier students from showing off, and the poorer students from standing out. But school kids throughout history have managed to figure out ways around any system of control. In Kingston in 1985, defiance exploded in, of all places, shoe laces. All the boys wore black shoes to school, and the expectation, by any reasonable adult, would be to use simple, nondescript black shoe laces. But the kids found shoe laces that were multicolored, or extra wide, or sparkly, or ridiculously long, or, if you were lucky, all of the above. You wore them to brag about your recent trip to visit relatives in Brooklyn or Manchester. You wore them to pretend they were nothing special and that you chose these over your other equally loud pairs because you just felt like it. You wore them to flout the rules, even though the dress code didn't address shoe laces, which is why you got away with it. And the schools debated how to respond. Most just shrugged, knowing that in the greater scheme of acts of defiance, this fad was harmless. But even with their fancy feet, Jamaican school kids were burdened. Since it wasn't usually safe to leave anything at school, most of the kids were weighted down with enormous knapsacks. They carried all of their books with them every day, a tough task considering some of their commutes.

The school kids mixed easily with the adults on the busy streets. While some seemed to wander, as if they were rediscovering their way to school each day, many rushed, dodging quickly between the slower paced adults, as if they were late for class, or, more likely, wanted time to talk to friends before the bell rang.

A few blocks south, South Camp Road intersected with North Street, originally the northern boundary of Kingston. In the 1980s, North Street was the start of a dangerous neighborhood, its narrow, twisting streets creating an ungovernable warren of intractable poverty, where rival gangs affiliated with the two major political parties fought a turf war that no one would ever win. The situation only got worse the closer you got to the waterfront.

Just a block in on North Street sat Holy Trinity Cathedral. As cathedrals go, it was an unusual design. Where most Catholic cathedrals soar to the heavens, Holy Trinity is as wide as it is tall, a massive white-washed stump of a building with a blue copper dome. The Cathedral property borders on St. George's College, separated only by the high wall topped by the barbed wire that surrounds the school.

St. George's collection of classroom and office buildings, a mix of Spanish-colonial and Jamaican poured-concrete architecture, covered about twenty acres. The red-roofed Spanish buildings provided grace and beauty. The concrete structures provided space and shelter. Just inside the main gate lies Winchester Park, the school's soccer field. The Jesuits had received a large donation from an alumnus, an "Old Boy" of the school, to dig a well and irrigation system that kept Winchester Park green all year round, not an easy feat in the dry climate of Kingston. The lush green field spread out in front of the large Jesuit residence. The residence, with its wide second story porch, and rocking chairs overlooking the field, gave the entrance to the school a colonial feel - either charming or disconcerting, depending on your view.

I walked up the main driveway through the campus to calls of, "Good morning, Sir," or, "Good morning, Mr. Sullivan." It felt odd walking out of Alpha as Mr. Solomon, and a few blocks away, walking into St. George's as Mr. Sullivan. But the shift in name was in keeping with the shift in identity and helped me with the change in purpose.

The St. George's boys were the future leaders of the country. They were smart, hoped to go to college, and expected to do well. Many had visited relatives in the U.S. or Great Britain, and had perspective on how people lived in more prosperous places. They were keenly aware of the decisions and the burdens they would face in a few years. Many were convinced they would become soccer stars, and many others had goals that shifted weekly, like all teenage boys. But even those who didn't know exactly who they would become, knew they would become someone – someone who mattered.

The teachers' offices at St. George's were located in a nondescript building behind the Jesuit residence, just past the tree Father Doyle passed each morning. Like many buildings in the tropics, the defining line between "inside" and "outside" was blurred. The only door to the building was open grillwork. Once inside the entrance, the main hall was a verandah, open to an interior courtyard on one side, where a statue of Mary stood amid large bougainvillea bushes. The offices ran along the other wall. I shared a small office with the other English teachers.

My focus was grammar, not literature. I started the year with 40 kids in each class, and 40 textbooks. The kids were from dozens of different neighborhoods in Kingston. The text books were from four different editions. I struggled for a few weeks and then decided I owed it to my students to try to get one complete set of books. Since Father Doyle taught English literature and composition and had been at St. George's forever, I figured he had books stashed in remote corners of the school.

When I arrived at Doyle's reading room, four or five boys sat quietly at the small table reading while another dozen browsed the shelves. A boy approached Doyle with two books in hand. "Mi a have dees two book, fadda?"

"English only here," Doyle said flatly, barely looking up from his own reading. Doyle acknowledged the child's Jamaican patois as a separate language, with its own grammatical rules and constructs. It wasn't less than English, or incorrect English. It was separate and legitimate, but it was not the language spoken at Doyle's reading room, or in his classroom.

The boy repeated his request, "May I borrow these books please, Father?"

Father Doyle pulled out a small notebook and recorded the boy's name and class, the title of the book and the date. Nothing was said about when the books had to be returned. Doyle flipped the pages of the notebook. It contained page after page of names and dates; none of them checked off. Doyle noted who took out books to create the illusion that there would be accountability. But he didn't keep track of whether a book was ever returned. He didn't care if the books ever came back, as long as the boy did. In fact, most of the books were returned, and timely. With a minimum of paperwork and a heavy dose of steadfast reliability, Doyle had created an efficient and effective library; one that dispensed ideas and knowledge and hope.

I showed him the pale green copy of Warriner's English Grammar text in my hand. "In one of my First Form classes, I'm using four different versions of this text. If I could get four more copies of this one, Father,

I would only have to deal with three different versions. It would make things much easier."

"I'll see what I can do," he said. His tone of voice reminded me of the tone I had used with Q when he had asked for string. I knew Fr. Doyle would come through for me.

I glanced at the boys enjoying their few moments of stillness before the day would start in earnest. Here, in the gathering energy of the morning, a select few boys were learning simply to love to learn. Some teachers at St. George's wondered if Doyle was more interested in providing an escape for himself more than an education for the boys. But if the boys benefited, why would Doyle's intent matter? Was this room any different from what I tried to create when reading bedtime stories? When you wield your authority to give someone what *you think* that person should have, is that being generous or being selfish? I thought of the Prayer of St. Francis, and my own version:

Let me not seek so much to be understood, as to understand,

To dictate, as to inspire,

To direct, as to respond.

The boys' behavior was the proof. If no one had come to the room, if Doyle didn't have "regulars," then his set up would not be meeting a need, and would die from lack of use. Since the boys kept coming, they clearly found value in what he had to offer. I wasn't sure they felt the same way about me, and the supposed value I added.

I thanked Father Doyle and headed to the Fourth Form Block, and the most challenging, and therefore most rewarding part of my role at St. George's. It was paramount that I arrive in time with the first bell of the day.

This school year I was not only teaching, but was the Fourth Form Supervisor, basically the Dean of Discipline for the junior class. I had been a disaster at disciplining my classes the previous year, allowing the kids to control the tone in the room and to dictate whether any learning would take place on a given day. But I had learned my lesson. At the start of this school year the Headmaster, Father Jim Hosie, needed a Form Supervisor, and since I knew it was as a disciplinarian that I had the most to learn, I volunteered.

For many of the boys, life was chaotic and unruly outside of school. They couldn't figure out the rules of the game, in part because the rules didn't exist, were not clearly defined, or changed on a whim. Therefore, I decided I would make an unspoken pact with them. I would promise them structure and discipline, and clear consequences if they stepped out of line. I would be consistent and fair. I would be present and on time every day and the rules would be spelled out for them and strictly enforced. In short, they could hold me accountable and I would do the same for them. And it started anew, every day, with each class. It sounded so simple in theory.

Most of the boys scrambled into their classrooms as I approached, but a few remained even as I climbed the stairs. "Let's go, gentlemen - in your classrooms."

All of the classrooms in the Fourth Form opened onto a low verandah shaded by an enormous twisted cotton tree. Each classroom had one door at the front, and another at the back. The wall in between was composed of open cinderblock, which allowed any breeze to pass through, but partially obscured the view so as not to distract the boys. Because the classrooms were all right next to each other, with open doors and open cinderblock walls, any boys wandering up and down the verandah after the bell rang would disturb other classes. Order was important, or no one would learn.

Four of the five homeroom teachers were present, but Mrs. Carruthers was missing again. Mrs. Carruthers was in her late fifties. Although she had been teaching for years, she was new to St. George's. As Form Supervisor, technically, I had authority to call her on her tardiness. As a twenty-three year old, I had barely outgrown pimples as far as she was concerned. In addition, as a white American in Jamaica in 1985, I was often mistaken for a Jesuit novice, a priest in training. In some instances, it gave me an unearned clout. At St. George's, that clout sometimes triggered an unearned resentment with other faculty. Mrs. Carruthers' dismissive tone and condescending smile whenever I spoke with her told me the conversation about her punctuality would be a regular feature of my year.

As I entered Mrs. Carruthers' class to take attendance, Derek Biggar was standing in the doorway, his arms folded, seeming not the least bit worried about my presence. "Take your seat please, Mr. Biggar." He turned his back, arms still folded, and sauntered back to his seat. Derek led the football team and carried himself with an air of entitlement. His younger brother, Eldon, sat in my First Form class, and had the same ego. By the end of September, I had already blown up at both of them. Their arrogance drove me nuts, especially when I thought about the boys back at Alpha. Then I learned that the Biggar boys lived by themselves. Their mother worked in New Jersey and sent money back to support them. Derek was fifteen, and responsible for raising himself and his twelve-year old brother. Although they were at George's, they were almost as orphaned as some of the boys at Alpha. By October, I had already learned to cut him some slack.

I took attendance and warned the boys to stay seated while I checked on Mrs. Carruthers, my first - but not last - wasted breath of the day. Fr. Hosie, the Principal, walked by as I stepped out of the room.

"Mrs. Carruthers is missing again," I reported.

Father Hosie stepped into the class, surveyed the situation, sighed heavily and wrote an assignment on the board to keep the boys busy. Mrs. Carruthers taught history and Father Hosie immediately crafted an essay assignment around exactly what her class should have been learning at that point. Had Mrs. Carruthers taught algebra or chemistry, Father Hosie would still have known exactly what to assign the boys.

The Fourth Form verandah ended at the door of Father Hosie's office. The Fourth Form at any Jamaican school was notorious for having the most difficult behavior problems, mostly because the boys were fourteen or fifteen years old, a particularly tough time in adolescence. Having the principal's office an ever-looming threat just outside their classes was no coincidence. The Jesuits were strategic thinkers and they thought of just about everything.

Father Hosie's office had a small reception area with four metal chairs against the outside wall. The Jamaican flag stood in one corner, and, in the other, the school's flag, with St. George atop a rearing horse, sword drawn to slay the dragon. Although the air conditioner kept the room from being too still, you could taste the ink from the mimeograph machine the moment you walked in.

Behind the long deep counter sat the two office secretaries. Mrs. Southern, the lead secretary, was a light skinned Jamaican who had been at the school long enough to "remember when these boys came from *good* homes and knew how to *respect* people. Now they're just a bunch of animals."

Mrs. Patchett, a petite, soft-spoken woman, had a son in the Second Form. Her nimble mind helped Father Hosie coordinate the schedules of the 1100 boys in the school. Her pleasant disposition and sweet tone stood in stark contrast to Mrs. Southern's sharp tongue.

Mrs. Patchett said that Mrs. Carruthers had not called in sick. She would spend the next twenty minutes figuring out how to cover Mrs. Carruthers' classes, an exercise at which she had plenty of practice.

As I left to head up to the First Form block to teach my first period class, Fr. Hosie returned to Mrs. Carruthers' class and gave them a longer assignment that would keep them occupied for most of the period. Another day was underway.

I taught grammar and composition, so I wasn't the favorite part of anyone's day. But Mr. Lund, my sophomore English teacher at Pleasantville High School in New York, had been my favorite teacher, and taught me not just the grammar rules, but to enjoy language for its own sake.

At times, teaching young Jamaican boys to focus on subject-verb agreement or whether to use a colon or semicolon seemed an absurd use of their time. But to form a sentence is to structure a thought. And to organize a paragraph is to build an argument. And to write a story is to put an event into context within a life. Teaching them to write was teaching them to reason. If I could play a small part in helping them accomplish that, it was worth the many battles over "that" and "which" and "its" and "it's." I wanted them to love to learn, just as I was learning to love being a teacher.

When I walked into my First Form classroom, all of the eleven and twelve year-old students scrambled to their feet to stand on the left side of their desks. The boys' desks were arranged in four rows of ten, each row connected by long wooden slats on the floor. The desks looked like they were U.S. surplus, something you would see in a picture of a classroom in Kansas during the dustbowl. At the front of the room was a raised wooden platform, about six inches high, with a small table for the teacher. The platform was just big enough to fit the table, so if you were in the habit of walking while talking to the class, you had to constantly watch where you were or you would either fall off the platform or trip over it as you walked around it.

The whole "desk-on-a-platform" thing was new to me. It felt oddly colonial, overly authoritarian, even somewhat oppressive. Part of me felt that if I needed the added stature of a platform to have any authority in class, I wasn't doing my job well. On the other hand, the room was so deep, it was helpful to have the added height to keep an eye on the boys in the back of the room.

A blackboard covered the entire front wall. No maps, posters, charts or pictures hung on the wall. The only decoration was a simple crucifix mounted high in the center above the blackboard. The cinderblock walls were painted dark green from the waist down and a lighter shade above. There was electric power in the rooms, but it only came on in the evening when the lights were turned on for adult evening classes. Otherwise, the bright Caribbean sun was considered strong enough to illuminate the process of enlightening the minds.

"Good morning class," I said.

"Good morning, Mr. Sullivan," they responded.

"In the name of the Father," I started, and on cue each boy joined in and recited The Lord's Prayer, then took his seat.

"Let's get started," I said. I introduced the lesson on pronouns. "Take out your Warriner's grammar texts, please." Most of the textbooks the boys had were hand-me-downs from schools in the States. "Those of you with the yellow books, the exercise is on page 43. Those of you with the green version, it's on page 48. If your book is orange, turn to page 40. And blue – you're on 51. While I collect your homework, everyone please answer the first five of the ten sentences in that exercise." I wandered up and down the rows of desks collecting essays and making sure each boy was doing the assignment. Five classes a day, three with the First Form and two with the Fourth Form. Two hundred students in all. Lots of papers. Lots of pronouns. Lots of perseverance and patience.

As children and young adults, even up through college, we spend a great deal of our lives in classrooms, but always from the perspective of the student. Being a teacher, up in front of the room, I felt as if I was standing out in the heavens, looking back on the planet I had grown up on, and I was amazed at the view. I had spent so much time my first year of teaching just maintaining discipline, I hadn't had time to appreciate the role. This year I gave myself permission to enjoy the experience. Looking out at my class, all the boys with their heads down, pencils in hand, working hard, I started to understand things that hadn't made sense to me as a child. In grade school, teachers seemed to like the smartest kids and the most difficult kids, and I had never been in either group. I was in the vast middle of the bell curve, the kid you notice occasionally but not especially; the kid who didn't stand out, and didn't speak up.

In my sixth grade class at Gardner's School in Swansea, Massachusetts, Mrs. Rose wrote a graduation play anticipating our twenty-year class reunion. Each kid returned as a huge success at whatever he or she had shown an aptitude for as a student. The boy who played the guitar came back as a rock star. The girl who aced the science fair came back as a scientist who won a Nobel Prize. Mrs. Rose cast me as the waiter in the restaurant where we held the reunion. I was dead center on the bell curve.

I realized from my new vantage point at the front of the class, that although some students get more attention, the teacher is aware of all of them. I knew which kids doodled on their text books, which ones never wore socks, and which ones picked their noses. And I was conscious of my awareness, conscious of how I was becoming more of a professional.

"Let's take a look at some sentences up here on the board. Brandon, please read me your first sentence."

* * *

I had the last period of the day free, so I sat at my desk in the faculty room correcting papers and talking with a few of the other teachers. When the final bell rang, I headed to the Fourth Form block to run the detention room for any Fourth Form boys who had gotten into trouble that day. As I passed the tree of many trunks and vines, Father Doyle walked past carrying his papers and boom box.

"Stop by the reading room tomorrow, Jay. I'll have something for you," he said as he pushed the door of the residence open with his back.

In the detention room, I helped a few boys with their homework, discussed with a few others why they had misbehaved, coached a few on how to write better essays, and generally killed forty-five minutes. Then I packed up my work and headed down the long driveway to the front gate.

I had an odd feeling of excitement. The school year was underway, and I felt I knew what I was doing. I would still make mistakes, but the kids would learn. Teaching wasn't hard. The hard part was getting the mood in the classroom right so that learning could take place, and I felt as if I was off to a good start. As I left school that day, I felt as if I was in my first real grown-up job, doing something that mattered. At St.

George's, my responsibility was tangible. I had a title and a defined role. My success could be quantified by my students' success. I could be held accountable, and that made the job real. But I was twenty-three, and grateful that my "real" job was over for the day, and that I could head back to my pretend job at Alpha.

St. George's main driveway was bordered on one side by the Fourth, Fifth and Sixth Form blocks, and on the other side by Winchester Park. Before the school day started, and in the afternoon, after classes let out, dozens of boys would sit on the low wall that bordered the field and watch the soccer team practice, or play cards with friends, or just wait for their parents to pick them up. As I left school that afternoon at my usually full-out New Yorker pace, one of my First Form students called out, "See you tomorrow, Mr. Sullivan." I waved in acknowledgement.

Shortly before classes let out for the day, Mr. Shipman arrived with his coconut cart just outside the main gate. He had already covered his usual stops along North Street; the shady side of Bustamante Hospital in the morning, across from The Gleaner at lunch time, and at George's by mid-afternoon. He always positioned his cart so the hibiscus flower painted on the side faced the school's main gate. Mr. Shipman's wife had painted the flower. He thought the painting made his cart seem more inviting.

As I passed through the gate, Mr. Shipman smiled warmly, and gave a thoughtful nod of his head as I passed. "Come, fadda," he waved me over to him. "You look like you need a drink today."

I stopped at his cart and nodded a hello. He picked out a large green nut, about one and a half times the size of a man's head. Holding it in one hand with the narrow end of the coconut pointing up, he grabbed his machete and with three deft strokes, he chopped the husk into a point. Then, he repositioned the coconut in his hand, and with one smooth stroke, cut the point off, to open a small hole in the nut buried inside the husk. Mr. Shipman was quite skilled and could open the hole without spilling a drop of the water inside. The first few times I bought a coconut,

Mr. Shipman would offer me a straw, but I always refused. I enjoyed the feel of the occasional wayward drop of coconut water running down my chin and neck.

Had I taken a job in Boston or New York after graduation, or gone directly on to law school, my afternoon break would have been at the water cooler in some office, not out of a coconut shell. My fair Irish skin prevented me from being much of a beach person, but that didn't mean I couldn't enjoy living in the tropics.

After I drained the coconut, I handed it back to Mr. Shipman who shaved off a hand-sized disk of the husk. He placed the coconut on the chopping block on the back of the cart and with one quick stroke of the machete, cut the coconut in two, exposing the inside of the nut. Depending on how ripe the coconut was, the inside of the nut had either a thin layer of clear jelly, barely more than liquid, or a thick layer of white coconut meat. Today it was somewhere in between, a cream colored, sweet-tasting jelly that I could scrape off the inside of the nut using the wedge of husk that Mr. Shipman had cut for me. Even though the coconut water was warm, it was refreshing and a wonderful treat on a hot afternoon. It's odd how quickly the extraordinary loses its sheen; how quickly we forget to be amazed at our surroundings. My afternoon coconut was my reality check, my reminder to say a soft, "Wow."

* * *

Richard followed close by Q's side to deliver a set of keys to Mr. Herman, who ran the front office. Magdalen usually chose Q for quick errands because she felt most comfortable that he wouldn't get into trouble or wander off along the way. Richard snuck along, eager for a break from the routine at Junior Home. Richard fixed his eyes on the dirt path in front of him, avoiding eye contact with anyone who might challenge why he was leaving the Junior Home grounds. As they walked by the Senior Home refectory, they could hear strains of Jamaica's national anthem as the band began afternoon practice. They veered off course to sneak a peek. Both Q and Richard wanted to be in the band, Q hoping to play the trumpet, and Richard the drums. They peered around the doorway to see the band leader waving his arms, but not for more than a few beats before he would have to stop to correct a boy. There were always new boys joining the band, so the levels of experience differed dramatically. Q and Richard watched for only a minute before a Senior Home boy walking by called to them.

"What you two doing there?" he asked.

"Nuttin," Q said, defiantly, while Richard stared wide-eyed.

The older boy took a quick step toward them, feigning a punch. Q and Richard ran toward the office, with the laughter of the Senior Home boy ringing in their ears.

Mr. Herman's office was off the reception room, just inside the verandah. In the reception room a pair of couches faced each other, flanked by two side chairs to form a conversation area. The double doors that opened onto the verandah formed most of the front wall. The tile on the floor had a faded gold vine forming a pattern on a maroon background. Two of the Senior Home boys had the job of cleaning the floor by hand each day. As with many jobs at Alpha, polishing the floor was more about keeping so many boys busy and out of trouble than with a fastidiousness about cleanliness.

On the right, flanking the door to the small chapel, stood large display cases of trophies and awards received by the boys over Alpha's hundred-year history. Honors received by the band shared the shelves with pictures of a much younger Marie Therese standing next to Edmund Seaga when he was Prime Minister, and next to the Honorable Florizel Glaspole, Queen Elizabeth's Representative on the island. In decades-old black and white photographs, groups of boys stood smiling on the steps of one of the school buildings flanked by four nuns. The picture that always stood out to me was taken in the Senior Home refectory. All of the boys were seated at their tables with their dinners in front of them.

Every one of the hundred boys in the picture sat upright with his hands on the table, his focus on the camera. Along the side of the room stood more than a dozen nuns in long habits, each with her hands folded neatly in front of her. I tried to imagine what it would have been like to live at Alpha in those days, when nuns were plentiful, and peace and order reigned supreme. I imagined that the nuns in that picture expected that this world they had built for the boys would endure in that form forever. But that could have been nothing more than my naïve assumption. They were wise woman and knew the world changes constantly.

When the boys arrived at the reception room, Q stopped in the doorway of Mr. Herman's office, to wait for him to finish his phone conversation. While Q waited, Richard looked at the display cases in the waiting room. Among the pictures of Old Boys and other memorabilia, was a shiny silver plate, a gift to Alpha from someone for whom the band had played. Even through the inscription on the plate, Richard could see his reflection. There were no mirrors at Junior Home. In fact, there was almost nothing breakable in either dormitory. Magdalen had created an almost indestructible world where the boys could eat and sleep, play and learn without worrying about smashing anything. There in the waiting room outside Mr. Herman's office, Richard saw his face for the first time in more than a year. Two scars descended from the corners of his mouth, almost to his jaw line. Although they were flat, not raised, they were wide and unmistakable. They gave his face the appearance of a ventriloquist's dummy. He parted his lips and stared at his misshaped teeth. The combination earned him the nickname "Mushmouth."

Richard ran his fingers down the scars, feeling the smoothness of the skin. Ms. Irene always told him how much she loved it when he smiled and he wanted to see what she saw. He didn't like the image. He couldn't do anything about the scars, but he could try to hide his teeth. He tried to smile without parting his lips, but the scar tissue pulled his mouth taut and he could barely get beyond a grin before his lips would separate.

The scars reminded Richard of his mother. He remembered the

softness of her cheek, the warmth of her arms, and the soothing tone of her voice at night as they curled up together on the sidewalk, or in the shell of an abandoned building. He also remembered her loud rants at nothing in particular, the fits of rage when he would ask for food, the crashing blow of her fists, and the horror of seeing her slapped and beaten by whatever man was in her life at the time. He realized that he was starting to forget what she looked like. He wondered if she would ever be in his life again. Even at ten, he knew it felt odd to long for her and fear her at the same time.

"Richard," Q said. "Come. We go back to Junior Home now. Sista waiting."

Richard took a last quick glance in his reflection in the plate, and tried to smile again. When his lips parted and his misshapen teeth showed again, he hung his head and yearned again for his mother's consoling touch, and cursed at her for destroying his face.

6
DEDICATION & DUCK SAUCE

By early afternoon on most days, the boys at Alpha had finished with school and chores and were playing football on the field, a dry pebbly expanse of dirt - nothing like Winchester Park at St. George's. Between the dry Kingston air and the number of feet trampling it daily, there was no chance that grass could grow on Alpha's field. There was no sprinkler system; at Alpha, well water was needed to grow dinner. I headed up to Junior Home to set out games in the dining room and see who would show up for checkers and chess sets, playing cards and board games. The playfield was usually alive and chaotic. Today, there was an eerie silence from the empty expanse.

All ninety-six Junior Home boys stood on the verandah in two quiet rows. At one end of the verandah sat a strikingly handsome couple in their mid-fifties. The woman sat at a table with a pile of index cards. The man sat next to another table with sets of instruments beside him. He wore a short sleeve light blue polo shirt and khakis. She was dressed in a conservative white blouse and long denim skirt. Her blonde hair was pulled back away from her face. Her makeup and jewelry were simple and perfect. They both looked like they would have been just as comfortable sitting at a country club in the states.

I stopped on the concrete plaza a few feet from the verandah and surveyed the line. "Hello, boys."

"Hello, Mr. Solomon," they all mumbled, some with more energy than others.

I was relieved to be back to "Mr. Solomon." Now it was official - the hard part of my day was over.

"Jay, you're home!" I turned to see Sister Magdalen coming up from the convent to Junior Home. She was followed by Plunkett carrying a tray of glasses, which were covered by a dish towel. The sisters covered everything in clean dishtowels to keep the dust out, a valiant but ultimately futile effort in Kingston. "Come. I will introduce you to the Checks." She led me up the steps, motioned for Plunkett to put down the tray on one of the tables next to Mrs. Check, and made her introductions.

Betty Check smiled broadly and shook my hand. Dr. Tom Check nodded, and held up the dental instruments in his hands, as if to say, "I would shake your hand, but...."

Magdalen explained that the Checks came to Jamaica for a week each year. On the first day of their visit, they would examine all two-hundred and fifty boys. Then, for the next two days they would fill cavities, or pull teeth. Magdalen pulled one of the Junior Home boys out of line and over to her, "Open your mouth. Show me your teeth," she ordered.

The boy said, "Yes, Sista" and opened as far as he could.

She cupped her hand under his chin and tilted his head back. "Some of them have such bad teeth." She shook her head as she held his jaw and peered deep into his throat, like a vet peering into a horse's mouth. I wondered what she was looking for. "Have you ever been to a dentist before?" she asked the boy.

"Yes, Sista." I think I went once before."

"Well then, you are better than most of the boys." She turned him around and patted him on the shoulder as she directed him back in line. "After the Checks work here, they will head up to Mandeville, to St. John Bosco Home, and will work on the boys there."

As each boy approached, he would hand a dental card the size of a large index card to Mrs. Check, who would read his name, smile at the boy, and say a few words to help him relax.

"Well, hello again, Alfred," she said to Q, patting his hand. Q, Alfred

Poyser, had arrived at Alpha before his baby teeth had fallen out, so he had better teeth than many of the boys who were new to the home. He was pleased to be remembered, and muttered a weak, "Hello, Ma'am," under his breath. Betty Check's soft voice had years of experience soothing nervous patients. But Q was eight years old, and at that age, everyone is afraid of the dentist. He sat in the chair and opened wide. Dr. Check grabbed a clean dental mirror and pick and in less than two minutes checked each tooth in Q's mouth for cavities. He called off each tooth and any evidence of decay. Mrs. Check quickly marked the cards. Q's exam went without incident, better than most. Later that evening the Checks would sit in the library at Alpha and triage who needed the most immediate care.

During the twenty years the Checks had been visiting, they had set up a dental office on Alpha's property, down toward the girls' high school, Alpha Academy. They persuaded the Ministry of Health to provide a dentist two days each month to service all of the boys at Boys Home, the girls at Alpha's Academy, and the young children at the primary and nursery school. But they knew the need for care couldn't be met in that time frame, so they still came themselves every year. Whatever work they couldn't finish at Alpha in the next two days would be handled by the dentists at the clinic over the ensuing weeks. It was only later in my life, when I had family commitments of my own, that I imagined the hurdles they must have faced in creating the clinic, and the conversations they considered. "This year, what if we just went to the Bahamas for a vacation, instead of Alpha to work?" And yet every year they came.

Nurse walked down the long verandah from the pantry with another tray. The dental instruments under the dish towel clanked as Nurse placed the tray on the table to the right of Dr. Check. She gathered the used instruments he had placed to his left and carried that tray to the kitchen where she had a pot of boiling water on the stove. While the instruments boiled, she returned and emptied the small garbage pail full of slightly bloodied gauze and tissues. Given the number of boys and the number of instruments, she had clearly walked miles that day back and forth down the verandah from the Checks to the pantry.

"How can I help?" I offered, eager to add, "Ad Hoc Dental Assistant" to my list of odd-job titles.

"Oh, we're fine at the moment," Mrs. Check replied, offering me the same pleasant smile she gave the boys.

"Come," sister said to me. "Let them do their work. You will see them tonight. We will all have dinner together in the library. I need your help in here." I followed Magdalen into the Junior Home dormitory. Like Ignatius and Marie Therese, Magdalen wore the same thing every day. True to form, however, Magdalen had her own style. Rather than wearing the beige tunic and habit of the other sisters, Magdalen wore a simple zippered white polyester dress that came to her knees, the same white sandals, and no habit. "I couldn't wait to get rid of that thing," she once said. Her salt and pepper hair and dark-rimmed glasses also made her look younger than the other sisters, but it was her frenetic pace and unwavering energy that really set her apart.

The back corner of Junior Home dormitory was Magdalen's space. Magdalen was from Malta, a tiny island in the middle of the Mediterranean. She joined the Sisters of Mercy when she was sixteen, and completed her studies while in their care. At eighteen, she was sent to Jamaica and had worked in a half-dozen Mercy schools before being sent to Alpha. She was fluent in Spanish, English, French and Italian, and, after more than forty years on the island, spoke all with a Jamaican accent. Her office was piled high with supplies for Junior Home – new sheets, books, shirts and shorts and toiletries, and projects in various stages of completion.

Off to the side of her office was her bedroom and private bath. Her bedroom was the smallest room I had ever seen. It fit her twin bed against the wall with just enough space to walk next to it. At the end was a toilet, sink and a stall shower. Basically, her bed was wedged into the entryway of a bathroom. There was a small window at the end, but it was completely covered with heavy drapes for privacy. It was, after all, on the first floor of a dormitory with almost 100 boys. She needed privacy more than air.

"The connection from the TV to the video broke today and I want the boys to be able to watch a movie tonight so we can enjoy our dinner with the Checks. I need you to help me fix it. The boys' hands aren't steady enough." I had hoped to open the game room, but since most of the boys were still in line to get their gums prodded and their plaque scraped, the game room could wait for a bit.

"I thought I would read to them tonight while you enjoyed some time with the Checks," I said.

"You should join us. The boys will be fine, and we never get to break bread with you. The boys will be here tomorrow, trust me."

She cleared her desk and pulled out her soldering iron. She kept it on the shelf next to her tool kit, her first aid kit, and her blow torch, which she used to fix the bed frames when they gave way to metal fatigue. Back home, my father had a t-shirt that read, "He who dies with the most tools wins." Sister had my father beat by a mile.

She plugged the soldering iron into the long extension cord that was, in turn, plugged in clear on the other side of the room, behind a bookcase stacked with extra clothes for the boys. It was the only outlet in the room. Back when the space was built, who knew electricity would catch on?

The small metal tab that attached the VCR cable to the TV had snapped off the end of the cable. "Hold this," she said as she handed me a thin scrap of metal about the size of my fingernail. I held the metal tab against the end of the cable, while Magdalen tried to place a drop of molten metal on the connection. Within two minutes she burned my fingers, her fingers and the tablecloth she accidentally dropped the iron on. She unplugged the iron in disgust. "They can just read books tonight. Or better yet, I can have Benjamin lead them in saying a novena. They all need to pray more anyway."

"I'll go open the game room for the boys who have finished their dental exams, sister. I'll see you at dinner." I left her office and walked down a row of cots to the dining room at the other end of the dormitory. The sleeping area at Junior Home was separated from the dining room and Mr. Estig's classroom by a makeshift wall of chicken wire stretched across an open frame of 2 x 4s. It created the illusion of separate rooms and gave some definition to the spaces. Off the dining room, or refectory, was the pantry, which contained a simple counter and sink. All of the food for Junior Home was prepared down at the kitchen adjacent to Senior Home and carried up to the Junior Home pantry. In the pantry the plates, bowls, cups and utensils were stored between meals and washed afterwards by whatever boys were on kitchen duty. Today, a cooktop and gas tank had been brought up and placed on the counter so that Nurse could boil Dr. Check's instruments.

I opened the game room cabinet and set out a few board games and decks of cards. The boys started to arrive and I sat with a few to play checkers.

Within half an hour, the room had at least twenty boys playing Chutes & Ladders, CandyLand, Concentration and checkers. Magdalen came by and proudly held in the air the repaired cable.

"Once you left I was able to get it done," she boasted. "Your hand was shaking too much and it was driving me crazy," she laughed.

"Well if you hadn't scorched my thumb, I wouldn't have been so shaky, Sister!"

"Oh, my brother Louis, back in Malta, he is just like you. He is an architect," she said with a mixture of pride and derision. "He is all thinking with his head. He designs beauuutiful buildings, but he can't tie his own shoes."

"I know a hammer from a screwdriver, sister," I said, offering a weak defense. Despite my protests, I was keenly aware that I was of questionable value at the moment. I wanted to be more than a glorified babysitter that afternoon. But my drive to be more, to add more, kept butting into the fact that today, nobody needed a hero. They needed a glorified babysitter.

She laughed as she pat me on the arm, "Don't worry. You will be a successful lawyer one day back in the States and you will hire someone like me to fix things. For now, play checkers." She waved at the checkerboard on the table. "We should each stick to what we're good at. I remember once, when…" Her attention got diverted to a commotion outside. She spied one boy pulling a smaller boy by the ear along the walkway. "Hey, what you doing there!" she said as she ran out on the verandah and down the steps.

"Sista," the taller boy started his defense. "This boy took my kite string," he said with great indignity.

"Mi nah do it Sista. Mi find it on de ground!"

"Listen here," she said grabbing the string and waving it at the taller boy. "You don't touch the smaller boys. What kind of nonsense is that." She turned to the smaller boy, "Here, I have some string." She pulled a handful of stuff out of her pocket but no string. "Here, take this," she said to the younger boy as she handed him a rubber band. He went off happy. As she returned the string to the taller boy, she wagged her finger, "I'm watching you. Do not touch the younger boys. I will not let the older boys pick on you, and I won't let you hurt someone else. Got it?"

"Yes, sista." Then she cuffed him gently on the back of the head, "Now, go play."

As I watched her actions and listened to her tone I could hear my own mother breaking up fights between my siblings and me. Yet here there was something different. There was a desperate attempt to be conscious with the boys about what she was doing for them. She wanted them to understand the "why" behind her actions, and the implications of their own. She knew that every conversation she had with the boys might be the only point in the day during which this child, this child of God, would speak directly with an adult. This exchange might be her only chance to give this particular boy more than just a bed for the night and a warm meal at dinner. She could impart a lesson. I realized the tone she had used with the two boys was the same tone she had used with me in her office not a half-hour earlier when she insisted I join the sisters and Checks at dinner. I wasn't sure of my place yet, but Magdalen knew exactly what I needed.

Magdalen came back in the game room, "Now, where was I? I was telling you about something. I can't remember. Oh, well...next time. See you at dinner." It was one of a hundred incomplete conversations we shared, of unfinished stories and interrupted afternoons. Life always seemed to get in the way.

That evening, Sister Ignatius played host, getting all excited when Mr. Johnson, Alpha's driver, arrived with the dinner from Golden Palace, the Chinese takeout place in Liguanea, a suburban neighborhood. Although she was instinctively frugal and hated to see anything in excess, Ignatius was also conscious of being a good hostess, and always over-ordered for guests. More than a dozen white containers of various sizes created a miniature cityscape on the table.

"The food there is wonderful. The General Tso's chicken is just lovely," she said in her perfect, slow paced diction, as she lined up the cartons on the table off to the side of the room. She organized a few Senior Home boys to set up card tables and chairs as one long table in the center of the room. I brought my tape deck out of my bedroom so we could have some music. The ceiling fans hanging from the white rafters spun slowly to create a gentle breeze and keep the mosquitoes at bay.

The Checks were from just outside of Philadelphia. Dr. Check had heard about Alpha through some local Sisters of Mercy connections. He had made his first trip years before and had decided to make Alpha and its brother school, St. John Bosco, his personal mission. With the help of other dentists in the Philadelphia area, he raised enough money to build the dental office. The Checks would be two of many people with whom I would cross paths that year.

The last to arrive at dinner was Magdalen.

"Sorry I'm late. This is the night I go over the prayers for Mass with the boys. They never quite get it, and I never quite give up trying." We stood around the table waiting for Magdalen to prepare her plate.

When we were all ready, Sr. Marie Therese said, "Ignatius, why don't you say the blessing."

"Dear Lord, we are grateful for this food that you provide and for bringing the wonderful Checks to us and for all that you provide for the boys. Amen."

"And please don't let any of the boys bite Dr. Check tomorrow," Magdalen added.

"Amen!" Dr. Check said, "Although it's never happened yet, I must say."

"How did today go?" I asked as we sat down to eat.

"Just fine," he replied. "Most of them have never seen a dentist before coming here and they're scared. When I tend to the cavities tomorrow, they'll scream bloody murder, but I'll have them on so much Novocain they can't possibly feel anything. "

"We all have our fears and our struggles," Marie Therese said as she fumbled at a piece of chicken with her chopsticks.

"I know I was certainly afraid the first time we came to Alpha," Mrs. Check said, smiling at Marie Therese. "But you all made us feel very comfortable here." She turned to me. "Tom had come down here for... what was it, Tom...about three years, before I had the nerve to join him. By then, he knew the sisters well. Sr. Philomena was the nurse at the time, and Sr. Aine ran the trades. Marie Therese was in charge, of course, even back then." She leaned toward Marie Therese, sitting next to her, and they both smiled.

Marie Therese wiped her mouth carefully with her napkin and said, "You seemed so cautious when we met you out at Manley." Norman Manley Airport in Kingston is named for the once and future Prime Minister. "You seemed overwhelmed by the heat and the noise and bustle of Jamaica all at the same time. You were looking around yourself so quickly, like you were afraid someone would steal your purse. I remember thinking you may not last the day, let alone the week. And here we are, so many years later, and you are still part of our family."

"You were right to worry about your purse," Ignatius interjected. "The riff raff at the airport are terrible. The authorities try to do something about it, but they can't."

"I'll never forget that first trip," Mrs. Check offered. "I couldn't get over the heat. I think I started to perspire as I walked down the stairs from the plane and didn't stop until we were back in the air. Tom knew enough to get mosquito netting for the bed in the visitors' apartment."

"Yes, Jay," Magdalen interrupted. "The mosquito netting over your bed is the one Dr. Check bought all those years ago."

"The toughest part for me that first trip was leaving. At the time, our boys at home were teenagers and I couldn't help but see their faces in the boys here. It just broke my heart to leave them all behind." There was silence for a moment, and Ignatius and Marie Therese looked down at their plates. Dr. Check's eyes widened. My eyes darted around at everyone at the table, trying to figure out the problem.

"I'm sorry, Sisters," Mrs. Check apologized. "I didn't mean to suggest that they don't have a good life here."

"Not at all," Ignatius offered. "We provide what we can. But every child deserves a home and a family. We give them structure and we feed them and cloth them and educate them. But you are right to feel that they deserve better."

Magdalen jumped in, "I remember the first time I came to Jamaica. Looooord it was hot as blazes! And muggy like you wouldn't believe!" she said as she stood up. "Plunkett, come here." Plunkett and Wilbert had been sitting on chairs off to the side, in case we needed anything. Wilbert nudged Plunkett aside, and rushed to Magdalen first, thinking she was going to tell him to fix himself a plate. The boys had already had supper with the other boys at Senior Home, but teenage boys exist in a perpetual state of hunger.

Magdalen handed him two large bottles, with long thin necks. "Run to the pipe and fill these up. Hurry." Wilbert looked disgusted, and

Plunkett smiled and stared at the floor as Wilbert shuffled out the door.

"I first came here by ship," Magdalen continued. "When the ship came into the harbor I couldn't believe how greeeen the island was! And so hilly! Malta has small hills but is very dry and dusty. Here, the way the green mountains all crash down to the sea! I thought it was sooooo beautiful! They say that when Christopher Columbus returned to Europe and people say to him 'What Jamaica look like?' he crumpled up a piece of paper and threw it on the table to show the mountains, and said, 'Here. Dis Jamaica!'"

"I can't imagine coming here back then," I said. "The thought of not knowing when you could go home, of maybe never seeing your family again."

"You just did it. It was your calling. It was the life I chose. You left your family. You left your home. You joined a new family and went were you were told. Would you please pass the marmalade, Mrs. Check," she said, waving at the packets of duck sauce in the middle of the table. "It's such a treat having marmalade with supper."

And just like that, she went from the philosophical to the mundane. *I followed my calling...please pass the duck sauce.* Magdalen was like a fortune cookie message with "Life will bring you great things," on one side, and "Brush your teeth," on the other.

"And so you traded in one small island for another. And you never looked back?" I asked.

"I was on the ship with many other sisters from Malta and Italy, Spain, England, and Ireland. The three from Italy kept saying how they were soooo happy to be doing God's work. And the two from Spain kept offering up their seasickness to God - like throwing up was the same as suffering on the cross. They kept saying, 'God, grant me the strength to do your will.' I kept thinking, 'God, get me off this ship – I just made a big mistake leaving home.' But I was the only one who spoke Italian and Spanish and English, so they needed me to translate what everyone had to say for everyone else – except the Irish sisters. I couldn't understand anything they said. And they thought I was craaaazy," she said with her Italian-Spanish-Maltese-Jamaican accent.

"I can't imagine," Ignatius said softly as she spun her lo mien onto her fork.

"I don't know how you had the strength to make that commitment at that age," I said. "I don't know that I could have done it."

"When you are *called*, you are called," Sister Marie Therese said softly but firmly. "You have to choose *to hear* the call, but if you are open to hearing it, it's not your decision to make. It is God's."

The conversation continued in the same vein, alternating between the sacred and the mundane, until Marie Therese indicated it was time for us all to turn in, as the Checks had another busy day ahead of them tomorrow.

The others left and Magdalen and I stayed to clean the library.

"Plunkett. Wilbert. Get the other office boys. Finish this up."

Wilbert rushed forward for a plate. Plunkett went to the door and called out for the others. Within seconds Worldhead and Michael came crashing through the door. Michael's twisted leg didn't seem to slow him down much.

"Do you boys like Chinese food?" I asked.

"Yessir."

"They like anything they can chew," Magdalen said, rubbing Plunkett's head. "Go. Eat," she ordered.

The boys piled food onto their plates. Wilbert kept pulling the containers closer to him. Plunkett kept warning him politely that he needed to save some for the other boys. I watched as Plunkett slipped some of his share back into two lo mien containers he positioned carefully on his chair, between his legs.

In less than ten minutes they finished off the considerable amount of food that had been left. After they gorged, they sat back in their chairs holding their stomachs and moaning with delight. For the next few evenings as they played checkers or cards on the office verandah, they would brag about how much they had eaten and whether they preferred the lemon chicken or the sweet and sour pork. They had eaten so fast, I wondered how they could possibly have tasted any of it.

While the office boys and I cleaned up the library, I noticed Plunkett stash one of the paper bags from the Chinese restaurant in his back pocket. Plunkett was the last to leave that evening. We talked more about him and his brother as we folded and stored the tables and put the chairs back against the wall. Once we finished, he seemed to stall, as if looking for some reason to linger. Since my room was off the library, I would have to lock the door behind him after he left. I knew he had stored two containers of food behind the couch and needed to sneak them out before I locked up. I wanted to give him an opportunity to exit gracefully.

"Plunkett, I have to go into my room to get the keys to lock up. Why don't you head out now? Thanks for your help, and have a good night."

"Yes, Mr. Solomon. Good night to you too, sir."

I went into my room and waited a moment, while I heard him dash across the room to collect his stash, and then head for the exit. I thought it was so inconsistent with his overall honesty and dedication to be stealing food, particularly since he had eaten so much at dinner, but I knew I would never truly know the world view of these boys, and who was I to judge their behavior.

A few minutes later, Plunkett arrived at Junior Home. He placed the paper bag with his two containers of food in the shadow on the side of the bench on the verandah. He opened the screen door to the dormitory and motioned to Benjamin, the Senior Home boy on duty. "Send my brudda Wayne out 'ere," he whispered.

Benjamin shooed him away with his hand, looking too tired and lazy to get up from his chair.

"Do it, now!" Plunkett implored.

Benjamin pulled himself up from the Adirondack chair and came to the door. "What you want him for?" he asked.

"Mi need to talk to 'im," Plunkett said.

"You have food for 'im, don't you?" Benjamin said, squinting. "I'm 'ungry too ya know. Leave me da food and I'll give it to 'im." It wasn't the first time Benjamin had shaken down Plunkett, but Desmond was ready.

"I brought you some too, so send him out now or I'll never bring you more," Plunkett demanded.

Benjamin was more than a foot taller than Plunkett, and was still carrying the thin stick he used to intimidate the smaller boys. In one motion, he raised the stick over his head and took a quick step toward Plunkett. Plunkett instinctively raised his arm to protect his head, but deep down, he knew Benjamin wouldn't hit him. He had too much to offer.

"Where's da food?" Benjamin said, still in a whisper.

"Send Wayne out and you'll get yours," Plunkett replied.

Wayne had heard Desmond's voice and had propped himself up on his elbows in bed and was watching the exchange.

"*You* get 'im," Benjamin hissed at Plunkett, as he brushed by Desmond to the verandah.

Desmond made a quick gesture to Wayne, who rolled off his cot and walked quickly to the door. The brothers stepped out on the porch, where Benjamin had already found the bag of food. He took the larger of the two boxes for himself, grabbed the only fork in the bag, and sat at the far end of the bench and devoured the contents. When he finished, he tossed the empty container at Desmond's feet as he walked by the boys and back into the dormitory.

Wayne opened the container of lo mien noodles with chicken on top. He reached for the first piece with his fingers, but Desmond stopped him, pulling a fork from his pocket. Desmond kept watch for the few minutes it took Wayne to finish his late night meal. It was less dangerous than the lookout he had had to keep when they lived at home.

Wayne said a quick, "Thank you," before heading back to bed. Plunkett refolded the paper bag, which he knew might come in handy, even if just for bartering. He washed out the two Chinese food containers – again, valuable in their own right. Plunkett slept soundly that night, knowing he could protect and provide for his brother.

* * *

Morris didn't eat that night. He still found it uncomfortable to walk, and hadn't slept well since the attack. He had been groggy and irritable the entire week. He managed to steal an occasional piece of food, but had often resorted to sifting through the trash, trying to get something edible before the goats found it. Normally, when he came upon other boys hunting for food, he would join with them, knowing they had a better chance to eat if they worked together. But this week, when he came upon a smaller boy in a trash pile near the main square, he threw a rock at him to chase him off.

7
THE LEPER DILEMMA

The plans for Friday evening changed five times before the week ended. Instead of meeting at the Carib, I met the other BC teachers for dinner first at Mrs. Creighton's, the house Irene shared with the five other BC grads from 1985. Mrs. Creighton's house was, by Jamaican standards, huge. It had a large living room and dining room, a good-sized porch, a tight but manageable kitchen, and four large bedrooms. Mrs. Creighton herself lived in a small attached apartment, a common feature of Jamaican homes. She had been renting to BC teachers for a number of years already, which provided her with reliable income, and BC with an easy way to provide accommodations for each new batch of teachers.

One of the mixed blessings of the house was its large, flat, poured concrete roof. The roof provided a great place to sit out at night, easily accessible by a set of wrought iron stairs just outside the porch. Unfortunately, because the ceiling was only about nine feet high, the large concrete slab trapped the heat in the rooms below, which often made them oppressive.

Irene hadn't met any of her roommates until shortly before she arrived in Jamaica, but they were all getting along well, sharing the challenges. Peter, Doug and Brian worked at St. George's with me. Melissa worked at Immaculate Conception with Irene. Karen worked at St. Anne's, a primary school in one of the toughest sections of Kingston.

The other volunteers, those from my year, lived in a few places around Kingston. Although we all usually saw each other on the weekends, I preferred to eat at Ms. Creighton's, mostly because of Irene.

Barbara, a friend of Karen's, had come to visit for a week. Over the course of a year, more than a dozen friends would visit. Some came expecting a week on a beach, and usually left confused and disappointed. Others came expecting an "authentic Jamaican experience" and instead found an authentic "American-expatriate-in-Jamaica" experience, but not knowing the difference, felt fulfilled.

Doug made dinner, priding himself on what he was able to prepare given our limited budget and the even more limited offerings at the local market. It took a large pot of rice and beans and two chickens to feed us all. Most chickens in the market in Kingston were scrawny compared to those at American grocery stores. The pot of rice always included a few sprigs of thyme for added flavor. A side plate of fried plantains provided more starch. No matter who cooked, most dishes tasted overwhelmingly of Pickapeppa sauce, a spicy Jamaica Worcestershire Sauce.

Karen had set the table on the patio, which always included lighting a bug-repellant candle. Since Karen worked at St. Anne's, by far the most difficult place to teach, she always had the best stories. "It was insane this week," she said through a mouthful of rice. "I don't know how any learning goes on there at all, except in our small classroom." Unlike the green and open campuses of St. George's and Immaculate Conception, both high schools, St. Anne's consisted of a single two-story square structure on a crowded city block. A twelve-foot high concrete wall surrounded the school's small paved play area. The wall kept the kids in, and the occasional gunfire out. The school was just two blocks west of the Kingston Hospital, and the sound of sirens punctuated most lessons. The main floor of the school building was one large open room. Movable blackboards separated the space into four "classrooms." There was no way to control the noise level, and with many of the kids sitting on the floor because of a shortage of desks and chairs, most days seemed like endless bedlam.

"Franklin, one of my first-graders, is always sniffling and congested," Karen started. "Today I saw him sniffing something out of a small brown bottle. When I asked him about it, he handed it to me and told me his mother gave it to him so he could breathe easier. I took a whiff. It was pure ammonia! His mother is having him sniff ammonia to clear his sinuses!" She shook her head. "No wonder the kid is half brain-dead."

Karen and two other BCers who worked at Anne's had a small shack in the back of the yard, furthest from the school entrance, and about thirty feet from the main building. The relative quiet was not without a price, since the shack - and it was literally a shack – sat right next to the bathroom. From their small outpost they would tutor the kids who had the greatest difficulty learning. It was a last-ditch effort to keep struggling kids in school. In fact, more learning probably took place in the shack than in the entire main building, given the ridiculous set up.

Karen continued. "I honestly think Sister Agnes has lost it. Not that I blame her, working in those conditions. But the way she yells at the kids is unbelievable. And she talks to the teachers the same way. I'm not sure I can last a whole year at that place."

"It seems that lots of the teachers and administrators we run into at these schools have succumbed to Jamaican way of dealing with kids, which is just yell at them and hope they get in line. It's so counter-productive," Peter added.

Melissa interrupted. "First of all, most of the teachers and principals *are* Jamaican, so I don't think they have *succumbed* to anything. I also don't think they think that their way is inferior to the way you and I do things. There are a number of girls at Immaculate whose parents moved *back* here from New York because they were more confident about the education system here. They feel there is more discipline."

Although we usually referred to ourselves as volunteers, we were paid by the Jamaican Ministry of Education as salaried teachers. In fact, because we all had undergraduate degrees, we were paid on a higher scale than most of the local teachers. In addition, as expatriates, we did not pay

Jamaican income tax. As a result, we made significantly more than our colleagues, albeit, far less than any of us would have made if we stayed home in the States and had even minimum wage jobs. Nevertheless, we often spoke of our contributions at our schools with an air of superiority, a self-righteousness borne of youth and inexperience. Every once in a while we would catch ourselves in our arrogance. In fact, we all knew how much we had to learn, and how much we were learning from our Jamaican colleagues. But that didn't stop us from sounding overconfident from time to time.

Karen continued, "In spite of the ridiculousness of St. Annie's, I love it here. I think the people are warm and friendly. Everyone seems to appreciate the work we're doing. The whole thing is just great."

Melissa shook her head. "I don't get you. One minute you're packing your bags and the next you go all Pollyanna on us. When you're done hugging all the cockroaches and washing the lovely smell of diesel fuel out of your hair, it's still just a hot muggy place to live, if you ask me," Melissa added.

Karen put a cup of coffee in front of Barbara, her visitor from home. "Is this Jamaican Blue Mountain Coffee," Barbara asked eagerly. "I've heard it's great." She lifted the top of the sugar bowl, her spoon poised, but let out a shriek and dropped the lid on the table as she pushed back in her chair. "Oh! There's a dead cockroach in the sugar!"

"It's the Caribbean. There are dead cockroaches everywhere," Peter said flatly.

Barbara, feeling sheepish and suddenly silly, tried to regain her composure, "I'll wash out the bowl and get more sugar." She stood and reached for the sugar bowl gingerly, a look of disgust on her face.

"Don't bother," Karen said. She grabbed the sugar bowl, scooped out the cockroach with her spoon, and then put sugar in her own coffee. Barbara's eyebrows disappeared up into her bangs as she stared at her friend, who six months earlier had been a neat freak in a BC dorm.

Karen noticed Barbara's reaction. "Look, the first six times I found a cockroach in the sugar, I threw out the sugar and boiled the bowl. The next few times, I threw out the sugar and rinsed out the bowl. Eventually I just threw out the sugar each time, but then we kept running out of sugar. Now I just throw out the cockroach and enjoy my coffee with a side order of 'pretend-that-didn't-just-happen.'"

"That's nice," Barbara said. "If you don't mind, I'm gonna skip the coffee."

After dinner, we scrapped the idea of going to the movie altogether. The Jedi would have to defeat the forces of the Dark Side without us. Instead, we hung out, talked and played cards.

After a few rounds of Red Stripes, Barbara went to the bathroom to take out her contacts. As she opened the medicine cabinet to grab the saline, the small green lizard that was gripping the inside of the cabinet door fell into the sink, scampered up the side and jumped over to the toilet. Barbara shrieked, turned to run and slammed straight into the closed bathroom door. In the living room, we heard Barbara's shout, then the thud. We all looked up from our game, but no one, including Karen, moved. Within a few seconds Barbara was back in the room, rubbing her forehead, this time more angry than sheepish.

"Okay. Just tell me what else I need to be prepared for. Bats? Mice? Flying monkeys? I'm not a wimp. I would just like some warning."

Peter stared at his cards. "Yes and yes, on the bats and mice. Not sure on the monkeys."

After another round of Red Stripes, more to calm Barbara's nerves than out of thirst, Melissa got up from the table. "I've had enough, guys. I'm turning in."

"This early?" Doug asked.

"Karen, Barbara and I are going running in the morning, and we want to go early, before it gets hot."

"There *is* no time before it gets hot here," I said.

"That's why we go at six o'clock, before the sun is fully up and before all those cars on the street start belching out their filthy exhaust."

"You go running that early? Is anyone on the street?" I asked.

"No it's nice and quiet," Karen said. "No traffic. No cat calls from the guys sitting in the doorways, no chance of accidentally running into one of our students."

"You realize that people here don't exercise the way they do in the States, right? And you realize it's probably a little dangerous for women to be running when it's still dark out and no one is on the street, right?" I asked. I thought of the Prayer of St. Francis again, and my own version.

Where there is ignorance, let me sow awareness.
Where there is stupidity; judgment.

"Don't bother, Jay," Doug said. "We've had this conversation with them already. It goes nowhere."

"We're perfectly safe," Karen said. "Everyone here has been so friendly to us. Everyone knows we're here to help. We'll be fine."

"Well, I just think…" I started, but Irene put her hand on my shoulder, and I took the hint to stop talking.

"Why don't you grab a couple of beers and I will get a blanket and we can go sit up on the roof?" she offered. It was all the encouragement I needed to drop the subject. I went in the kitchen for the beer.

The roof at Mrs. Creighton's was wide and flat, the perfect place to sit on a hot evening. Kingston is dry and dusty, and the roof was always coated with a thin layer of grit. Irene laid out a blanket, and we sat down with our beers.

After a few minutes of just listening to the crickets chirping I said, "I thought about what you said the other night at Alpha…that it's all just about making the small differences every day. I'm not sure that's enough for me. I love what I am doing at Alpha, but sometimes I feel like I want to make big changes. Some days I want to save the whole world and feel like I am wasting time where I am." I lay back on the blanket.

"The other afternoon in the gameroom, that adorable Richard Burns asked me to read to him," Irene said, leaning back on her side, her head propped up on her elbow, facing me. "So I read to him. The whole world didn't ask me to do anything. When the whole world asks, I'll think about responding. Right now, I can just about handle the needs I hear from my students, my housemates and the boys at Alpha."

I put my hands behind my head. "You know, I just realized something the other day. After more than a year at Alpha and St. George's, the only children in my life are black, or at least a lot darker than my family. When I have kids, chances are they aren't going to look anything like these kids, and that seems strange.

"I know what you mean. Our frame of reference right now is that kids are black. But it's just a frame of reference. Having pasty-faced white kids will feel right when we have them."

"Everything with you is so logical."

"And everything with you is so loose and dreamy, with your 'what ifs' and your 'wouldn't it be great ifs'. Well, 'what ifs' don't walk the dog, buddy. You have to deal with the world you're in at the moment."

"What if I want to change the world I'm in?"

"Oh, geez! Don't you think you make a difference to Plunkett and Wilbert and Richard and Worldhead, and Q and all the others?"

"I know I do. But that just doesn't seem like enough."

"*Enough* for *who*? Are you down here for them or for you?"

"I assume I'm down here for them, but obviously, I enjoy being here, too, so I must be getting something out of it for myself. Don't you enjoy being here?"

"Of course," she said. "Look, there are some things I do with my students at Immaculate that are for them, like putting together good lesson plans, and keeping discipline in the classroom. And there are clearly some things I do for me, like coming to Alpha.

"But you coming to Alpha has a terrific impact on the kids, and you could easily find something just as rewarding closer to home, instead of an hour bus ride with two transfers."

"Probably, but it wouldn't be the same, and with the game room, you've made it easy to work with the boys. Look, I'm just saying it's important to recognize why we do what we do. Have you ever been out to St. Monica's?" she asked, mentioning the home the Sisters of Mercy ran in Spanishtown for the elderly and lepers.

"Yeah. I went a few times last year on weekends. I needed a break from working with kids." In retrospect, it sounded absurd to say that when I needed a break from working with orphans I would visit a leper home. But at the time, it made sense.

"I went out there once last year too. And I thought 'never again.' It's a great place, and Sister Kate does a great job providing for those people, but they're all gonna die. Any time I spend out there and any impact I have is going to be over soon. I need to work with kids because I feel like I can change their lives and that it will have a lasting effect on them and their children and grandchildren."

"I don't see myself going back either, but for a very different reason," I said. "Have you met Miss Mahalia?"

"I'm not sure," she said.

"The leprosy has eaten her fingers, so her hands look like little paddles. When you sit with her, she holds your hands between her palms. Her skin is surprisingly soft. She's blind in one eye, so she has trouble reading. We sat on the verandah outside her room and she told me about how grateful she was that they had opened St. Monica's. She didn't say much about her life before, and I can only assume it was pretty miserable. She wanted me to read to her from her prayer book. She is so filled with joy, to have someone there with her and to have a safe place to live. She was so at peace."

"And yet you haven't been back."

"Right. But not because any impact I have will be short-lived. I don't go back because I have nothing to offer. She has what she needs and is at a peaceful place in her life." I sat up and took another drink.

"I think you're full of crap. I think you don't go back out there because it's a pain in the ass to get out there and because you have more important work right here in Kingston." She paused. "And I don't think there's anything wrong with admitting that. It's human nature to want to take the easy route, and you have the same need to be productive as I do. You're more valuable to the kids than to Miss Mahalia."

"O.K. You're right. It takes about two hours to get out there and it's hot as hell in Spanishtown and that bus ride is miserable. I have better things to do at Alpha and while Miss Mahalia is peaceful and reassuring, the kids make me laugh more. And after all, it's all about me, right?"

"And in a world of limited time and resources, it's as good a reason as any, I guess," Irene said. "Now, Magdalen and the sisters are a different story. Their dedication is complete."

"I thought so too, until I realized that they could be reassigned tomorrow by their Mother Superior to another ministry. They could be pulled out of Alpha on a moment's notice and would have to leave the boys and never look back. What kind of devotion is that?"

"It seems like the ultimate devotion to me," she said. "They didn't commit themselves to the boys. They committed themselves to doing 'God's work,' however their order might define it. How much more complete devotion can you ask of someone? Don't you think if the Sisters of Mercy reassigned Magdalen she would be heartbroken to leave Ignatius and Marie Therese? She has worked with them for years now. And yet she would accept a new assignment with the same kind of devotion she gives to getting those kids in line for dinner every night. That's amazing to me."

"And so what are we devoted to?" I asked.

"For the time being, I'm devoted to doing the best job I can teaching the Immaculate girls math, and helping the boys at Alpha have a few laughs."

I finished my Red Stripe and lay back on the towel. "Well, I'm devoted to enjoying this nice breeze tonight and to finishing a few more beers. And, for now, that'll have to do." I lay back on the towel and Irene lay perpendicular to me, her head resting on my chest.

"Have you been to Hope Gardens yet?" I asked. "It's on the way up to the university."

"Haven't been there yet," she said, seeming to drift off.

"I take groups of boys up there on Sunday afternoons. We usually arrive around 1:00. I would be great if you could join us some Sunday.

"I'll let you know." Her tone said she just wanted to relax and enjoy the moment, not talk about work. We stared at the stars and enjoyed the breeze while we listened to dogs barking in the distance.

* * *

Morris Mathers scored big that night, or so he thought. He had wandered into New Kingston, where two large American hotels anchored the newest business neighborhood in the city. He sat on the curb of the parking lot behind the Pegasus Hotel watching the back door of the kitchen. In a short span of time, a busboy, actually a grown man, had come out of the heavy steel door three times carrying a large black garbage bag and disappeared into the fenced-in area containing the hotel's dumpsters. Each time, Morris could hear a grunt and the slamming of metal as the man heaved the bag into the dumpster and let the lid bang down. After the busboy emerged and retreated again, Morris felt confident he had enough time to make his move. He dashed to the enclosure, threw open the latch and slid inside. The edge of the dumpster towered over him. With his hands extended he barely reached the lip. But Morris was used to that problem. The dumpster was only two feet from the wall of the hotel. Morris wedged himself between the two structures and, bracing his feet on whatever crevice he could, he scaled the side of the dumpster. With one foot on the edge of the dumpster and another leaning on the wall, Morris bent over and lifted the lid, which fell back and slammed on the top of the dumpster with a tremendous bang. Morris knew he needed to work quickly. The dumpster was full, so Morris had no problem grabbing the bag on top. Lifting it was another matter. As he leaned into the dumpster to gain a solid hold on the bag, he could hear the rustle of rats moving beneath the other bags. It took all of his strength to the hoist the bag over the edge of the dumpster and drop it to the ground. He scampered to the ground and dragged the bag outside the enclosure. As Morris dragged the bag across the parking lot to a spot behind a truck, the bag started to tear, leaving a trail of garbage. Once behind the truck, Morris tore open the bag and sifted through the contents for a meal. He picked clean the first three chicken bones he came across, and polished off every crust of bread, all the while stuffing into his bag everything that looked edible. The clanging of the cans at the bottom of the bag intrigued and excited him, but they also masked the footsteps of the busboy who had noticed the trail of garbage across the parking lot. The man's broad smack across the side of Morris' head sent him reeling onto the pavement. "You miserable 'tief!" the man yelled. "Look at de mess you make!"

Morris lay on the ground for a second, rubbing his left ear. The man knew the boy had to eat, and he wasn't interested in punishing him, but he was angry at the work Morris had created for him. "G'won! Git out a here!" the man yelled, giving Morris enough time to grab his bag and run. Although his ear smarted, Morris knew he had enough food for a few days and felt the smack upside the head was worth it.

Morris was unfamiliar with New Kingston, its stores, its alleys and its gangs. But he knew that whenever you're away from home, you're in someone else's, and that was dangerous. Morris needed to get back to the familiar streets around the Central Market, but he couldn't control his impulse to take stock of his loot. He leaned against a wall in an alley next to the Royal Canadian Bank, a few blocks from the Pegasus. As he pulled each item from his bag, he smiled, especially when he realized he had grabbed a dozen sealed packages of crackers, which would be good for a few days. As he stood to leave, he saw three boys, only slightly larger than himself, coming toward him down the dead end alley. Morris scanned the ground for a weapon, but all he could spot was a piece of rubble from a cinderblock. Before he could grab it, Morris was surrounded by the three boys. The first stepped forward, screwdriver in his hand and slammed Morris into the wall. The jolt to the back of his head brought tears to his eyes, just as the throbbing from the busboys smack was subsiding. One of the other boys grabbed Morris' bag and, just as quickly as they appeared, the three boys walked back down the alley. Not a word had been exchanged.

Morris squatted for a moment, knowing his hard work and earlier scuffle had now been for naught. He would have nothing further to eat tonight, and would have to hunt and fight again tomorrow. He was disgusted with himself, and angry at the other boys. Morris picked up the broken piece of mortar and hurled it out of the entrance to the alley. The rock slammed into the side of parked car and the car's alarm started blaring. Trapped in the alley, Morris ran for the street, but a policeman wielding a bully club stepped out and blocked his way.

"You go to jail fi dat', ya know!" the guard said as he grabbed Morris by the collar and hauled him into the street. Morris struggled to pull away, but after the first blow to his back from the policeman's club, he stopped resisting.

8
PONTIUS PILATE

Sister Magdalen was not by nature a morning person. So when her alarm clock rang at 6:00 on Sunday morning, she lay in bed for a moment, took a deep sigh, and before she threw back the covers, said her morning devotion. "For you, Lord. Only for you." After a quick shower, she stepped into her white polyester dress with the zipper up the front, and, since it was Sunday, pinned on her simple silver dove broach, the symbol of the Sisters of Mercy. She opened the door from her bedroom to her office and then from the office to the dormitory, and glanced out at the sleeping boys.

She kept the door open while she dealt with a few small projects at her desk. She preferred giving the boys a chance to wake up to the sounds of familiar activity, rather than the sound of a morning bell. Then she took a large ring of keys from her desk drawer and walked to Craig Frasier's bed. Craig was a morning person and he had started to stir when he heard Magdalen open the office door. Magdalen said a soft, "Good morning," as she dropped the keys at the foot of his bed and returned to her office. Craig was eager to be in involved in any activity. He was restless, cheerful, engaging and talkative, and was helpful or a nuisance, depending on your perspective. After a quick stop at the bathroom, Craig scurried to the four large wardrobes at the back of the dormitory, jangling the keys along the way. He opened each tall cabinet and swung back the large paneled doors, exposing row upon row of cubbies, each with a neatly folded set of Sunday clothes for the boys, along with a clean t-shirt and shorts. Most of the cubbies contained a pair of shoes as well, and a select few even had a pair of socks. Craig took a quick inventory. He himself had locked the cabinet the previous Sunday afternoon, so it was unlikely he would find anything missing. Even boys who would steal just about anything won't steal dress-up clothes. But Craig took his task seriously and didn't report back to Magdalen until he had checked all ninety-six cubbies, counting out loud as he did so; more activity to help wake the boys. He knew which shelf belonged to which boy and occasionally mistakenly called a boy on the play field by his cubby number instead of his name. Craig knew everyone's business, and he often hung out with Q, O'Brien and Richard. Even at ten, he had become part of the institutional memory of the place. He remembered boys that had been at Alpha for only a few days, when they had been there, who they hung out with and where they had gone.

As Craig returned the keys to Magdalen at her desk, she handed him two tubes of toothpaste. He slipped one in each pocket of his shorts, like a gunslinger fully loaded. Craig and Magdalen barely spoke, but that was the beauty of it. He knew he had a relationship with her that the other boys didn't, even if it lasted for only a few moments each week. Their routine made him special.

When Magdalen was ready, she stood up from her desk in her office and said a simple, "O.K. Let's go."

Craig went to the door of the office and in a clear voice meant to show authority announced, "Time to get up. Up now…ya hear. Time for church." Many of the boys had already been lying awake by this time, but Craig would have to repeat his announcement three more times. Some boys woke up the last few stragglers themselves, in part just to silence Craig. Two rows at a time the boys filed into the bathroom holding their toothbrushes. Craig stood in the bathroom doorway with a tube of toothpaste in each hand, doling out the smallest dollop to each boy. Even though Craig, one of the younger and smaller boys, was the only authority managing the process, the boys remained remarkably quiet and in control, more likely because of the early hour and the ritual nature of the task than because of Craig's posturing.

When each boy finished in the bathroom he headed straight to the wardrobes where Magdalen handed him his clothes. During the week, the boys kept their shorts and t-shirts folded at the foot of their beds. And no matter how disciplined she kept things, the process of getting the boys ready for Mass never stayed on cue. Once the boys were dressed in the long pants and, in some cases, crisp white dress shirts, they lined up on the verandah for their walk to church. Meanwhile, Ignatius had been taking the boys at Senior Home through their almost identical routine, although some teenagers were easy to rouse in the morning, and some were impossible.

The younger boys paraded silently from Junior Home in two lines, led by Magdalen. As they passed through the alley between Senior Home and the refectory, the Senior Home boys fell in behind. I took the front of the line and Magdalen hung back to check on any stragglers.

We proceeded past the garage, which was rarely used, and then passed the open square formed by the trade shops and Senior Home classrooms. Ignatius referred to the square as the "parade ground," and in some distant past, the square probably was used for band demonstrations and routines. She was the only one who used that term now. At the far end of the square began the quarter mile walk down a road bordered on each side by large hibiscus bushes. The road connected the boys' school at the north end to Alpha Academy, the girls' high school. In between, along the hibiscus way, were a primary school, a small grade school, a day care center, the dental clinic the Checks had built, a business school for women who had already graduated from high school, and the gardens the boys tended. The Sisters of Mercy had been busy over the years, responding to educational needs as they developed.

The main convent and the attached chapel dominated the center of Alpha Academy's eclectic group of buildings. A dozen sisters lived at the convent and worked at the various schools on the compound. The boys were never allowed near the girls' school when girls were present.

When we arrived, we stopped at the door of the chapel and waited until Magdalen arrived from the back of the line. Then, without words, and with only a swift wave of her hand, she motioned for the boys to proceed inside.

The chapel was shaped like the letter "L", with the altar at the joint, facing the shorter side of the chapel, where the nuns from the convent sat scattered in the pews. The boys squeezed into the longer side of the church, facing the side of the altar. Since the two congregations could not see each other, Mass had an odd, separate-but-together quality to it.

In our area, the Senior Home boys sat on the right side of the aisle and the Junior Home boys on the left. Sister Ignatius stood at the front of the aisle and as the boys filed in, she determined when each row was full. After all were seated, Magdalen would walk down the aisle again, this time pulling out those that she knew couldn't sit still for the entire service. The half-dozen boys she removed sat in the second-to-last pew, just in front of Magdalen and me.

Sister Ignatius always sat at the back of the Senior Home boys, with the same watchful eyes. Today, she was joined by Dr. and Mrs. Check, who had returned the day before from their work in Mandeville, at St. John Bosco Home.

Most of the boys at Alpha were not Catholic. Nevertheless, they all were expected to follow along with the Mass. Each Tuesday evening, Magdalen would spend fifteen minutes with the boys just after dinner to recite specific prayers and explain the process and the symbols, so that the service would have more meaning for them. At the age of twelve, each non-Catholic could ask to become Catholic. The sisters never pushed the faith on any of the boys, and only a handful chose to convert each year.

Even before Mass began, Waldemar, sitting just in front of us, began squirming in his seat and poking Craig sitting next to him. Sister quickly tapped him on the shoulder. Before the end of the opening prayer, she had to tap him again. By the opening of the first reading, she grabbed his arm firmly and told him to behave. By the close of the first reading, she cuffed him in the back of the head, and then looked at me and rolled her eyes in disgust, more with herself for hitting him, than with him for misbehaving. Finally, Magdalen held Waldemar's shoulder firmly and steered him out of his pew and into ours, sitting him in between the two of us. He seemed pleased with this result and behaved for the rest of the service.

Father Henry Williams always processed in from the sisters' side of the chapel, flanked by two altar boys from Senior Home dressed in ornate garb. Rather than a simple white robe with a rope belt, each boy wore a long crimson robe that trailed to the floor. Over the robe each wore a long sleeved white linen shirt edged with six inches of lace. The outfit looked more fitting to a cathedral in Europe than a chapel in Kingston, and seemed miserably hot in the Jamaican heat.

To some of the sisters, Fr. Williams was the pride of Alpha Boys School. He had grown up at the school and was one of the few graduates to go on to college. When he entered the seminary, some of the sisters felt their entire life's work had come to fruition in this one man. He now lived on the grounds of the school and was the chaplain for the entire compound. He was a kind and gentle man, but an awful homilist. Each week the boys heard how wicked they were, how condemned for eternity we will be if we don't mend our ways, how sinful mankind will always be. Even though he always made the point about salvation through Christ, that tag line always got lost in the fire and brimstone. It was during father's homily that I noticed Sr. Magdalen close her eyes and start to chant to herself, "Christ was crucified by Pontius Pilate. Pontius Pilate. Pontius Pilate." It was a line from the Apostles' Creed, the prayer said just after the homily in which Catholics reaffirm the main tenets of the faith. But this seemed like an odd line to choose to meditate on. After all, Pontius Pilate was the Roman prelate who oversaw Jerusalem at the time of Christ's crucifixion. Depending on how you read the Gospel, he was a symbol of abandoned responsibility or outright cowardice, neither of which deserved the deep devotion Magdalen seemed to be showing. And yet she kept repeating, "Pontius Pilate. Pontius Pilate," her eyes closed tight and brow furrowed.

Eventually, Fr. Williams ran out of ways to berate all of us for our sinfulness. He pleaded for us all to beg God for His mercy. And then God granted mercy to all of us, by ending Fr. Williams' sermon. We began to recite the Apostles' Creed. Magdalen's chant of "Pontius Pilate," though soft, grew more intense. At the key moment in the prayer, the moment she had been waiting for, when Catholics worldwide recite, "And Christ was crucified by Pontius Pilate," at least a dozen boys in unison, in a beautiful Jamaican lilt, said, "And Christ was crucified by bunch of violets."

Sister hung her head and sighed heavily. Then she looked up at me, smiled weakly, and said, "Next week. They'll get it right next week."

I thought again of the Prayer of St. Francis.

Where there is doubt... faith.
Where there is despair... hope.
Where there is let-down after let-down... steadfast persistence.

At the end of the service, Ignatius strode slowly to the front of the aisle. Usually at this point, she would start directing the boys to file out of their pews into the center aisle, and to process out of the church. Today however, she stood still, waiting for silence. The boys' light chatter died down.

"Boys, I would like to thank Dr. and Mrs. Check for being with us this week." Ignatius gestured to the Checks who walked to the front of the church and turned to face the boys. They knew the routine, and solemnly bowed their heads. The boys each stretched out an arm high in the air toward the Checks, each palm open and facing down. In unison, and without prompting, they began to sing.

May the Lord bless and keep you.

May His face shine upon you.

May the Lord bless and keep you all your days.

They had raised their voices loudly during the service, in some cases butchering the lyrics, but in most cases hitting every note beautifully (another way to tell that they weren't all Catholic). But now, with their simple prayer of thanks, they sounded downright angelic.

Blessed be the Lord.

Blessed be the Lord.

Blessed be the Lord for all his good.

Blessed be the Lord.

Blessed be the Looooooord.

Blest be the Lord for all his good.

When they finished, the boys lowered their hands as the Checks raised their heads. As they walked back down the aisle, Dr. Check nodded appreciatively to the boys and Mrs. Check mouthed a soft 'thank you,' as sincere as the boys' blessing had been. It was a blessing that would sustain them for another year.

What the Checks accomplished at Alpha was tangible and had a lasting impact. This was not an adventure to them, a quick jaunt to the tropics to work with the poor before getting on with their lives. This was their life. The relationships they formed with the boys and the sisters were integral to their own identity. Having grown up moving from town to town, and school to school, I had always had the luxury of closing the door on the past, ignoring old relationships and moving on. Watching the boys bless the Checks, and feeling the passion with which the Checks approached their commitment to the boys, I started to worry that it wouldn't be so easy to close this door once I left.

* * *

"BE CAREFUL! BE CAREFUL!" Sister Ignatius' voice called out from just outside my bedroom window. She sounded cautious, but not panicked. I got up from my table where I was correcting essays and hurried outside. Sister Ignatius was staring up into the branches of the sixty foot mango tree that towered over the library. Her left hand shielded her eyes from the sun and occasionally gathered her habit, which was blowing in the breeze. Her right hand pointed to different points along the lower and mid boughs of the tree.

"Over here. There are wonderful looking ones over here," she pointed. About fifteen feet above Ignatius, Wilbert slide his bare feet along a wide bough while he braced himself by holding onto a branch overhead. In other parts of the tree, Plunkett and Worldhead did the same. Each boy maneuvered gracefully through the tree, finding some clusters on their own and some with direction from Ignatius. As they reached the fruit, they would twist each firm and waxy delight until is separated from its stem. Three other boys on the ground jockeyed for position below their brothers to catch the treats as they were tossed from above. The sky was raining dessert. The boys on the ground deposited their catch into two large metal buckets.

Sister wandered slowly around the base of the tree, pointing and suggesting places, and the boys moved accordingly – an aerial ballet choreographed from the ground.

"Mr. Solomon," Wilbert called down. "Catch!" He dropped two mangoes in quick succession. I caught the first but fumbled the second.

"Don't worry," Ignatius offered, about the missed fruit. "Most of them aren't ripe yet anyway so I'm sure it will be fine. Just toss it in the bucket with the others. After catching another dozen mangos I noticed that Worldhead had climbed considerably higher in the tree, going after some clusters of mangos.

"Sister, is that safe?" I asked. "He seems to be climbing a bit high."

"Nonsense, Mr. Jay," she said, still looking upward. "They grow up doing this. Their feet know the branches and they know to be careful," she said calmly. "THAT'S FAR ENOUGH, WORLDHEAD," she called out. "YOU'LL HAVE TROUBLE GETTING DOWN IF YOU GO FARTHER."

"Or he'll have a very quick trip down," Magdalen said as she walked up behind us. "Ignatius, we'll need about three hundred. That will give each boy one with supper tonight, if they're ripe enough, and still give Cook enough to use in her recipes this week."

In spite of Ignatius' warning, Worldhead climbed even higher. He had spotted a large clump of mangoes directly above his head and didn't want to lose the opportunity. Unlike the steady boughs at the base of the tree, the branches on which he now walked swayed and creaked under his weight. In addition, Worldhead found himself brushing aside the now frequent smaller branches that poked in his face, and there were more of them the further he got from the center trunk of the tree. After he tossed down the mangoes, and with Ignatius' calls to climb down still in his ears, he paused to take in the view. Worldhead had grown up in small shack in the country well outside Kingston. His home had been just sheets of zinc tied together, and braced with tree branches. No one in his yard had anything but a shack, and certainly, no one had a two-story home. Until this day, up in the mango tree, the upstairs porch on the convent was the highest Worldhead had ever been in his life. Now, from the highest branches of the tree, he looked down on the convent porch, the roof of the library, even over the top of Senior Home dorm and across the field toward Junior Home. He was sure none of the other boys had ever shared this view, and his unique perspective made him feel special. Over the tops of the small classroom buildings he could see the band on the parade ground, instruments by their sides, practicing their marches to the shouted instructions of the band master.

"Worldhead!" Ignatius called again. "Come down now, before you fall."

"Yes, sista. Coming, sista." He slid along the branch only slightly, just to give the appearance of complying, but pivoted and stared across the gully, and over the tops of the building just across South Camp Road. Worldhead didn't get many opportunities to leave the property. Leaving the ground was the next best thing to leaving the grounds. He could see the zinc rooftops of the neighborhood just across the street, and the mottled silver and rust colored panels reminded him of home. When he turned slightly to the north, he could see the tops of the high rise hotels in New Kingston. He remembered being in the backseat of Magdalen's Volvo running errands one day, and seeing an ice cream shop near that pink hotel. He wondered if he would get back there and what kind of ice cream he would order if he did. Worldhead couldn't see forever, but when you don't get to see much, even a limited view feels like you're suddenly Columbus discovering the New World.

His escape ended abruptly. The other boys had followed Worldhead higher into the tree, making Ignatius nervous.

She glanced at the tin buckets at the base of the tree. "All right boys," she said. "We're about half done. Start working your way down the tree. There are plenty of bunches on these lower branches."

I had never been adventurous as a kid or daring as a teen. Watching the boys climb so high, I felt both nervous and jealous. They seemed too high in the tree to be safe, and the sisters seemed so irresponsible to let the boys climb so high, and yet boys climbing trees, trees providing food, and mothers with limited means finding a way to provide for those in their care – nothing could have been more natural. So I watched, and I caught fruit, and I carried buckets of mangos to the kitchen. Half an hour later, all the boys were safely back on the ground, and Ignatius was ready for the next project to occupy her Sunday afternoon. As she directed the boys to carry the brimming tins back to the kitchen, she carefully placed three mangos in my hands. "Do you know how to cut a mango, Mr. Jay?"

"I've learned since I've been here," I assured her.

"Good. This is a very old tree and these are some of the best mangoes on the island. Leave these on your table for a few days. When they are a bit softer to the touch, they'll be ready. You'll enjoy them," she assured me.

I already had.

9
DESMOND DE RAT-KILLER

Waldemar arrived in the gameroom carrying a large piece of cardboard. "Look, Mr. Solomon. Mi make a board to play checkers. Can mi use it today? Do you want to play on it wit' me?"

"Of course, Waldemar. Let me spend a few more minutes on this puzzle with Q." Q had been working on a large puzzle of the Eiffel Tower for more than a week. After two games with Waldemar, I stepped out to the verandah to enjoy the late October afternoon breeze. Craig sat on the bench near the door reading slowly to himself. On the plaza in front of Junior Home, Richard and O'Brien wielded two long sticks, sword fighting. O'Brien jabbed at Richard, poking him in the shoulder. "O'Brien, careful. You'll poke him in the eye" I warned.

As Richard and O'Brien ignored my comments, two new faces approached across the plaza. Both boys were short, and deep shades of brown.

"Well, hello," I said, extending my hand. "Who are you?"

"Them the new boys, sir," Craig tilted his head toward them.

The smaller of the new boys looked at Craig with puzzled look, as if to say, "I can speak for myself." He extended his hand warily, "I'm Morris Mathers." His eyes narrowed as he peered into mine.

"Well, Morris. Welcome to Alpha. I am Mr. Sullivan. And you?" I said, looking at the other boy.

"Winston, sir," he mumbled, dropping his gaze to the ground.

"Well, welcome to you too, Winston. Let me introduce you to the gameroom." I showed them inside and explained the simple rules. "This is the game-room. I open it as often as I can. Everyone is invited. The only rules are that you have to play by the rules of whatever game you are playing; you must say 'please' and 'thank you' whenever appropriate; and you must respect each other, so no yelling or hitting. Are those rules clear to you?"

"Yes, sir," they replied hesitantly. Craig pushed passed us, having had enough of reading for the afternoon. He interjected with specific rules for particular games, and warned the two new-comers not to drop any puzzle pieces, because, "It ruins the puzzle if you can't find that last piece." Most of the tables in the Junior Home refectory were occupied. We could hear the usual accusations of someone cheating, and the occasional, "Mi win!" One of the boys showed Winston how to play Concentration, and he was soon involved in a game. But Morris Mathers stood off to the side, taking in the scene.

I returned to scaling the Eiffel Tower with Q. It was a five-hundred piece puzzle, well beyond the ability or attention span of most eight-year olds. But Q could concentrate for longer than most. And the longer the puzzle took, the more time he got one-on-one attention from an adult. At least three times, Craig stopped over for a minute or two, tried a few pieces, got bored and return to his fifty piece puzzle of Donald Duck and Goofy. When I looked up from the puzzle I saw Morris still standing by himself. "Come on over, Morris. Join us."

Morris walked over hesitantly. As he approached the table, he didn't look at the puzzle. He kept his eyes on me.

"Why don't you sit down and help us build this puzzle."

Morris sat across from me at the table. He picked up one puzzle piece and examined it. He studied the picture on the box. He tried the piece in a number of places. He tried the same with two other pieces. Then, without saying anything, he left the table and walked around to see what the other boys were doing. He had a serious, watchful look on his face and seemed intent to take it all in.

I had learned not to pump the new boys for too much information too quickly. They needed to get used to the place before they would open up. If they were coming to us from home, chances are their situation had not been pleasant and they would be reluctant to talk about it. If they were coming to us from the street, getting used to the structure and the discipline was the hard part.

By the time dinner approached and it was time to close the game room, Morris had stood next to each table, seemingly studying each game, but not playing any. Later that night, as the boys gathered around my chair to listen to stories, Morris again came to check out what was going on, but stood off to the side, not sure if he belonged, or wanted to. He would need a few days, and then he would participate fully, I was sure.

I locked the game room cabinet while the boys on kitchen duty prepared the room for supper. They set out tin cups and utensils and stacked the plates in the pantry. Their efforts were noisy, but noisy the way all family activity is noisy. As I stepped out on the verandah, Silent Malcolm came and stood by my side and held my hand. We watched as two of the older Junior Home boys carried an enormous pot of food from the kitchen at Senior Home up the path to the Junior Home pantry. They struggled as they walked sideways facing each other, holding opposite handles of the hot pot with thick dishtowels.

Mr. Estig called out to the three or four stragglers on the soccer field, hailing them with his stick. Most of the other boys were in lines on the plaza in front of the dormitory verandah, facing sideways, toward the bath area. The outdoor bathroom area at Junior Home was a large open-air rectangle, about twenty feet wide and thirty feet long. The walls, about ten feet high, were punctuated with open brick work that allowed the air to flow freely through while still providing privacy. Wide back-to-back sinks of poured concrete formed an island in the middle of the space. At one end were the showers, four simple pipes sticking out of the outer wall, each with its own single knob. A shorter wall a few feet away from the outer wall provided privacy to the boys showering, but created the sense of openness to discourage any of the boys from trying to abuse the smaller boys. At the other end of the space were the toilets, again separated from the main space by a low wall, and separate from each other with partial cinderblock walls. Benjamin, from the senior home, stood guard at the entrance to the bathroom controlling the flow to the sinks, where they would wash their hands and faces before dinner. Later in the evening, when it was time to go in for the night, he would cycle them through the toilets, then the sinks, then the showers. With ninety-six boys to move through the process, no one was long in any one place. Benjamin held a long switch in his hand that would make a loud "whack" when he slapped it against the wall to make the slow-pokes move faster. He was under strict orders from Magdalen never to hit one of the boys, but she knew he needed to threaten a beating in order to have any authority with them.

Malcolm's hand always felt somewhat gritty, as if he hadn't washed in a while, but his grip suggested he was in no rush to join the others in line for the bathroom. From the back of one of the lines, Waldemar called out.

"Mr. Solomon," he waved. "I passed my reading test today!" It was great to see him so excited about school, even though his reading skills were still significantly behind where they should be.

"Malcolm," Waldemar called. "Come down before Benjamin beat you with a stick." Most of the boys did a good job of looking out for Malcolm. In fact, I had never seen anyone at Alpha taunt or try to take advantage of Malcolm. His innocence seemed to bring out the best in all of the boys.

Malcolm smiled and stared blankly out at Waldemar. "Go on," I said, releasing his hand. "You had better get in line with everyone else." He smiled meekly and walked down the steps of the verandah and got in line in front of Waldemar, who stepped back and, grabbing Malcolm by the shoulders, adjusted him in place in line.

Just once I wanted to hear Malcolm's voice; hear him say anything.

I thought if he could just form a word that there might be hope. I knew thoughts passed through his brain. I knew he could be happy or sad. I knew he could follow rules, or at least follow the crowd. But without language, what hope would he have? There have been many great men who have been "men of few words." But I don't know of any functioning adults who get by as men of *no* words. All I could do most days was to hold his hand and smile back.

Once the boys were washed and ready for supper, they snaked single file through the Junior Home pantry. Each boy would take a tin plate from the stack at the end of the counter and hold it out in front of whatever peer was doling out the food, usually under Mr. Estig's watchful eye. An adult had to monitor the process to make sure no child got slighted. Each boy received some boiled calaloo, boiled cassava, a small shred of chicken and a slab of buttered bread. They each took their plates to their assigned table. Older boys walked around pouring milk into the small tin cups. Less milk was spilled this way. The one-liter milk cartons had "UHT" stamped prominently on the side. Milk pasteurized at ultra-high temperatures did not need to be refrigerated and could last for months if unopened. It is the perfect product for a tropical climate where keeping milk cold is impossibly expensive. It was often donated in bulk to Alpha. The boys said a solemn - if rapid - grace and then dove into their food. Nurse, Cook or I would stand watch to make sure every morsel was eaten. The boys were not allowed to save food for later in the evening. It was too easy for an older, larger boy to bully a smaller boy into saving some of his dinner and handing it over later

I walked back to my room to grade papers before my own dinner would arrive. The wisps of clouds in the sky over Long Mountain were beginning to change color as the sun settled lower in the sky. The older boys were lined up outside of Senior Home refectory, waiting for their dinner. A more casual mood prevailed at Senior Home. The lines were not quite as straight, the talking louder, the jostling for position in line a little more aggressive. It was the natural order of things. There was less control on the older boys, in part because they needed to learn to start fighting their own battles.

When I got back in my room, I laid the essays from the day's classes on the table, one folder for each of the four classes. 160 essays. My goal was to grade forty of them tonight. I took off my shirt, grabbed a soda from the fridge and started grading. Thirty minutes and ten papers later, I went for another soda. As I closed the fridge door and turned toward the table, out of the corner of my eye I saw a movement at the other side of the room. Then, silently, a large rat dashed from under my bed to under my wardrobe. The soda spewed out of my mouth as I jumped up onto the chair, which wasn't easy since the ceiling in the room was less than eight feet high. My heart was racing. The rat was at least the size of a small dog. I was paralyzed for a moment, and then realized how ridiculous it was for me to be standing on a chair like a woman in an old TV sitcom. I slowly started to get off the chair when I heard the rat moving, which ended any thought of stepping on the floor. Instead, I reached over and maneuvered the other chair into position so that I could step from one chair to another and then over to the low chest at the foot of the bed. As I reached the bed, the rat ran out from under the wardrobe and into my small bathroom. I reached out from my perch on the bed, tangled in the mosquito netting, and slammed the bathroom door shut.

I jumped off the bed and, without thinking, pushed a chair in front of the bathroom door. I pulled on a shirt, and hustled to do what any red-blooded American man would do when faced with a rat in his room. I ran to get a 62 year-old nun to kill the rat.

Magdalen was in her office in Junior Home with a half-dozen boys crowded around her.

"Sister, mi want a soccer ball."

"Sister, mi need the key for the pantry."

"Sister, mi can have the thing for the thing?"

I interrupted. "Sister, there's a rat in my room."

She seemed surprised, but not astonished and dealt with my crisis with the same sense of urgency as the other requests I waited patiently as she handled each of us in turn, if you can call pacing nervously looking in other corners for rats "waiting patiently."

"Okay," she said after what must have been two whole minutes. "So you have a rat," she said, folding her hands calmly in her lap. She was almost smiling, as if this would be a nice distraction from the typical routine of the evening. She turned to little Waldemar, who happened to be standing closest to her, "You. Run down to Senior Home kitchen. Get me one of the new cats they have there. Meet me in Mr. Sullivan's room."

"Yes, sister," Waldemar replied as he darted out of the room. "Mi go with him," Craig insisted.

In the doorway, Waldemar shoved the soccer ball Magdalen had just given him into Richard's hand, excited that he had a special errand to run. Richard thought he had won the lottery, receiving a soccer ball without even asking..

Magdalen turned to Desmond, who was off duty at the office and in line behind me hoping to get another ball. "Do you know how to catch a rat?"

"Yes, sister," he said eagerly. Two other boys in line also claimed to be experts at catching rats and mice and other vermin. In two years in Jamaica I never heard a teenage boy admit that there was something he couldn't do.

"Good. Come with us." She turned and winked at me. "Let's go catch your rat."

As our little parade walked from Junior Home to my room, sister asked, "So you saw it in the bathroom?"

"I saw it run in the bathroom and I closed the door, so I assume it's still in there." I already regretted having put the chair in front of the door, knowing how ridiculous it was going to seem in a minute. Before we reached my room, Waldemar showed up with the smallest of kittens.

"Sister, *that's* the cat?" I said. "This rat is three times the size! I'm telling you, it's a *huge* rat!"

Magdalen rolled her eyes. As we walked by the office, she grabbed a broom that was leaning in a corner.

Now five of us were standing at the door of my room: me, Magdalen with a broom, Waldemar with the kitten, Craig with a big grin, and Desmond with an ego about to get him into trouble. I fumbled with the keys a bit, took a deep breath, slowly creaked open the door, and immediately stepped to the top of the chest at the foot of the bed. I turned back and started to say, "Okay, the coast is clear…" but Magdalen had walked right past me to the door of the bathroom with her army of boys in tow.

As I sheepishly hopped down from the bed, she looked up at me and pointed to the chair propped up against the door.

"What's the chair for?" she asked.

"Well, I…never mind. Let me get it out of the way. How can I help, Sister?"

The door to the bathroom opens out into the room. As Magdalen reached for the knob, I said, "Sister, is that a good idea?"

"Well, Jay, how do you think we're going to get rid of the rat if we don't open the door?"

"Okay. Right. Open the door."

"Thank you," she replied raising her eyebrows.

Five of us tried to get a peek in as Sister opened the door a crack. Immediately there was movement in the bathroom, and we could all see the rat hiding behind the toilet. From the rat's perspective, we must have looked like an odd five-headed totem pole in the narrow opening of the door, with Waldemar's head at the bottom, then Craig's, Desmond's, Sister's and mine. Sister closed the door.

"Give me the cat." Waldemar handed her the little kitten who was about to learn that you have to earn your keep in this world. Magdalen tossed it in the bathroom and quickly closed the door. The sounds on the other side of the door were ungodly. The shrieking and screeching went on for about thirty seconds, and then, silence.

"That poor kitten," I said.

"The cat will be fine," Magdalen admonished. "This is what God made it for." She noted my look of concern. "Don't worry. He gave you other talents," she chuckled.

She opened the door and we peered in. The kitten and the rat were in a stalemate on opposite sides of the base of the toilet. As the kitten, its back arched high, fur on end, approached the rat on one side, the rat would move to the other, its teeth bared. What had been a cute little kitty a few seconds ago, was now an intimidating predator.

Sister closed the door again and turned to Desmond.

"You. You said you know how to catch rats?"

Desmond suddenly realized that Sister's seemingly innocent question back at Junior Home had actually been a job interview. His eyes grew wide and he started to back off his bravado.

"Well, I helped my grandmother catch one once a long time ago," he hesitated, "but it may have just been a mouse."

"Good enough," she said, as she handed him the broom.

"Sister, don't make him go in there." I said. "I'll do it."

Desmond was eagerly handing me the broom when Magdalen turned him by the shoulder. "You can do this," she said. "Just poke at the rat with the broom. The cat will do the rest." She opened the door again, and pushed the frightened boy into the tiny bathroom.

This time the screeching was louder, and included Desmond's voice, but didn't last more than a few seconds.

"Okay, sista! Okay!" Desmond yelled from inside the bathroom. Magdalen quickly opened the door and we all stared in. Desmond, wide-eyed and breathing heavily, had the rat wedged in the corner with the broom and the kitten had the rat by the throat. I stepped in and helped Desmond finish the job.

"Well. That ends that," Magdalen said. "Don't touch the rat," she warned the boys. "I know I don't have to tell *you* that," she said to me laughing. "Craig, run and fetch a shovel for Mr. Sullivan."

"Yes, sista," he turned and ran quickly out of the room.

"Jay, the garbage pile is out behind the garage behind Senior Home. When Craig brings you the shovel, can you throw the rat on the pile?"

"Of course, sister. Not a problem."

"You," she pointed to little Waldemar, "Bring the cat back to Senior Home and tell Cook to give it some milk. And you, my brave rat-killer, you did well." She patted Desmond on the back. "Come, I'll give you a treat too."

"Desmond de Rat Killer!" Waldemar said admiringly, looking up at Desmond. I found myself looking at him with the same sense of admiration. I couldn't imagine my parents putting me in charge of killing a rat as a young teenager, and I couldn't picture myself eager for the challenge.

"Sister, how do you think the rat got in here?" I asked, obviously concerned that others would follow.

"I don't know. Sometimes they come up through the shower drain." She pulled back the shower curtain, "Look, there's no drain cover. I'll have Mr. Maxwell take a look at that tomorrow. I have to get back to Junior Home now and get the boys ready for bed." We walked to the door of the library. "Dinner should be up from the convent soon, Jay," she said over her shoulder as she walked out and along the verandah by the office.

"Okay, Sister. Thanks for your help."

As usual, Magdalen had turned a chance opportunity into a teaching moment. She often referred to each boy as "you" and gave the impression that she couldn't remember all of their names. And I am sure she couldn't at times. She easily could have handed me the broom to kill the rat, or would have had no difficulty in doing it herself. But she knew that the boys needed to be taught to take care of things: to not shy away from taking action. Every chance she got, she made sure they took on responsibility. Desmond had started the day as just "Desmond." Now he was "Desmond the Rat Killer." Magdalen would make sure he had a special meal that evening. But his real treat was bragging rights. Desmond would live on this victory for a long time, telling his story and feeling special. More importantly, soon he would be moving to Senior Home. He would need more confidence there, particularly when being pushed around by the older boys. But Desmond the Rat Killer was now better prepared for that move. He had faced one of life's little challenges and had emerged the victor. Magdalen had made Desmond a winner.

But what identity had the incident created for me? Although I still couldn't define what role I wanted to fill at Alpha, I certainly knew I didn't want to be a burden. Magdalen had better things to do with her time than take care of a grown man afraid of a rat. I needed to either step up my game, or leave. The only thing I knew for certain was, if another rat got into my room, I now had two people I could run to.

As Magdalen rounded the corner of the office she was almost knocked off her feet by Craig racing around the corner with a shovel. Craig and I went back to my room, where we scooped up the rat and brought it around to the pile. "Have you ever killed a rat before, Craig?"

"Yes sir. Just now. Mi an expert at killing rats. And cleaning up from killing rats too."

After we threw the rat on the garbage pile Craig returned the shovel and I returned to my room. I stood in the doorway of the bathroom. After staring at the shower and the open drain for a few minutes, I went into the library and took an unused shelf from one of the bookcases. I got a cinderblock that was used as a door stop for one of the library doors. I put the shelf over the drain and the cinderblock on top of the shelf. I would have no more visitors that evening. For about a week, until Mr. Maxwell was able to install a drain cover, I would move the block and shelf each time I used the shower and replace them immediately afterward.

10
THE RAINS

"Please copy the sentences on the board. They are part of your homework for this evening," I started my last class of the day at St. George's. The First Form classrooms were much brighter than those for the older boys. They had the same wall of open brick-work facing the verandah, but a full wall of windows on the other side. The windows faced the school's rarely used tennis courts - courts with no nets but lots of weeds – and in the distance, the hills that surrounded Kingston, and the Blue Mountains beyond.

My First Form students would soon be identifying subjects, underlining verbs, and drawing boxes around direct objects. But for now, they were engaging in an exercise at which they would all succeed 100% - rewriting sentences. As I stared at their down-turned heads, I thought about the difference between these boys, those at Alpha and my classmates at BC. Different abilities. Different opportunities. Different expectations for what life would make available to them, and for what they would contribute in return. What we all shared was a need to define our own paths and make our way in the world, in essence, to define our calling.

I had begun my experience in Jamaica thinking that the boys at George's would be my focus, but they had become a means to an end. I still owed them my energy in the classroom, my passion for them to learn, whatever intelligence I could bring to the process. But they were just my ticket to be in the country, while my true vocation had become their brothers at Alpha. The George's boys were work. The Alpha boys were family.

Jamaica has substantial Chinese and Indian populations, and both groups tend to be wealthier and better educated than the general population. As a result, there were far more Chinese and Indians at St. George's than at Alpha, where almost all of the boys were of African descent. But because races had intermingled in Jamaica for so long, many of the faces in the class and at Alpha represented an amalgam of humanity. Not only did skin colors run the gamut, but the boys' features combined in dramatic ways. The boys were Indian-Chinese, or Caucasian-African, or Indian-Caucasian. To my eyes, the most beautiful were the boys of African-Chinese descent, in part I think because of how exotic they seemed. These boys of the amazing faces didn't know at the time that they represented the future of the world, and the hope that people can transcend the superficial to focus on the substantive. It was 1986, long before the corporate world invested millions in "diversity programs," long before America had its first mixed-race president, long before everyone had a biological or adopted family member of a different race. Each morning at St. George's, the diversity wasn't just in the class, but in each boy. And every day in the classroom I was given the gift of seeing how much more beautiful we were becoming as a species.

October through December is the rainy season in Kingston. You experience rain in Jamaica with all five senses. First, you feel a single wisp of a breeze, just enough to cool the hair on your arms, but not enough to ruffle the papers on your desk. Within moments of the breeze, you notice a new scent; a nutty, earthy smell caused by all of the dust in the air suddenly settling to the ground at once, unable to stay suspended in the rapidly growing humidity. In a few seconds, that scent is replaced by a dampness in your mouth that tastes of hibiscus flowers. Then, the first drops land with loud "plops" in the dust just off the verandah. The isolated drops continue for only a minute before the skies open and the deafening downpour begins. The rain can be so heavy at times, you can barely see from the First Form block to the cafeteria, about twenty yards from the verandah, and you don't bother walking out into it unless you absolutely must. I had experienced hurricanes and nor'easters in New England. I was used to heavy rain accompanied by driving winds. But except for the initial breeze, the afternoon rains in Kingston were different - just water, tons of it, unloaded from the heavens without the accompanying dramatics of gusting winds or thunder and lightning.

The view of the hills from the First Form block allowed a view of the changing sky. The clouds always rolled in around 2:30. After that, it was anyone's guess if the rains would start before the 2:50 bell dismissed classes for the day.

If the rains held off, the bell would prompt the boys to make a mad dash for the door and across the campus to waiting parents or drivers, or a fast trot out the main gate and in many directions to catch buses home. If the rains came before the bell, the boys were stuck.

Today, the clouds and breezes rolled in on cue. As the sky darkened the boys started to pack up their books and papers.

"Just what do you think you're doing, gentlemen?" I asked.

"But, sir, class is almost over and we want to be ready to go," Barrington Lee explained to nods of agreement from his classmates.

"Class is over when I say class is over. You can pack up when the bell rings. We have a few more sentences to finish." The boys groaned in defeat. As I wandered up and down the aisles, I noticed how some had stealthily slipped their papers and pens in their bags. Others had strategically laid all of their materials on their desk poised to sweep them into open book-bags the minute the bell rang.

The next breeze brought with it the smell of the dust settling. I explained the homework assignment, and read off the names of the boys who I thought deserved honorable mention for a paper well done, a test aced, or a grade point average brought up. The first drop of rain plopped outside the classroom. Then silence. Then a few more plops. Then the bell rang. The immediate bustle and chaos as the boys raced for the door was comical, and it was always hard for me to keep a straight face watching them become so desperate to leave. In the seconds it took the boys to reach the verandah, the downpour had begun. The bottleneck at the doors kept some of them in the room.

As I packed up my own papers, I announced facetiously, "Well, since you can't go anywhere for a while, why don't we do a few more exercises?" A few of the boys looked at me with panic, but most just ignored my comment, rolling their eyes and kissing their teeth as they looked back over their shoulders from the doorway.

One boy pulled a deck of cards from his school bag. Others plopped down in nearby desks to read comic books or play with their Gameboys.

After fifteen minutes, the rain subsided to mere monsoon level and many of the boys rushed for the front of the campus. I was in less of a hurry, knowing my Fourth Formers who had detention would wait for me. Not interested in getting wet, I sat at my desk for another ten minutes correcting papers and listening to the rain.

* * *

Back at Alpha, Mr. Estig was finishing his afternoon lessons with the boys. Morris could not read, and could not understand how reading would help him find food once he left Alpha. You didn't need to read to forage in a dumpster or swipe food from a higgler at the market. When Mr. Estig dismissed all of the boys, he ordered Morris to stay put in his seat. Morris had been at Alpha for only a few weeks, and still didn't know what to make of the people and the processes. The minute he was alone with Mr. Estig, however, he started to get nervous. He had been beaten and abused by enough adults that he was wary of any private interaction. In fact, he could not remember ever being alone with an adult where he didn't end up worse for it. But Mr. Estig's classroom was open to the dormitory, where a steady stream of people passed, making Morris feel less isolated.

Mr. Estig pulled a chair up to Morris' desk. He turned the boy's small hand-held blackboard toward him so he could read his work. The slate was empty.

"All right, Mr. Mathers. Let's start from the beginning." Mr. Estig, in his perfect diction and patient pacing, taught Morris the alphabet in a single afternoon. Morris remained tense, knowing that when he let down his guard was usually the moment when an adult would reach out to take advantage of him. But Mr. Estig just kept working through each letter, forcing Morris to repeat, and more importantly, to understand why he was repeating, each symbol. Morris didn't like the repetition, but began to like the attention.

Once the rains started, Morris found it difficult to concentrate. He had always enjoyed the downpours when he lived on the street. Heavy rains create chaos, and chaos creates an opportunity to steal. Sometimes he found himself helping the street vendors cover their wares, knowing they would show him gratitude afterward. Though he found the gifts rewarding, it was easier just to steal. In either case, when it was raining, everyone else was too busy to yell at him, or kick at him. Morris liked the hour after the rain let up most of all. In spite of having to always be on the lookout for danger, and in search of his next meal, he enjoyed the reawakening of the city after the deluge. Puddles on the sidewalk and in the street always had a film of oil or grease, just enough to catch the sunlight and form a swirling rainbow. Morris occasionally allowed himself time to marvel at the colors. Today however, Mr. Estig was keeping him from enjoying the rain. Morris hadn't noticed that his apprehension at being alone with Mr. Estig had dissipated, turning into impatience with having to concentrate rather than have fun.

He shifted uncomfortably in his seat as Mr. Estig asked him questions and tried to get him to sound out the letters and a few short words. Mr. Estig started to get frustrated and his voice became shrill and commanding. But after a few minutes, the sound of the rain hitting the metal louvers on the windows of Junior Home made the lesson impossible anyway, and Mr. Estig sent Morris on his way. As Morris raced through the dormitory he noticed a poster on the wall with The Lord's Prayer on it. He couldn't read the text, but he immediately noticed the capital letters "O" and "F" from the words "Our Father" at the top. Under his breath, and almost subconsciously, he mumbled the sounds of the letters softly. Morris reached the verandah just as the rains subsided. The puddles on the plaza reminded Morris how much he preferred the outdoors, and he promised himself he wouldn't get stuck staying after class again.

11
ALL FOR A GOOD CAUSE

Sr. Marie Therese sat in her small office upstairs in the convent. Her desk was a simple table with a stack of cubby holes on the back holding various envelopes, office supplies, large rings of keys, prayer cards, and programs from events at which the Alpha band had performed. On the left side, a six-inch cross of Blue Mahoe wood made by one of the boys in the woodworking shop served as a paperweight for the pile of bills that had to be paid. On the right were stacks of ledgers. On the floor next to her were other stacks of folders and papers no one had looked at in years.

She had just sent Plunkett to Mr. Herman, who worked in the office downstairs, to get the current ledger that would tell her the head count for the orphanage. The number of boys as of the first of the month would determine the amount of support Alpha would receive from the Jamaican government. Different government ministries provided funds for housing, education, and the trades, but it was never enough. To make up the difference, the sisters had learned to be creative.

Marie Therese had been at Alpha for more than twenty-five years. For many years she had lived at the main convent at the Academy and had come up each morning to teach the younger boys. When it had become clear to her that Alpha would be her life's work, she moved to the smaller convent above the office and took charge of the Senior Home. A few years later she stepped into the role of school administrator.

Marie Therese cared deeply for the boys. She was both confident in their goodness and worried for their future and the future of Alpha. The arthritis in her hands and knees had gotten worse in the last year, and she occasionally felt light headed. In the last few months, in an effort to limit the number of trips she needed to make up and down the stairs, she had begun working in her upstairs office for most of the morning, not coming downstairs until about eleven to meet with Mr. Herman and Mrs. Donegan, the book-keeper.

Plunkett brought her the ledgers. There had been two hundred and forty-two boys at Alpha on November 1: ninety-six at Junior Home, and one-hundred forty-six at Senior Home. The government paid slightly more for the care of teenagers than for smaller children, knowing that teenagers ate more. Nevertheless, the state was about three months in arrears. Older boys may eat more, but apparently they could wait three months for their dinner.

Marie Therese would spend the better part of October putting together her budget for the next year to share with the leadership of the Sisters of Mercy. She was an excellent administrator, and she knew she needed the fund-raising expertise of her order's larger organization to keep Alpha afloat. Each day she sat at her desk, put her hand on the cross on the top of the pile of bills and said a quick prayer before facing her challenge.

* * *

As I walked by the office, having just returned from St. George's, Plunkett came scurrying around the corner. "Afternoon, Mr. Solomon," he said quickly, nodding as he hurried by me. "I have to bring these keys to Sr. Ignatius, sir," he said holding up a large ring of keys, as if apologizing for not stopping to talk.

Magdalen walked out of the office finishing a conversation with Mr. Herman.

"Jay. You're back from school. Good. Are you busy this afternoon?"

"Well, I was going to open up the game room, but if you need something, I'm sure that can wait a bit."

"Irene arrived early today and opened the room, so you don't need to worry about that. Would you join Marie Therese on some errands this afternoon?"

I hesitated since I hadn't seen Irene in a few days. "Of course, Sister. Whatever you need." The truth was, the sisters rarely asked anything of me. I was always free to decide how I spent my time at Alpha. I dropped my bag in my room, ran up to Junior Home for quick hello to Irene, and then back to the office.

Marie Therese slowly descended the stairs from the convent. Like Ignatius, Marie Therese spoke with perfect diction, but with a less clipped and more motherly lilt to her voice. Everything about her – her smile, her voice, her hands, her words - was warm and comforting. The skin on her face and hands was the warm light brown of cashews. Of medium height and a slightly stooped posture from her arthritis, without the habit, Marie Therese would have looked like many of the older Italian women I knew growing up. Her face reminded me of my Great-aunt Sally Cervini.

"Mr. Jay. I hear you are joining us for our adventure this afternoon. I'm so glad." Marie Therese made everyone she met feel like they were the most important person in her day, which may be why she reminded me of Aunt Sally. As a child, I only saw Aunt Sally once a year, at Christmas. The dozens of gifts under her tree were each wrapped in a different type of paper, making each one feel unique. When she approached me with my gift, she would hug it close to her chest as if to say how important it was to her, and how she remembered picking it out just for me. All I wanted to do was tear into the paper, but I knew I'd have to wait for her to cup my face in both her hands and plant a big wet kiss on my cheek. The smell of her Jean Natě bath water permeated the wrapping paper, the ribbon and the room. Sr. Marie Therese did not use Jean Natě, but I smelled it whenever I was around her. "Come then," she said. "Mr. Johnson is waiting."

Mr. Johnson, the driver, pulled the van around to the front of the office, from back behind the Senior Home where it was usually parked. Alpha's van was about ten years old. It sat about fifteen people, legally, but could take up to as many as twenty when necessary. Mr. Johnson had been the driver for many years. In addition to taking Sr. Marie Therese on her errands, and picking up Chinese food for special occasions, he would drive the band to its many concerts to help raise the school's profile, and some much needed cash. Concerts required two or three trips, since the twenty-some boys in the band couldn't fit with all of their instruments.

As Marie Therese walked by the front of the office, she turned to Wilbert and said, "Wilbert, I may need your help."

Wilbert went dashing from his perch on the bench by the office, turning to flash a bragging smirk to Worldhead, who stood in anticipation, hoping he too would be called.

I put out my arm to walk Marie Therese to the van.

"Thank you Mr. Jay. We don't get to spend any time together. This will be nice," she said in her slow careful speech

"Sister, do you think we might need Worldhead's help, as well as Wilbert's?" I looked over my shoulder as Worldhead's eyes grew large and he stood up from the bench.

"Well, that would certainly be fine," she said. I nodded to Worldhead who dashed past us to jump into the van.

"Worldhead," I called. "Why don't you walk sister to the van?"

"Yes sir," he replied, quickly turning back. He grabbed sister by the other arm and started to pull her toward the car.

"Worldhead, just put out your arm like this," I said. "That will allow sister to hold on to you, and move at her own pace."

He nodded, "Yes, sir. Yes, sir." Sister smiled, knowing she was a merely a prop for a lesson on how to be a gentleman.

As we got to the van, I said, "Wilbert, get out and help Sister up, please."

"Yessir," he said quickly, jumping out and running to the back of the van. He brought around a small step-stool

Once we were all in, Mr. Johnson put the van in gear and we drove the short distance to the main gate. Even though the senior home boy guarding the gate was on his way to open it for us, Mr. Johnson still honked twice as if to tell him to hurry.

As the boy opened the gate, a rail-thin woman who looked to be in her thirties, started crossing the bridge over the gully. The bridge was barely wide enough to accommodate a person and the van at the same time.

"Mr. Johnson," Marie Therese said, "please see what this dear woman wants."

Mr. Johnson rolled down his window and spoke briefly to the woman.

"She looking for a job, sister," he said.

"Please tell her to speak with Mr. Herman in the office, Mr. Johnson. I know he is looking for someone to help with the cleaning and to help Nurse."

Mr. Johnson again exchanged words with the woman, who suddenly stood up taller, thanked sister through the open window, and walked through the gate.

We turned right onto a busy South Camp Road, which ran from the military camp down to the harbor.

We headed north, through the Crossroads intersection and into an industrial part of town I had not been to. Wilbert and Worldhead were both staring out the windows as avidly as I was.

The narrow streets were crammed with small delivery trucks and flanked by high walls and solid gates, making them feel like chutes, with no way out.

We pulled up to a tall steel gate, rusted a deep red. "Peters' Bakery" was painted in faded black letters on the concrete wall next to the gate. The guard sitting in front peered at us, but when he saw the school's name in light blue letters on the side of the van, and Sister Marie Therese in back, he opened the gate and we drove in. The smell of fresh baked bread mixed with the diesel fumes. Once we parked, Wilbert jumped out and positioned the step-stool.

"Mr. Jay, boys, come with me please," Marie Therese said as she slowly climbed down.

As we arrived at the foot of the loading dock, I stepped ahead to help Marie Therese, but she brushed me off, and her back seemed to straighten as she pulled herself up the short flight of steps and into the industrial bakery. The foreman was busy yelling at some poor hapless worker stacking trays of bread on rolling racks. As soon as he spied Marie Therese, he stopped yelling and hurried over.

"Sister," he said warmly, taking the hand she extended. He didn't really shake her hand, as much as just held it. He was almost bowing.

"Mr. Peters," she said in her perfect diction. "So good to see you. How is Mrs. Peters?"

"Very good, Sister. Very good. Thank you so much for coming to see her after the funeral for her brother. That meant a lot to her, Sister."

"He was such a good man. What an awful thing with that minibus," she shook her head.

"What can I do for you, Sister?"

Marie Therese introduced me to Mr. Peters, who was about to be hit by a bigger bus than had flattened his brother-in-law.

"Mr. Peters," she started. "You know we have always bought our bread from your bakery."

"Yes, Sister. And I appreciate it."

"Well, I'm not sure your driver appreciates the relationship we have shared over the years. Our delivery has been short by about ten loaves each delivery. We are trying to feed so many poor boys." She turned and gestured toward Wilbert, pulling him in front of her. She didn't introduce him. He seemed to know intuitively it was his turn to be a prop, and tried his best to look thin and pathetic. "As you know, the Ministry is always late with their checks to us and we run a very tight ship. The Ministry is late with us, but we always pay our bills on time."

"I know, Sister, but I can't believe my driver would short your delivery," he said, genuinely amazed.

"Mr. Peters, one of our staff members monitors the delivery very carefully and she has had to correct the driver every time. On the few occasions that she hasn't been on hand when the delivery arrives, we note we are an entire tray of bread short."

"Well, Sister, I will promise you that will never happen again. I am sure it is not intentional."

"I am sure it isn't, Mr. Peters, since your driver is such a polite man. Nevertheless, I would appreciate it if you could make sure it doesn't happen again." She started to walk along the loading dock. "What smells so lovely this afternoon?"

"Well, Sister, we send out the bread in the morning, but in the afternoon, we deliver the donuts."

"Oh, donuts. Business is good then, if people can afford donuts. I am so glad for you." She ran her hand along the rolling tray stacked with boxes of donuts.

"Here now, you two," Mr. Peters snapped his fingers at two workers standing nearby. "Bring these to Sister's van." He gestured to two tall stacks of trays.

"Oh, Mr. Peters, you are too generous."

"Not at all, Sister."

The two men rolled the stack of trays over to the van, where Mr. Johnson had already opened the back hatch. They loaded two trays of donut boxes into the van, and then stopped and looked at poor Mr. Peters. While still staring into the warehouse, but sensing they had stopped loading the car, Sister said, "We have 250 boys at Alpha," she said softly.

Mr. Peters nodded to the two men, who filled the back of the van with the entire rolling cart of donuts.

"Mr. Peters, are those pies?" Sister asked, nodding at another rolling cart in the warehouse.

"Yes, Sister," he said with less enthusiasm than when he had greeted her.

"They look lovely," she said.

"Sister, I would be glad to give you some pies for the boys this evening." He turned to his workers. "You there, put two trays of pies in Sister's car."

"Oh, you are too generous, Mr. Peters," she said smiling.

"If you will excuse me, Sister, I must get back to the office now," he said, again, bowing and tucking his clipboard under one arm.

"Mr. Peters, you are such a generous benefactor of our school," she said warmly, this time, taking his free hand in both of hers. "Please give this medal of the Blessed Mother to Mrs. Peters, and tell her we will say a special novena for her dear brother tonight at evening prayers."

"Yes, Sister, it is so good to see you. And I promise, there will be no more short deliveries."

"Of course not, Mr. Peters. I am sure it was just a mistake. And we will be calling soon to place our special order for Christmas, as we always have done. Now, we shouldn't keep you from your business. Come, Wilbert."

Wilbert took Sister's arm as she descended the loading dock stairs.

Because the back of the van was now full of donuts, we all got into the van first, and then Mr. Peters' workers stacked boxes of pies on our laps.

The guard pushed open the gate and let us out of the parking lot. Tight security hadn't stopped this self-inflicted robbery.

"Sister, that was quite a negotiation."

"Mr. Peters is a good man and simply wanted to help us feed the poor boys in our care. He is a generous and good Christian," she said. "Wilbert, stop drooling," she added. "You and the office boys can have a box of donuts as soon as we get home. Mr. Johnson, please take me to the supply store in Liguanea where we get the supplies for the printery."

A few minutes later, we pulled into the public parking lot in a small strip mall. "I think we need to pay a visit to Mrs. Friendly. We need another ink delivery for the print shop. Wilbert come with me...and bring a pie."

Four stops later, Sister had arranged for donations of extra ink for the print shop, extra milk and a trial order of cheese from the dairy, four bolts of fabric to be delivered for the tailor shop and two cases of chalk from the school supply store...all for the cost of five of Mr. Peters' pies.

"Sister, you managed to get quite a bit done today," I said as we headed back toward Alpha.

"Yes, it was a good day, Mr. Jay. So many people want to help us help the boys. Sometimes it's just a matter of giving people the opportunity."

She was so kind and generous about other people's motives it seemed impolite to challenge her assumption. And I was pretty sure she knew she was ascribing her own motives to others. It was part of her graciousness.

When we got back to Alpha, just before dinner, Mr. Johnson dropped Marie Therese off at the office. "Mr. Jay, thank you for coming with me today. I hope you got to see another side of Kingston."

"Absolutely, Sister. Thank you." It was the other side of sister that I saw that I found more interesting.

"Mr. Johnson, please pull around to the pantry. Magdalen should be there now preparing dinner. Unload the donuts right away or they will disappear. And take a pie for yourself and Mrs. Johnson."

"Yes sista. Thank you sista."

"Can I also impose on you to give a pie to each of the teachers who are still here?" she asked.

"Yes, Sista. Gladly, Sista. Thank you."

We drove around back to the kitchen and unloaded the van right into the storeroom. The donuts would be cut in quarters, and the boys would have donut pieces for dinner that night, breakfast the next morning, and dinner the following night. Mr. Estig, Nurse and Cook all went home that night carrying a pie and a smile.

That evening I reflected on my own naiveté. It had never occurred to me that someone would try to rip off a convent or an orphanage. Whether it was Mr. Peters or his driver didn't matter. What mattered was that someone consciously tried to take advantage of the nuns and the boys.

It seemed cruel and bizarre to me. From my own narrow perspective, I had assumed everyone would think of Alpha as a wonderful place of good will and good works, and that people would want to help the place provide refuge and care for the boys.

As one of the few adult males at Alpha, I wondered about my role as protector. To what extent could a taller presence, a stronger back, a deeper voice, a firmer stance help secure the peace and ward off threats? Had there been barbarians at the gate, I could have helped more. But the threats to the boys and the sisters and what they had built were much more subtle, and the sisters' wisdom, tact and emotional intelligence were more important armor than what I had to offer. Firm resolve was more important than a firm handshake, and hands when folded in prayer were stronger then when clenched in fists. Testosterone told me to act, and do, and accomplish. But I wasn't being asked to contribute in any of those ways. Most of the time, I was asked to simply be present, and it was starting to drive me nuts.

* * *

That afternoon, the boys enjoyed the breeze on the field behind Junior Home. Q and Richard stood close by O'Brien as he took his turn maneuvering the kite they had built and rebuilt a dozen times that fall. They kept marveling at how small it looked the higher it rose in the sky. They were beyond proud, knowing that theirs was the largest kite on the field. Because the plastic bags that formed the skin were translucent, whenever the kite passed between the boys and the sun, it glowed like a stained glass window. Richard acted as navigator, shouting to O'Brien to reel in or let out the string, and to keep moving back from the other boys so the string would not get tangled. His active participation helped him stave off his burning need to take control of the kite himself. After fifteen minutes, he couldn't control himself any longer and badgered O'Brien long enough to get him to hand over the reins. Now O'Brien acted as guide, shouting at other boys to stay out of the way, and cautioning Richard to watch his step as he kept backing up. By the time Q had his turn the afternoon was wearing on, and part of the kite was wearing out. The largest single panel, a broad red swath in the middle, had developed a tear that spread quickly, creating a gaping, creepy smile on the kite's surface. Q knew they could find a few sticks to strengthen the panel, and that he had a section of a plastic bag that would cover most of the damage. As he reeled it in, wrapping the string around his small arm, he watched carefully to make sure the tear wasn't growing. When the kite was about ten yards off the ground, a mild breeze blew it in the way of two other kites. The strings became tangled and all three kites plummeted to the ground. At first, it seemed very exciting and Q, O'Brien and Richard laughed as they ran to assess how their kite fared in the crash. The boys who had been manning the other kites were already cursing and kicking at the ground at the sight of the fractured twigs and torn plastic – the remnants of all of their hard work. The three younger boys immediately changed their attitude. One of the older boys shoved Q to the ground and kicked dirt at him, yelling at him for his foolish error. The older boy ignored Q's protests that the wind, and not his skill was at fault. Q got to his feet while the other boy further assessed the damage to his kite. Q's kite was the largest of the three involved, and therefore had the most structural damage. As he, Richard and O'Brien examined the sticks and skin, they were already figuring out how to fix the problems.

"Gimme dat!" the older boy said, grabbing their kite. As the younger boys protested, the older boy stripped three large pieces of plastic from the kite, and twisted off a few of the twigs that formed the frame.

"You cannot do dat!" Q shouted. Mi a tell sista on you!"

The older boy threw what remained on the ground and took a step toward Q. "Go ahead, Q. Just try and run to sista. See what happens the next time she not around." The older boy walked away, cursing.

Morris Mathers had been flying the third kite, having begged a turn from other boys, who were now busy inspecting the damage to their toy. He watched the whole scene carefully making note of Q's limited defenses. Morris stepped toward the three boys. Morris was only an inch or two taller than them. "Gimme dat string, now, ya hear!" he demanded.

Q had already endured enough for the day. "G'way. Mi nah give you anyting," he said with a quick snap of his wrist.

O'Brien, Richard and Q were devastated. Q could feel the tears welling up in his eyes. He knew the day would come when the protection he enjoyed from Magdalen would come to an end. He seemed to be on the verge of that moment now. He also knew he was defenseless against an aggressive older boy. He had come to Alpha at such a young age, he didn't have the street fight instincts of some of the others. The three boys gathered the remnants of their kite and tried to figure out what to do next. O'Brien wanted to give up entirely. Q was too angry to think creatively. Richard just looked at the other two and didn't know what to do without their direction.

After supper, the boys had calmed down. Their boredom led them to start to rethink their kite. If they designed a smaller version, they would be able to control it better and they wouldn't need many more supplies. They had almost completed the skeleton when the bell rang for them to line up for their showers.

The smaller boys always entered first. After Q brushed his teeth he entered the shower area and took his usual quick rinse. It was now late fall and the water was getting cooler in the evening. He would start taking even shorter showers in the coming weeks. While he was drying off, Morris Mathers appeared next to him, naked. "Gimme your bottom, Q," Morris demanded, pointing at Q's waist. Q pulled his towel tight around him, and looked puzzled. Morris grabbed at the towel, "Turn around and bend over." He said again, this time in a whisper.

Q stepped back, more in shock that out of fear. He had never been told to do such a thing. He wasn't sure what Morris wanted, but he knew it wasn't a good idea to give it to him. Even without O'Brien and Richard to back him up, Q knew he could hold his own against Morris.

"Git away from me!" he said confidently.

"Den you give me de kite string or I'll take your bottom next time," Morris threatened.

"G'way! You trouble, Mathers!" Q walked toward the hooks where his shorts and shirt were hung and quickly pulled his clothes on, watching over his shoulder.

Morris Mathers stared at him over the short wall that separated the shower area from the sinks. Now that he knew Q wasn't afraid of him, he would need to find other boys to intimidate.

12
NUANCES

One Friday afternoon, Richard sat on the cool tile of the verandah, his legs spread wide, bordering a large square of cardboard. His thumb and forefinger squeezed hard on the stub of a green crayon in his right hand. He leaned forward over the cardboard, concentrating to keep his lines straight, as he carefully traced a grid – eight squares by eight squares. He was tired of waiting for an available checkerboard during the afternoon gameroom, and was determined to make his own. To color in every other square, he started by drawing a face - two round eyes and a short vertical line for a nose. Eventually, he had thirty-two incomplete faces on his checkerboard. Then he started on the mouths. He tried straight lines, open mouths, frowns and smiles. None seemed to please him. He stared at his faces for a long time, and then scribbled over each, banishing all the smiles and frowns beneath a thin layer of green crayon until all that was left was a checkerboard.

* * *

That evening, after we closed the game room, Irene and I strolled up to *You Must Come In*, the bar up the corner from Alpha. Although we had been dating for a while already, most of our time alone together was on the roof of her house or in my room after working with the boys. We were never far from kids or colleagues. We didn't get many opportunities to go out together. At the bar, the young girl with the broom was nowhere to be seen, but the throbbing reggae filled any possible void in the room.

The tables on the street were too close to the traffic, so we chose one inside, by the window.

I had felt out of place on my first visit to the bar, but now, with company, I relaxed. As the large bar matron put the Red Stripes in front of us, she leaned back, pulled the towel off her shoulders to wipe her hands, and smiled, "So what brings you two 'ere?"

"You mean, we don't look like we just moved into the neighborhood?" Irene asked.

"Ha! Da neighborhood? You both so pale you look like you just got to de planet!" She roared at her own joke.

Elisabeth, the barmaid, introduced herself and then stayed at our table talking. She told us how both Alpha Girls' School and Immaculate Conception High School were too hard for her to get into when she was a teen. She did fine at school, but finer when she met the man who owned the bar. When he died, his wife kept his house, but she, Elisabeth, got the bar, which the wife thought was fair since Elisabeth had borne two sons and a daughter to the man. However, when a third woman showed up at the funeral with two children in tow, the wife threw herself at the coffin, wailing not in anger, but in frustration that her husband had needed more than she could provide.

"Well, here's to meeting Mr. Right." Irene raised her beer, and Elisabeth quickly grabbed mine and threw back a long swallow. They toasted and Elisabeth laughed and went to get me another Red Stripe.

Irene came from a stable, loving home on Long Island. I came from an equally wonderful, boring home life – no complicated lines of relationship, no regular hysterics, no great tales of deception or betrayal. Our days seemed dull after listening to Elisabeth's life history, and our families, mundane in comparison. As with many of our conversations in public, when we compared our lives in the States with life in Kingston we kept our voices low, in case we might offend someone. I wonder if being "culturally sensitive" meant not thinking in the same ways we had been taught to think, or just knowing when to keep our opinions to ourselves.

By the time we finished a second round of beer and a plate of chicken wings, it was time to head to Alpha. At Junior home, the boys were in the midst of their bath ritual, brushing their teeth and washing before bed. We stayed out of the way, sitting on the steps of the verandah looking out over the field toward Senior Home.

I shared with Irene how Marie Therese handled Mr. Peters. She told me how Magdalen had not only stopped by the game room while I was out, but had actually sat and played a game of checkers with the boys. "You should have seen how the boys gathered around her! They were so excited. Of course, she could only play one round and then had to go. And as she stood up, laughing, she scolded another boy for having gotten into a fight in Mr. Estig's class today. How she stays on top of it all is beyond me."

"She seems to have achieved the right balance between being an authority figure and a loving presence in their lives," I said, wishing I knew how to accomplish the same.

As I stared into the dusk, a small figure appeared walking from Senior Home, carrying a bag on his shoulder.

"Well, hello, Francis," Irene said warmly. Francis had been sent to see his family because his grandmother was sick. He had been gone about a week. Francis was one of Irene's favorite boys, and he always lit up when he heard her voice. He was ten years old, and small for his age. He had a round face, and a great smile that showed off one of his missing teeth.

Francis walked up the middle of the stairs, forcing Irene and me to scoot apart, as he squeezed in between us and sat himself down, plopping his bag at his feet.

"How was home?" she asked.

"It was fine, miss," he said smiling.

"How is your family?"

"My grandma's not so well, miss. That's why my mother called for me. I think she's going to die."

"I'm very sorry, Francis," I said.

"Tank you sir," he said, looking warily over his shoulder at the door to the dormitory.

"How is the rest of your family?" Irene asked.

"My mom is good, miss. I like her cooking. Sista gave me a pie to bring her when I went, and she really liked that. My older sista isn't there anymore. She live in country with my auntie. My mom didn't want her around the boys in the yard anymore." He continued to look over his shoulder at the door.

"Okay, Francis," I said, "Why don't you go get ready for bed now."

"Yes sir," he said, but didn't move right away.

"Francis," Irene said. "Mr. Sullivan and I were just watching the stars come out. Sit here with us for just a few more minutes?"

"Yes, miss," he said eagerly, and settled into place with a deep sigh.

We stared out as the sky grew dark. Francis shared more details about his visit home, and even told us about some trouble he had gotten into with his own friends in his yard that had landed him at Alpha.

Eventually, Irene said, "Okay, Francis. It's time you headed inside. We'll be there in a minute to read stories."

"Yes, Miss. Thank you, Miss," he said as he stood, stretched, and headed in.

"That was nice," I said. "I don't get to spend much time talking to the boys alone. I'm always surrounded by at least three or four of them. It's nice to get some one-on-one time."

"Actually, I asked him to stay out here for his sake, not yours," Irene said.

The puzzled look on my face clearly begged for an explanation.

"He just came from being with his mother and grandmother, who he obviously loves very much. He just came from *home*. Once he steps through those doors," she gestured to the screen door of the dormitory, "once he steps through there, he is back here again. As long as he was out here with us, he wasn't back yet. I thought he needed a little more time to make the adjustment."

"How did you get to be so smart?" I asked.

She smiled. "Stick around. It'll rub off."

When I read stories that night, Irene sat at the end of one of the beds, with Francis sitting at her feet, pressed to her left leg, and Richard Burns pressed to her right. After we tucked them in, to the strains of George Winston's *December*, we walked out to the road and took a cab to her house, where we had dinner with her roommates and spent the evening talking about our purpose in the world, in Jamaica, and in the lives of the kids, all over more rounds of Red Stripe.

* * *

"One...two...three...four...five...six," Q counted to himself slowly, and then Orvis, the boy in the next bed, breathed deeply once again, and Q began his count from the start. Orvis, sound asleep, had been breathing at the same pace for a while already, and keeping track had given Q something to do while he stared at the ceiling. During his count, Q could also hear Patches occasionally growl, the distant sound of the music pulsating from *You Must Come In*, and the occasional rooster crowing, regardless of morning still being hours away. Normally Q slept soundly. But there were plenty of nights when he would wake up when Sister Magdalen came back to Junior Home for the night.

He liked sleeping closest to her door, and the sounds coming from her room and office were the closest he had ever known to the familiar sounds of a home pulling up the covers and settling in for the night. Q stared at the ceiling. He thought about the evening. Mr. Solomon had read a story about Anansi the Spider. It was one of his favorites. At the end of the story, after the mother explained to her son and daughter why Anansi was a good omen, she gathered them both in her arms and hugged them close before putting them to bed. She tucked in the sheet around them and kissed them each on the forehead. After the story, Mr. Solomon had walked around again and thumb-wrestled with many of the boys. Q wondered what it would be like to live in a home with only a mother and maybe a sister or brother. He wondered what it would be like to have someone have only him to tuck in. He tried to imagine being one of two, instead of one of two hundred. As he stared at the ceiling, he hugged himself , but it left him empty, and he knew a real hug must be different, like when Ms. Irene would put her arm around him, or even when he and Richard and O'Brien would sit shoulder to shoulder, crammed at Mr. Solomon's feet to hear stories. But he imagined a mother's hug to be different. In the Anansi story, the boy notices the sweet smell of his mother's skin, a combination of flowers from their garden and spices from the dinner she had prepared. Q could still smell Sister Magdalen's scent from when she walked by. She smelled like Sister Magdalen, familiar, just like Nurse or Cook, but not sweet, and not special. He stared at the ceiling.

October 28, 1986

Dear Jay,

I just love hearing from you! Thanks a lot for your letter. Knowing how you must be busy over your books, I appreciate it all the more. But please do not worry if you are too busy to write. I can understand, as I am always too busy to write!

At present I am at Gordon Town for 4 days of rest. I love this place. All I do is sleep, eat and pray, and write letters in between. Yesterday I slept until 11:00 a.m. It is such a wonderful feeling to know you can stay in bed as long as you please! After almost 40 years in Religion, I still cannot get used to getting up 5:15 every morning. And if there is nothing to help me to get to heaven, this only or this alone should provide me with a free ticket – non-stop – to the pearly gates.

This reminds me to give you the sad news of my mother's death. She was 92 on Sept. 27 & she passed away on Sept. 30. But I prayed that the Lord will take her – she was bed ridden for 9 months – and the Lord answered my prayers. I feel she is closer to me now, but my family miss her very much. There is so much to thank the Lord for. He has given me such a wonderful mother & let the whole family enjoy her for so many years. I was glad I saw her last year when she was quite well when I left her. I have that last impression of her. She was a good woman – it is a pity I do not take after her – but we cannot all be angels!

Please give my love to your dear mother & all your dear ones at home. You know you have my love always.

God Bless you.

Sr. Magdalen.

13
THE TRAVAILS OF TRAVEL

In early November, a local charity contacted Sister Marie Therese and asked if there were any boys at Alpha with a physical handicap. She immediately thought of Michael, the office boy with sickle cell and the twisted right foot, and Anthony Gayle, whose withered right arm and significant limp made running impossible, but somehow didn't impede his spirit.

The charity organizes trips for handicapped Jamaicans to visit the shrine at Lourdes in France, where many people believe miracle cures occur in the name of the Blessed Virgin. Jamaica is a nation of many faiths, where people believe passionately in their god and are devoted to their church; but where following a particular religion doesn't exclude finding hope and comfort in others. Just as bloodlines had mixed on the island for centuries, eternal truths blurred as well. So the sisters registered no surprise that the leader of the charity was a local Jewish businessman.

Marie Therese knew the trip would be a defining moment in each boy's life. But she was concerned about building up their hopes, particularly since the trip wouldn't happen until the spring, and a lot can happen in five months. She knew that even the best of intentions didn't always result in tangible outcomes. So when Michael and Anthony met with the representative of the charity, they were told the interview was because the man was interested in supporting Alpha.

Anthony was one of the few actual orphans at Alpha. He had been abandoned at Kingston General Hospital as an infant, and lived at Primrose, an orphanage, to the age of six. He lived with a foster family for two years, but when that family emigrated to the U.S., they turned Anthony back to the child care system, and he arrived at Alpha.

The sisters kept Anthony in the Junior Home longer than most because his physical limitations and his complete lack of guile made him an easy target. But he had been in the Senior Home for two years at this point. He was doing well and had decided to become a tailor. He had enough dexterity in his good arm, and enough control of his withered arm to do the job. In addition, there was rarely anything associated with tailoring that required speed, a quality he lacked. Because he was unable to participate in the band, and because he didn't have any family, Anthony had rarely left the Alpha compound in the seven years he had been at the school.

On a Tuesday morning in early November, Magdalen took Michael and Anthony to get their pictures taken for their passports, again, telling them the pictures were needed for other reasons. They were dressed in their Sunday dress shirts, slacks and shoes, rather than the usual shorts, t-shirts and bare feet. Anthony was almost giddy at the thought of going in the car, and heading out on the streets of the city. His smile engulfed his face and he was so eager he almost stepped out in front of the blue Volvo as Magdalen was pulling it around to the front of the office.

"Dear Lord," Magdalen said to herself. "If he's this excited about a ride in the car, he's going to burst when he finds out where he's going!"

Michael, being older, immediately took the passenger seat, leaving the back seat to Anthony, who was so grateful he would never have thought to ask for more. As the boys piled in, Desmond ran from the convent steps and handed Magdalen an envelope. "Sister Marie Therese said to give you this. It's the money for the pictures," he said in the car window to Magdalen.

"Plunkett, why don't you join us?" Before Plunkett could even answer, Magdalen yelled out to Mr. Herman who was standing in the office doorway. "Mr. Herman, tell Sister Ignatius I have taken Plunkett with me. I might need him." Magdalen enjoyed Desmond's company, since he was quiet when she needed to think, listened well when she told her stories, and spoke up when engaged. She never knew what might come up when she was out on the road and he might come in handy.

Anthony awkwardly scooted over as Desmond climbed into the back seat behind Magdalen. As she put the car in gear, she honked twice to signal the boy at the main entrance to open the gate. She pulled out onto South Camp Road and headed north toward Crossroads.

Years of British colonial rule left Jamaica with an English accent on its patois, pith helmets on its occasional traffic policemen and British driving rules, which meant driving on the left side of the street. Sister was short and drove slightly hunched over. She didn't wear sunglasses, so she was always squinting. Magdalen chatted with the boys about all the construction going on in Kingston, and how some projects seemed to take forever and other buildings went up so quickly, but that in spite of the buildings, nothing really important in the country seemed to change. Michael agreed readily. Anthony didn't really follow the conversation; he was too busy watching the whole world go by his window.

Plunkett felt himself viewing the trip differently. He enjoyed his frequent errands with Magdalen. Although they always involved chores, the trips were certainly better than the tasks Sister Ignatius had the other boys performing. But this time, felt different. Magdalen had told Mr. Herman that she might *need* him. He liked being needed, and being needed was different than being given busy work.

As they pulled to a stop at the intersection of Old Hope Road and Oxford Road, a man in rags approached Magdalen's window. "Please, sista. Mi beg you some money."

"Sorry. I have no money for you today," she replied. "But here, take these sweets." She reached under her seat for the bag of hard candies she kept there for just this purpose. As she did so, the man spotted the envelope on the seat beside her, and rightly assumed it contained cash.

While Magdalen was pitched forward, the man leaned in the window and thrust his arm behind her, reaching for the envelope. Magdalen cried out as her shoulder was forced against the steering wheel. Michael and Anthony froze. The man kept pressure on Magdalen's back, preventing her from sitting up. Plunkett quickly leaned forward and tried to push the man's head back out of the window and get him off of Magdalen. Just as the man was about to grab the envelope, Plunkett knocked it on the floor of the car at Michael's feet, out of reach of the thief. The man started to pull back out of the window.

"Drive sista! Drive!" Plunkett yelled.

"What you trying to do," Magdalen yelled at the man as she sat back up. "You think I don't deal with boys like you every day!" She pushed his face out the window as she took her foot off the brake. The man fell back into the street as the car rolled forward. Magdalen sped toward the next intersection.

Michael and Anthony sat dumbstruck. When they reached the next light, Plunkett asked, "Are you all right, sista?"

"Yes, Plunkett. I'm fine," she replied, rubbing her shoulder and the back of her neck. After she gathered herself and could feel her heartbeat slow, she looked over her shoulder at Plunkett, "You did a good job making sure he didn't take our money." Plunkett felt himself smile slightly at his quick reflexes, but was still too shaken to fully enjoy the compliment.

"I told Mr. Herman I might need you today, but I didn't realize it would be for protection. Now you're my bodyguard," she chuckled.

At the photographer's Michael and Anthony didn't ask any questions as they sat for their passport shots. What they thought would be the most exciting part of the afternoon, had become a non-event. In fact, they would completely forget about the pictures for many months, until the spring, when the sisters would finally tell them about their trip.

After the errand, the group drove home by a different route. By dinnertime that evening, Anthony and Michael had retold the story of the attack so often, other boys were asking Plunkett how many gunmen had attacked the car and how he learned to fight like that. Although he didn't like the attention, he found himself laughing when one Junior Home boy asked him, "Did you really bite the man's thumb off?" Plunkett lay in bed that night, looking at the crosses on the wall, and found himself less afraid of moving on to Senior Home.

14
THE VISITATION

Thursday of the third week of November, Mr. Herman, the office manager, sorted Alpha's files so he could start work on the end-of-year report on the boys in Alpha's care. Mr. Herman had been with Alpha for almost thirty years. He moved either slowly or with a steady pace, depending on your perspective. The overhead fixture in his office was weak, and most of the light in the room came from the four tall windows that looked out at the side verandah toward the grape arbor and the concrete stairs that rose to the convent. People passed by his windows all day, but Mr. Herman never seemed to lose his concentration. Dozens of times each day the boys would bring notes or keys or requests from the sisters. It would have been very easy for them to stop and conduct their business with him through his windows, but a Jamaican sense of courtesy and decorum always trumped brash efficiency. So, the boys would walk around the building and into the reception room of the office.

Mr. Herman wore horn-rimmed glasses, although lately he was prone to pushing his glasses up onto his forehead and leaning forward squinting, bringing his eyes within a few inches of whatever form sat in his black Royal typewriter. As he organized his files, the phone rang. He always seemed to wait until the second ring before reaching for the receiver on the large heavy black phone on the far corner of the desk. He listened intently to the call, "Yes, ma'am…Yes, ma'am…Yes, ma'am. 5:30 this evening, at the Archbishop's residence….Yes ma'am. I'll tell Sister right away, ma'am." He wrote a quick note and hit the bell that sat next to his phone. Worldhead appeared in an instant.

"Bring this upstairs to Sister Marie Therese right away, now," Mr. Herman said. Worldhead ran out of Mr. Herman's office, through the reception room, and around the building, passing by Mr. Herman's windows and up the stairs to the convent where he could be heard rapping on the gate at the top and calling out to sister.

* * *

I arrived back at Alpha that afternoon to more commotion than usual. Mr. Johnson had parked the van by the row of poinsettia bushes that lined the entrance to the office. The leaves had already turned deep red, nature's signal of the start of the Christmas season. Sister Thaddeus' bike was on the verandah Originally from Cleveland, Sr. Thaddeus had been in Jamaica for decades, and lived at the convent at the girls' school. She was in her late sixties, and rode a bike almost as old as she was back and forth between the two schools. Two days each week she met with boys one-on-one for counseling sessions, mostly to just let them talk privately with an adult. She was a kind voice, and knew how to draw the boys out of themselves.

"Mr. Jay," Marie Therese said, when she saw me walk by the office, "Are you busy this afternoon?"

"No, sister. Did you need me to shake down a few more bakers with you?"

"Not at all, Mr. Jay," she replied, not quite sure what 'shake down' meant. "Archbishop Carter is having a reception at his home this afternoon to welcome Mother Teresa. All of the religious houses on the island have been invited. We are leaving in a few minutes. Would you like to join us?"

"Mother Teresa? *The* Mother Teresa? What is she doing here?"

"Two sisters from her order began work in Kingston about a year ago. She is here to visit them," Thaddeus said, glowing.

"Well?" Marie Therese asked.

I was stunned. "Sure sister. That would be wonderful. Are you sure it would be all right for me to go?"

"Of course. You would be our escort. Sister Thaddeus is joining us because there is no room in the other van."

"I would be honored, sister." I threw my bag in my room and headed for the van. Magdalen was instructing two of the boys to make sure dinner was served properly up at Junior Home. "Sister, I can stay if you need me to, and make sure things go smoothly," I offered, hoping she would decline.

"Nonsense, Jay. They will all be fine," she said as she turned and we started toward the van together. "Personally, I would be fine not going, but Marie Therese feels we should *all* go. I think she and Ignatius are very excited, and I am intrigued to see her myself."

So Magdalen, Ignatius, Marie Therese, Thaddeus, Mr. Johnson and I piled in the van and set off to meet the saint. How strange and wonderful, I thought, to be going to meet someone world-renowned for her dedication to the poor, for her self-sacrifice, and for her inspiration to those she touched, with a group of women who meet the same description.

Archbishop Carter was a Jesuit, and an enormous man, well over six feet and close to 300 pounds. His official residence was a two-story colonial-style building with a roof of red Spanish tiles. The reception was out in the yard behind the house. It was an amazing sight. There on the lawn, were Sisters of Mercy, dressed in cream-colored tunics and black habits; Franciscan sisters dressed in light brown, Franciscan brothers and priests dressed in darker brown robes with long white cords wrapped around their waists; Silesian priests in powder blue shirts; Dominicans in black; Passionists in long white robes; Maryknolls in whatever moved them; Irish Christian Brothers in their black garb with ruffled ascots; diocesan priests in Roman Collars; three Brothers of the Poor, a new Jamaican order, in simple street clothes; and Jesuits in polo shirts and khakis. Many were greeting each other warmly, not having seen each other in a while. Given the tropical setting, it reminded me of being in a bird habitat, with all sorts of colorful creatures sharing a small space - beautiful individually, and magnificent together.

A low verandah ran the length of the back of the house. Unlike most houses in Kingston, the verandah was not enclosed in metal grillwork. The large wall around the yard was enough to keep out would-be robbers. The lack of the grillwork made the verandah and house look much more open and inviting. At exactly 5:30, Archbishop Carter came out from the double doors in the center of the verandah. The crowd grew quiet and gathered closer. The Archbishop was followed by three nuns dressed in long white robes with three royal blue stripes, two narrow and one wide, trimming their habits, the trademark of Mother Teresa's order, the Missionaries of Charity. The habits are especially noticeable because the nuns always stood with their heads slightly bowed, which caused their habits to drape down over their foreheads. While all three women were petite, one was particularly small. The archbishop welcomed the crowd and then introduced Mother Teresa, who was greeted with polite and sincere applause, and on many a face, a knowing smile. They treated her not like a rock star, but like a kindred spirit.

I wanted to feel in awe, but all I could think was, "Wow! She's really short!"

The polite applause would have continued for quite some time had Mother Teresa not motioned calmly for quiet. Rather than listen to what she was saying, I played with the focus on my camera to get the best shot. She briefly thanked the Archbishop and everyone who had in any way helped the sisters from her order to establish their ministry in Kingston, and then asked the group to pray the Hail Mary with her. When we all finished, Mother Teresa suddenly turned to go. The Archbishop, who seemed somewhat startled at her hasty departure, bent down close to her. Because of the difference in their sizes, he seemed to overwhelm her. He spoke softly to her, and she turned and stood by his side. Archbishop

Carter stepped to the microphone and announced that Mother Teresa would be glad to meet everyone.

The line snaked across the expanse of lawn. One by one, each person walked up the three steps to the top of the verandah to shake Mother Teresa's hand. The sisters from Alpha were at the back of the line. I stood off to the side with my camera, and as Magdalen, Ignatius, Marie Therese and Thaddeus each had their moment with Mother Teresa, I snapped a few pictures. I then quickly got in line behind them, and, fumbling to put my camera on my shoulder, walked up the steps.

Whereas everyone else had had the good sense to simply allow Mother Teresa to hold their hands in hers and accept the gift of a simple rosary and a soft, "God bless you," I awkwardly pumped her hand as if we were at a business meeting. I told her my name and that I lived at Alpha. That I taught at St. George's and was on the island with other graduates of BC. I guess on some level I was trying to impress her. By the time I realized I had spoken to her for longer than she had addressed the group, a little voice in my head finally told me, "Shut up, already! Just take the rosary and get out of her way!" I quickly concluded by muttering, "It's very nice to meet you," and walked off to the left and down the side steps of the verandah.

As I stood in the driveway at the side of the house, feeling elated and stupid at the same time, I realized that I had taken the last picture on my roll of film. I opened my camera and started to replace the film when someone touched me on the shoulder. I turned around to see a young Jamaican priest, dressed in a traditional black shirt and pants. "Would you please help Mother into the van?" he asked. I looked to his left, and down about two feet, and there stood Mother Teresa, who let go of the priest's arm, and took mine. This time I didn't fumble with the camera. I just dropped it on the ground. I walked Mother to the waiting van that I hadn't even noticed. Like in a movie where things move in slow motion, those few steps seemed to take forever. I was guiding *Mother Teresa* on my arm. Hours earlier, I didn't even know I was sharing a country with a woman revered in many circles as a living saint, and now she was holding my arm for balance in the same way my grandmothers had later in their lives. I remembered my father's lessons and gently put my hand on hers in case she should stumble. *Now* I was in awe. Sometimes fate throws you a curve ball, and sometimes it just plain old knocks your socks off.

As I helped her up into the van, she said a soft, "God bless." I stepped back as the driver slid the door closed. The van crunched the gravel in the driveway as it made its way to the gate, and as unceremoniously as she had arrived in my day, she was gone.

I stood on the driveway stunned by my bizarre good fortune. When I moved into Alpha, I thought I would volunteer my time, get to know a few children, and make some moderate contribution to their lives. I hadn't anticipated the chance encounters with so many strangers, let alone an international and historical icon. I not only met her, but helped her do something as mundane as climb into a minivan. When you meet Mother Therese, it should be while tending the sick, feeding the hungry or showing compassion to the dying, not while changing the film in your camera. The exchange should be eloquent, pithy and gracious, and in fact, she had been all three, with her thanks, her prayer, and her brevity, not wanting people to focus on her. I, however, had been clumsy, vapid and then clumsy again. And I struggled with how my behavior could possibly matter. Every one of the nuns I lived with had been serving the same God, with the same devotion, for decades before Mother Teresa was a household name. They had *been Mother Teresa* long before Mother Teresa was *Mother Teresa*. And she was just a servant of God, doing her job as best she knew how, just like the Checks, and Mr. Peters the baker, and Mr. Shipman, the coconut man. I had heard in Mass so many times that we should treat every needy soul as our brother or sister, willing to share our food, open our home, warm with our jacket. It occurred to me then, how easy it was to also see the *Mother Teresa* in everyone, each doing their share.

For their part, the sisters in the van that day didn't seem to mind that Mother Teresa got all the attention. They, of course, were not in it for the attention, but for the intention. They sacrificed for others, yet they saw that sacrifice as a privilege, not a burden. They were called as Mother Teresa was called. And a *calling* to them was both a gift and an obligation. If you were called to the religious life, how dare you not answer. If Mother Teresa was called to work in the slums of Calcutta, did she really have a choice to say "no"? If she was also called to be the poster child for unwavering devotion and self-sacrifice, did she have a choice to say "no" to that either?

What did I have the right to say, "no" to?

I picked up my camera and went to find the sisters. I found Magdalen, Ignatius and Thaddeus speaking with the other sisters from Alpha who had come in the other van. In a quick scan of the crowd I spotted Marie Therese bending the ear of the Archbishop. She didn't have any pies with her on this trip so I was wondering what she was bartering in exchange for what.

During the ride back to Alpha, the conversation about Mother Teresa lasted only a few minutes, most of which Marie Therese spent simply staring out the window, fondling the rosary in her hands. As we neared Alpha, Marie Therese said, "Ignatius, the Archbishop has promised to use our band more frequently in archdiocese events."

"How nice," Ignatius replied. "He is such a good man, the Archbishop."

"Yes, he is quite a good man," Marie Therese replied flatly. "Tomorrow, please check all the events listed on that calendar the archdiocese just published. Call the archdiocese office and ask them at which events they would like the boys to play. Tell them it is the Archbishop's suggestion."

"Yes, Sister. That does sound like a good idea."

There is an old saying in Jamaica, "If you want something done, ask a woman." The Archbishop had authorized more use of the Alpha band, but it would take Marie Therese's persistence to get the band the added work.

The conversation quickly turned back to the two boys who had gotten into a fight that day, finding a new math teacher, replacing some of the equipment in the print shop, and calling the Ministry to see why the payments were late again. The work of saints is never done.

15
GARDENS OF HOPE

At the end of Mass on Sunday, Sister Marie Chin, the Mercy Superior on the island, came to the altar. Sister Marie Chin was always referred to by both her first and last names, since there were far too many "Sister Marie's" to have the name mean anything on its own. Sister Marie Chin faced the nuns' side of the chapel.

"As many of you know, today is Sister Angela's 80th birthday."

There was polite applause.

"We have a special treat for you sister," Marie Chin continued.

With that, Dwight Richards, a Junior Home boy, walked up to the altar. I couldn't image what this petite twelve-year-old was going to do, especially since he couldn't speak clearly. His stammer was so debilitating that he struggled when he tried to utter even a single sentence. He found saying his own name a challenge. On the occasions when he would come to the game room, he would only ask for one game or puzzle because the request was so exhausting for him, his face contorted as he struggled to push out the syllables.

Dwight climbed the three marble steps in front of the altar, turned toward the nuns and drew a deep breath. His face grew serene as he closed his eyes, tilted his head back and let the first notes of the *Ave Maria* glide over his vocal chords. He did not sing like an angel. Angels don't have a Jamaican cadence, and they are accompanied by harps. Dwight sang a cappella, and at the sound of his soprano, choirs of angels would have turned in their wings and considered their talents cheap. His voice never cracked, never wavered, and not a syllable was repeated. When he finished, I was dumbstruck and could feel the tears on my cheeks. The nuns applauded and the boys erupted with shouts and hoots and enthusiastic clapping. Sister Angela hobbled forward on her cane, threw her arms around Dwight, and spoke softly in his ear, too softly for anyone to hear. As she released him from her embrace, he replied, "Th-th-th-th-thank you s-s-s-s-sista." His brief foray into the clouds was as abrupt as his return to earth. Nevertheless, he grinned ear to ear as he rejoined his pew.

As the boys filed out of church, many patted Dwight on the back. He glowed in the attention. When I congratulated him, his "thank you, sir" through his stammer took forever. He was entering adolescence, the time in our lives when we start to find our own voice. His would be cruelly limited. I am sure there is a clinical explanation for how someone incapable of normal speech can sing so beautifully, something to do with neuro-linguistic wiring or the way the brain processes music. But such explanations could never do justice to the feeling of listening to Dwight's singing. What he possessed was a gift. Not a gift of voice, but one of prayer.

As the boys formed their lines after Mass, I asked sister if I could take another dozen boys to the park and zoo at Hope Gardens. This would be my fourth trip this year. I was hoping to get all of the Junior Home kids out on a Sunday at least once during the year.

"That would be wonderful, Jay. You can take Michael House." Each row of the dormitory was considered a "house," a distinction that came in handy whenever sister needed to divide the boys into smaller groups. "But, of course, they have to do their chores first."

Of course. Chores always came first. Not because of a Catholic sense of duty before pleasure, but just because of reality. Things had to get done, and the boys simply had to do them.

Sunday was wash day. When we got back to the dormitory, the boys each washed their Sunday shirt and their school clothes: a pair of khaki shorts and a brightly colored t-shirt. Each house had a different color t-shirt. In the boys' bathroom area was a long row of concrete sinks. The front wall of each sink sloped in toward the drain, instead of dropping vertically to a flat bottom. Deep ridges had been carved into the slope, creating a built-in washboard for each sink. The boys rubbed their clothes vigorously up and down the ridges to scrub out the dirt. There were no clothes lines up at Junior Home so the boys had to figure out a way to hang out their clothes to dry. Around Junior Home the grass grew in scattered clumps, never enough in one place to have anything remotely resembling a green lawn. It was too dusty and dirty to lay clothes directly on the ground to dry, so instead, the boys shirts and shorts were draped over tree branches, hung from the swing-set bar, (which hadn't had swings on it for more than a decade), lain carefully over the tops of bushes, and propped up anywhere else the boys could find room. (Every time a new boy arrived, the others would encourage him to dry his shirt by draping it on the outstretched arms of the statue of the Virgin Mary that stood at the center of the Junior Home plaza, knowing he would get a major scolding from Sister Magdalen when she saw it.) By the time their Sunday morning washing was done, most of the Junior Home yard was covered in fabric. It looked like an enormous laundry bag had exploded in the middle of the property, scattering clothes everywhere.

By noon, the twelve boys of Michael House were dressed in a clean pair of khaki shorts and t-shirts that the bookstore at BC had donated. I had stopped in at the bookstore the previous summer and requested a donation of out-of-style shirts. Dan Fitzpatrick, the gruff but obliging store manager, gave me a dozen shirts with the BC logo emblazoned across the front. As soon as I returned to Alpha with the shirts, I had all ninety-six Junior Home boys congregate on the verandah for pictures. The twelve boys in front wore the t-shirts. The boys behind held up a large sign. In one picture the sign read, "Thank you BC." In another, "Thank you, Mr. Fitzpatrick." A month later, boxes of BC t-shirts arrived from Mr. Fitzpatrick with a note that read only, "For those other boys."

Each boy wore sneakers. Alpha was lucky enough to have a regular pair of shoes for each boy for special occasions. Sneakers were a much more precious commodity. There were probably twenty-five pairs on hand for the ninety-six Junior Home boys. Since we would be playing soccer in the park, Magdalen had taken the time to make sure the boys each had a pair that fit. Any adventure I conjured up for the boys always resulted in more work for Magdalen.

I led the boys of Michael House out the main gate and to the bus stop. For some, it was their first time off the school property in months. A few mini-buses came by, but were already crowded and we could neither fit, nor split up, so we waited. Eventually we caught one of the full-size buses that traveled the same route to Liguanea and up into the hills toward the university and Hope Gardens. There were other passengers on the bus, but still plenty of seats. I sat down next to Hubert, a new boy. I knew all of the boys by sight, and most by name, but only a handful well. The trips to the park were a way to get to know some of the other boys.

"Hubert, have you been to Hope Gardens before?"

"No, sir. Dis my first time."

"Well, it's quite different from Alpha. The ground is very green and the trees are huge and give lots of shade."

"It will feel like home sir."

"Where is your family from?"

"From country, sir."

In Jamaica, "country" means anywhere outside of Kingston. "Who is back home?"

"My mom and my grandma, sir. And I think my sister is still home, but I haven't been there in a long time, so I don't know."

As we spoke, I felt something moving slowly in my hair, never a good feeling, and in the tropics, usually an indication that an enormous bug had landed. I quickly swept my hand across the back of my head, and then turned around. In the seat behind us sat a woman and her small daughter, about six years old, both dressed in their finest, and clearly just returning from Sunday services. The girl was reaching out again to run her fingers through the hair on the back of my head. Her mother, who had been looking the other way, quickly grabbed her hand and gasped.

"Emily! I'm so sorry, sir."

"Momma, it's soft! And it looks like gold," Emily said.

"I don't think she has ever seen red hair before, except in pictures," the mother explained.

"It's okay," I laughed. I had grown accustomed to people on the street calling out to me, "Hey, whitey!" or "Hey, white boy. Come here." But this was the first time someone actually felt the need to touch.

When the bus pulled up to the park entrance, Irene was waiting for us. The boys were as excited to see her as I was.

We found a large expanse of empty lawn, and the boys immediately took off the sneakers Magdalen had spent so long organizing. Irene and I played soccer with them for a bit, but then put them into two teams of six, set out goals, and let them play by themselves. At Alpha, there are usually more than fifty boys on the field at a time, and the soccer ball is in sorry shape, if it is a real ball at all. Often it is just a wad of plastics bags wrapped tightly around each other until it is big enough to kick. The real treat for the boys today was to have a real soccer ball and to be sharing it among only twelve of them.

Irene found a spot in the shade nearby and stretched out the blanket she had brought. Even though the lawn was lush, you didn't want to sit down without a blanket. If you accidentally sat on a hill of fire ants, you could end up in the hospital, their bites were so fierce. We sat down and watched the boys play.

"I got my first rejection from a law school this week," I said. "So much for taking the "early decision" route."

"Sorry to hear that."

"It was a long shot anyway. Something will come through. I'll know in a few months."

"It'll be hard for you to leave here," she said.

"That still feels like a long way off. It's only December," I said, leaning back on my arms, scanning the field and counting the boys. "I'm sure it will be hard when the time comes. But I knew coming into this that it was for a limited time."

"How do you think they feel about it?" Irene asked, nodding toward the boys.

"They have a lot of people going through their lives. I'm sure I'm just one more on a long list."

"That's a crock. You know you matter to them. It'll just feel less painful to you when you leave if you pretend they don't care."

"Well, thanks. That's helpful – reminding me I'll disappoint a hundred little kids. What am I supposed to do about that?"

"Nothing. There's nothing you can do. But you have to be honest with yourself about it or the experience won't be genuine. Look, you can't be that close to all ninety-six boys. You're close to a few and you may be able to stay in touch with them. But your life moves on." As usual, she was right. I would lose touch with most, and stay connected to a few.

One of the boys kicked the ball off course and it came bouncing over to us. I grabbed it and threw it back. Then we sat quietly for a while.

"Are you all right?" Irene asked.

"I'm not sure. I guess hearing from the first law school really does have me thinking that my time here is short. I'm taking from these kids and then I'll leave and they'll be left behind."

"The place doesn't begin and end with us. Alpha was around for a hundred years before you arrived, and I think it'll survive a few more after you're gone."

"I know. It just doesn't make it any easier."

"Well, since we're only here for a short time," she said getting up from the blanket, "let's make the best of it." She pulled a Frisbee from her knapsack, and ran out onto the lawn. The boys hadn't used one before, but within fifteen minutes they were all throwing like pros.

After lunch we toured the modest Hope Garden Zoo, where the

largest animal was the caiman, a small alligator-like reptile with a narrow jaw and dozens of teeth. The boys were thrilled when it snapped at a fish thrown by a keeper. At the even-more-modest amusement park, some of the boys enjoyed their first ride on a merry-go-round and small roller coaster. Morris Mathers didn't like the spinning of the merry-go-round, and tensed at the sight of the small roller coaster. While Irene watched the others on the ride, Morris and I walked over to the ice cream stand to get treats for everyone. As we waited in line behind a woman with two small children, I noticed Morris staring at me. From utter silence, he asked clearly and without hesitation, "Why are you 'ere?"

I was startled by the directness of the question. "What do you mean?" I asked.

"Why are you 'ere," he repeated indignantly, as if the question were obvious on its face. "You're all 'ere for some reason."

I was stunned. "Where did you come up with that?" I asked smiling. "And who do you mean by 'you all'?"

"You white Americans," he replied. "You're all 'ere for a reason."

"Who else have you met before coming to Alpha?" I asked.

"Just people," he replied.

His tone had been as mature as his question, and I wasn't sure if I should engage him as an adult, or answer casually with platitudes. I generally do better with platitudes, but being challenged by someone who looked like a child but spoke like a man was disarming. "Well, I don't know why I'm here," I said. "I haven't figured that out yet." "Why are you here, Morris?" I asked.

"Mi at Alpha because the police sent me 'ere. Mi at dis place because sista told me I must come wit you."

"And why do you think we're here on earth?" I asked. If he was entitled to ask deep questions without warning, so was I.

He looked at me as it were the stupidest question he had ever heard. "Mi not know," he shrugged.

"Well, for today, let's say I'm here just to buy you some ice cream, and enjoy the park with you. And that will have to be enough for us both."

Morris continued to stare at me, but he didn't shrug, and he didn't question.

With that, the woman in front of us paid for her treats and hustled off with her children. Fortunately, there was no one behind us. As we placed our order for fourteen ice cream bars, the other boys came dashing over laughing, followed by Irene, who was holding hands with Waldemar, who was grinning broader that the caiman had been. Waldemar didn't ask challenging questions. He just accepted the day on its own merits, and Waldemar was having a great day.

That night, while I sat on the verandah, under the porch of the convent, watching Plunkett and Worldhead build puzzles, and listening to Wilbert and Michael Winters play cards, I thought about Morris' question. I don't know if he deserved a better answer, but I did know that I owed one to myself. I was three months into my year at Alpha and I hadn't yet figured out why I was there. Another few blinks and I would be packing to leave. I was happy, but it still mattered to me to define my purpose, to find my calling. Just killing time on the verandah wasn't enough, shouldn't be enough, couldn't be enough. I hadn't defined any special talent I could bring to enrich the boys' lives, any special wisdom I could share, any clear role I could fill. The TV upstairs in the convent went silent, and Sister Ignatius footsteps grew louder as she walked to the porch and called down to the boys.

"Another day is done, boys," she called. "Time to turn in. Plunkett, come walk with Sister Magdalen. Wilbert, come take these keys to Mr. Watchman. Mr. Jay, we will see you tomorrow."

As usual, everyone had a role except me. If I was to have a purpose at Alpha, I would have to define it myself.

16
TREATS ALL AROUND

Like any school, Alpha took great pride in its alumni. Sister Ignatius ensured that any Alpha Boy who left Jamaica, would always find a warm welcome when they returned. Any work involved in caring for an "Old Boy's" needs though, fell to Magdalen. "Ignatius treats some of these Old Boys like they are the prodigal son," she once said. They say they want to come back to see us to say hello, and Ignatius offers them anything she can think of. She is so proud of the few who actually make something of themselves, that she feels we owe them the world. I just do what I'm told." And so, when Simon Melvin came to town, Magdalen was on duty. Simon had become a band-leader in Miami and called Ignatius when he returned to Kingston to visit family. In the course of their conversation, Simon must have mentioned that he missed the beautiful Jamaican beaches, so Ignatius offered to have Magdalen drive him to Negril, an eight-mile stretch of beach on the far end of the island. Magdalen asked me to join them for the day, and although I'm not much of a beach person, I went to keep her company.

On Saturday morning, after she had prepared everything for the boys for the day, Magdalen pulled the Volvo around to the front of the office and introduced me to Simon.

"Simon is a very successful band leader in Miami," Magdalen said. "Everyone in the music world knows him," she continued. "He has many records out and is one of our most successful Old Boys."

Simon chuckled at the attention and stared at the floor, "Sister, you are too kind." He was in his late forties and had a deep baritone. I could easily picture this heavy-set man smiling broadly at the crowd and making everyone at the party feel as though they had hired Louis Armstrong to play at their event.

I sat in the front of the light blue Volvo with Sister, and Simon spread out in the back. Sister handled the car like a pro as we made our way west through the center of Kingston to the highway. Though I was strapped in tight with my seat belt, I held onto the door handle with my left hand, as my right hand gripped the edge of my seat. Each time the car in front of us slowed, I quickly slammed my right hand on the dashboard to soften the jolt as Magdalen slammed on the brakes. She wasn't a bad driver, but the Volvo didn't have power brakes, or power steering for that matter, and it took a great deal of strength to drive it.

"I like driving with you, Jay," Magdalen said laughing.

"Because you like to see me look nervous, Sister?"

"No, because every time you put your hand on the dashboard I know I should step on the brake," she laughed.

Kingston has the sixth largest natural harbor in the world, which facilitates much of the industry on the island. But the harbor is far too polluted to attract swimmers. Therefore, to enjoy the beach, you have to travel to another part of the island. Negril is about four hours from Kingston. As we drove through the center of the city, Simon talked about his early childhood before he arrived at Alpha.

"I grew up in Trenchtown," he said wistfully, staring out the window as we headed out Spanishtown Road. Trenchtown was a notoriously rough neighborhood in Kingston. "My mother and sisters and brothers and I all lived in a small shack. There were about seventy people in our yard," he said.

"Trenchtown has quite a reputation now," I said turning to look in the back of the car to Simon.

"T'was the same back then," he said. "It was so violent. The gunmen and the shooting, and the fights. It was awful." He shook his head in disgust. "I never understood why people did that." He was silent for a moment. "My younger brother was sitting in the doorway of our house in the middle of the afternoon one day. A fight broke out between two men in the yard. My brother was shot in the head. It just about destroyed my mother when he died. I can still see her kneeling on the ground holding him close to her and crying out, rocking back and forth." He rocked as he remembered her pleas. "It was just after that she sent me to the sisters at Alpha. I arrived the same day Sister Ignatius started to work at Alpha."

"Were you able to stay in touch with your family at all?" I asked Simon.

"My mother came to see me every few months for a while. Then she would come around Christmas. I went to see her once after I got out of Alpha, before I went in the army. Not much had changed. She had a real floor and the yard had been paved, so it wasn't as muddy as I remembered it. But that was about it. One of my sisters died when she was still a girl, but the others are still alive."

Simon moved to Miami after he got out of the army. He told us all about his band, The Verones.

"There are two other Jamaicans in the band. We knew each other from the army. We play at all of the most important weddings in Miami. Some very wealthy people," he said. "We put out a record a few years ago. It did very well. I sent Sister Ignatius a copy."

"Yes. She plays it all the time, Simon" Magdalen assured him, truthfully, I'm sure.

After we got outside the city limits, Simon fell asleep. Sister and I talked about the boys, something we rarely had a chance to do.

"O'Brien and Q and Richard are quite the team," I said. "They seem to hang out together all the time."

"It's good that the boys make friends," she said. "They don't have strong connections on the outside. They need to bond with each other. It's hard when they haven't had that experience with their own families.

And you have been good for them, Jay."

"Sister, when I leave at the end of the year, I will be just one more person abandoning them."

"You're leaving them with me," she said with a smile. "That's not quite *abandoning* them."

"You know I didn't mean that sister. It just feels like I am treating them like little play things for me while I am on some great adventure, and when I am done, I'll leave them and go on to something else. What lesson is that supposed to teach them?"

"It teaches them that they are loved and that you chose to spend your time with them."

"You have chosen to spend your whole life taking care of them. Your commitment is complete. Mine is a blink of an eye."

"My commitment is complete? I think you mean I should be *completely committed*," she laughed. "This is the life I have chosen. It's the life I was called to. You are called to something else. You are doing good while you are here. Don't be afraid of where you are called next."

"Is that what they teach you in formation in the convent?"

"We don't spend much time talking about such things in the convent. It's not like we're all theologians, sitting around thinking big thoughts. We *do* more than we *think*. But they *could have* taught us that. It would go right along with the whole obedience thing. I always found that difficult too. Just when I would get settled some place and feel like I was getting to know the routine, up and away I would go to a new place. Oh, I loved when I was in St. Catherine's," she said rolling her head. "We had a school right by the ocean. You could watch the waves crash on the rocks from the front of the school, and it was always a little bit cool. Of course in those days, it needed to be since we all wore the long veil and habit. It was so silly in this heat. I was so happy there. When I could see the water, it reminded me of Malta and of sitting on the stone piers with my brothers and sisters. It was so nice." I slammed my hand on the dashboard as she swerved to avoid hitting a goat in the road.

"But then I moved to Alpha, and I was happy here too. Not right away, but once I got to know Ignatius and Marie Therese and the others. It has been wonderful. I wouldn't change a thing. Except for that habit."

"Well, the boys need you here," I said.

"They need all of us. And then some."

"I met the two new boys – Morris Mathers, and Winston somebody. Morris seems oddly mature and experienced for a boy his size, and Winston seems awfully shy."

"I think Mathers is older than he looks. He carries himself differently. Winston's last name is Yardley. I think they have both had a rough go if it."

"Q and Richard and O'Brien seem wary of him," I said. "They are my only barometer on the other boys."

"Q told me that Morris Mathers told him to give him his bottom the other day. I had to tell Mathers that we don't allow that kind of behavior here. Mathers must have been abused on the outside. It's a shame when the boys come here with that kind of history. It's so hard to break them of it."

"Morris is only about ten. And he's smaller than Richard and O'Brien. I guess Q is the only one smaller than him. Is Q afraid of him?"

"I don't think so. And Q is more confident than the other boys. He would let me know if he was being threatened. When I talked to Mathers about it, I don't even think he knows what he was asking Q for. He just knows that's how you intimidate people."

Once we were out of Kingston, the activity on the roadside thinned to an occasional passing car, a small grouping of buildings at an intersection, and the seemingly random collection of food stalls that would dot the road every few miles. About two hours into the drive, sister pulled over at a set of roadside stands so we could grab a snack and stretch our legs. Simon and I walked around the back of the shacks to relieve ourselves. It turned out the shacks' location wasn't as random as it appeared. A pipe stood at the end of the row of shops, proving water for the burgeoning strip mall. One of the shop owners had scaled the nearest utility pole and managed to splice into the power lines, providing an added benefit for this shop owners. The first shop offered cold drinks and a small array of drug store products. The selection was impressive considering that his entire inventory could fit, and had to fit, in the trunk of his car, parked nearby. The next stall had a small fire burning in front. The shop owner was dripping clumps of corn meal into a frying pan of hot oil.

"You want some bammy?" she offered, referring to the cornbread sticks, a Jamaican staple.

"In a bit," I said, wanting to check out the other booths first.

The merchant at the next shop beckoned me over, just as he was settling up with Magdalen, who had three dishtowels draped over her arm. She thanked him and, turning to me, said, "We need these in the kitchen upstairs in the convent. I thought I'd pick them up while we're here."

After we checked out all of the stalls, I grabbed a soda and bammy and offered to do the same for Sister.

"Nothing for me, thank you," she replied, so we got back on the road quickly and headed toward Negril.

"Sister, this is a long way to go for a day trip," I mentioned.

"It is a long drive, but it's good to get out of the city every once in a while." She kept her eyes on the road.

"I'm surprised you didn't get at least something to drink."

"I gave up snacks and the only thing I drink between meals is water," she said

"Did you give up snacks for dietary reasons?" I asked.

"No. When I entered the convent," she said, never taking her eyes off the road.

"You gave up snacks forty years ago!" I said, astonished.

"Yes. When I was a child I used to love sneaking an extra piece of fruit from the kitchen, or a treat my mother would make. When I joined the Mercys, they told us we should make a sacrifice of some little thing that we liked enough that we would want it every day, but that it wouldn't be so hard to give up that it would be distracting or too hard to do without. I was only a teenager at the time, and didn't know much about the world, so I gave up snacks."

"And you have stuck to it for forty years?"

"Well, every once in a while I will have a little something, if I'm on vacation, or if there is a function where they have put out food. But I don't go out of my way for it."

"That's an amazing sacrifice, sister. I couldn't do that. I have too much of a sweet tooth."

"I really don't think about it anymore, quite honestly. Maybe I should come up with a new sacrifice since this one isn't costing me anything lately."

"And what about Ignatius and Marie Therese? What did they give up?"

"I don't know," she shrugged. "It's not something we sit around and talk about, you know. Who could live like that? You make your sacrifices in life and you get on with it."

We took the southern road across the island, avoiding going up into the mountains in the center of the country. The drive is flat and the land is dry and brown, with occasional palm trees, and, when the road dipped further south, a view of the blue Caribbean.

We talked for the rest of the trip: about the boys, the school, Jamaica and Malta. I told her how the boys as St. George's were so different from those at Alpha and yet still had so much in common.

"All children are alike," she said. "They need direction. They need guidance. Mostly they need parents. We give them a roof and meals and an education, but they need much more attention than we can provide."

"I think they do amazingly well given that they don't have their parents looking over their shoulder all the time. I'm twenty-three and I still count on my parents for guidance and support."

"I left my parents for the convent when I was sixteen. The Sisters became my family. They gave me structure and examples and took care of me."

"How could you have known at that age what you wanted? To decide at that point that you don't ever want to marry or have a family. It seems like such a tender age to be making such a decision."

"I've never regretted it, you know. And I did marry. You know, they call us 'brides of Christ.' Isn't that an interesting concept? We get to marry the Lord. Who could want a better husband?" She laughed. "He's a good man. He certainly listens better than most. He doesn't interfere. And he pretty much leaves you alone to do what you think is best. Overall, it seems like a pretty good deal to me."

"Whatever works for you, sister. Whatever works for you."

We arrived in Negril by one in the afternoon. Negril is a flat stretch of land on the western shore of Jamaica. Because it faces Mexico, rather than out toward the Atlantic, the water is always calm. Most of the resorts are modest: a simple collection of huts nestled in the trees just off the beach. It's a quiet place where people come for a cheap, no frills vacation in an "anything goes" atmosphere.

We pulled into a public parking lot and Simon went into the men's room to change into his suit. I bought sodas for the three of us and some Jamaican saltfish and bammy. Simon joined us at a nearby picnic table and we enjoyed a slow paced lunch.

It was an odd feeling to not have something pressing to do. Given how I was used to seeing Magdalen on the go all of the time, I was surprised to see how completely at ease she was being completely at ease. She wasn't looking at her watch. She didn't appear to be in a hurry. She understood what it meant to just relax. I, on the other hand, was already bored. My fair skin doesn't take the sun well, and I knew I would be fried the next day, no matter how well I tried to cover myself with sunscreen.

After lunch, Simon went to swim. Magdalen and I sat on one side of the picnic table staring out at the water and at Simon, who floated on the calm Caribbean. We sat in silence for a while, just watching the gentle waves. There was no one else at this public parking lot and only a few people strolling up and down the beach.

In the distance, a couple was walking toward us. They were white, and appeared to be in their late twenties. I thought they looked American. He wore a bathing suit that came almost to his knees, a big smile, and a pair of wraparound sunglasses. She wore a string bikini bottom, a gold chain around her waist and no top. (I didn't notice if she wore sunglasses.) My eyes grew wide at the sight of her naked breasts coming toward us, in part because I was sitting with a nun, and in part because they were naked breasts. I quickly turned to Magdalen who was still staring at the sea and tried to capture her attention, hoping she wouldn't notice the pair coming toward us.

"So Sister, tell me about Malta. What are the beaches there like?"

"Hmm," she said, somewhat distracted. She clearly had been thinking of something else. "What did you ask?" She refocused just as the couple was about ten yards away and about to pass directly in front of us.

I stared down at the table, averting my eyes and my embarrassment, "Do you miss home? Tell me about home and growing up in Valetta."

She was having none of it. I glanced up and saw her face was contorted as she stared at the young woman passing by.

"Look at her," she motioned when the woman was directly ahead of us.

I continued to stare at the table, "Yes sister, I know. It's disgraceful."

"Look at her," she prodded again, elbowing me and motioning toward the woman.

I looked up sheepishly, "Yes sister. I see," I mumbled.

"What's she showing off? She's got nothing up there. She's flat as a board. She walking around all proud," she said mimicking the woman's gait and broad smile. "If I was her, I would be covering up, not showing off. Look at that. That's ridiculous." She rolled her eyes.

"Yes, sister. It does seem ridiculous," I agreed.

"You can stop staring at her now, Jay."

"Yes, sister."

Ignatius or Marie Therese would not have reacted the same way. Both conservative Jamaicans, they would have been offended by this foreigner walking bare-breasted down their beach. But Magdalen, even though she had left Malta in the 1940s, had maintained a European open attitude toward the human body. The philosophy about the nakedness was Mediterranean; the blunt commentary and complete lack of awareness of my embarrassment was just purely Magdalen.

I changed into my suit and went for a brief swim. When I came out, Simon and Magdalen were both asleep on lounge chairs, Simon in his bathing suit and sister in here white polyester dress.

About an hour east of Negril on the way home, the main road across the island passes through Black River, a sizable town of a few thousand.

"If you don't mind," sister said, "I'd like to take a detour." Since she was behind the wheel, it wasn't really an option for Simon or me. She got off the main road and headed south toward the water. Once at the water's edge, we turned right and followed the road for a few miles through a few small villages, one looking pretty much like the next. "I know it's around here somewhere," she mumbled, mostly to herself.

"What are we looking for, sister?"

"I'll show you in just a minute," she said, peering out the windshield. As we came around a bend in the road she exclaimed, "Ah! There it is!" She pulled to a stop on the wide grassy strip between the road and the Caribbean and hopped out. Simon and I followed. I looked out at the ocean, not sure what I was supposed to see.

"What am I looking at, sister?" I asked peering out at the water.

"Not out there, silly. Over there!" She pointed across the street where a low stone wall surrounded a wide green lawn. A small herd of goats grazed in the shade of mango and palm trees. A large, three-story Jamaican-Victorian house sat back on the property. Its peaks, eaves, gables and wide porch were covered with decorative wood trim, like something from a small town in New England. The faded zinc sheathing on the roof and bright pastel colors made the house more Caribbean than

Connecticut. A two-story school building of cinderblock and poured concrete sat off to the side. "This is one of the first schools I taught at when I came to Jamaica," Magdalen said.

"Wow. What a great spot." It looked ideal. The breeze off the ocean helped the place feel worlds away from Alpha. The grass was much greener and more consistent here than in the spotty, faded clumps it grew in back in Kingston. Instead of the constant traffic on South Camp Road outside Alpha's gate, we could hear the waves hitting the rocks just beyond the grassy shore.

"I loved it here," Magdalen said softly. "That was the convent," she said, pointing at the large house on the property. "You know, Valetta in Malta is hot and dry and almost all of the island is paved, so you don't have cool green lawns like this. I felt there was so much space here. I was homesick when I first got here, but the other sisters were so nice to me, and the Jamaicans were wonderful."

"You were awfully young at the time," I said. "It must have been difficult to run a classroom."

"Actually, Jay, I wasn't much younger than you are now when I taught here. Fortunately, it was a grade school, so the students thought I was an adult." When you only know someone late in their life, it's difficult to imagine them as a young person, but of course, we each remember ourselves that way. I pictured Magdalen in a long tunic and habit. Her unfailing energy must have been even more pronounced when combined with a youthful exuberance, her personal brand of impatience and her gift for telling stories. She would probably have fit in very comfortably with the BC teacher crowd at Mrs. Creighton's.

"I was here for four years, and I loved every minute of it. Then they moved me to a school in Kingston, not Alpha, but another place we have. I have been in Kingston ever since."

"You did pretty well finding the place."

"Well, I came back a few times for vacations, but I never got to live here again. I was so sad when our Order decided to sell the school to the government and close the convent. I think part of me always thought I would get to come back here one day and enjoy the cool breezes again, and the smell of the ocean." We stood in silence for only a few moments longer. Then she said, "O.K. Enough of that. Then she said, "O.K. Enough of that. Thank you for letting me reminisce for a moment, boys. We should head back before it gets too late." On the way back toward the main road, sister pulled over to a small store front.

"I'll be right back," she said, getting out of the car. She emerged from the store a few moments later with sodas for the three of us and a bag of chips for herself.

"Today is like a vacation for me, so I thought a small snack wouldn't hurt," she said smiling. For most of the trip sister shared stories of her early days in the country, the kids she worked with and the sisters she lived with and had grown to love. All of the sisters at the school in Black Rock had been sent to other parts of the island, so she had never lived in that community again. But her memories were as fresh as if she were in college telling of high school escapades with her best friends. About an hour outside Kingston sister seemed to run out of stories. We drove in silence, until it was time to drop Simon at his hotel.

We arrived home after dinner. Ten hours in the car for a two-hour swim. It didn't make sense to me. There were so many things at Alpha I didn't understand. But I thought I was beginning to understand Magdalen.

17
FITTING IN

At the far end of Alpha, at the edge of the girls' academy, sat three two-bedroom identical houses. Fr. Williams lived in the first. The second was a guest house. The third had been occupied for more than a dozen years by the Lopez family, who had fled Cuba for Florida, but somehow ended up in Jamaica. In Cuba, Mr. Lopez had cut hair, and Mrs. Lopez worked in a tailor shop and made lace at home. When they arrived on the island, he tried unsuccessfully to set up his own barber shop and she supported the family by making dresses. The Lopezes were devout Catholics and Mrs. Lopez soon made a name for herself for the fine lace and embroidery that she made to decorate altar cloths as her donation to her parish. One of the Spanish-speaking sisters at Alpha met Mrs. Lopez through a local church. When the school's grounds-keeper passed away, the school hired Mr. Lopez for the role and gave his family a place to live. Their faith was more important to the sisters than any proven ability as a maintenance man on Mr. Lopez's part.

Their small house had served them well as a place to raise their young son. How the younger Mr. Lopez had fared during his teenage years being the only male on a campus of a girls' high school is known only to the younger Mr. Lopez. Mr. Lopez senior and his wife spoke almost no English. But Fr. Williams spoke Spanish fluently, and on many evenings he sat with the Lopezes in the small garden that ran behind the three houses sharing a drink and each others' company. They were yet another small community within the greater Alpha family.

Mr. Lopez had grown up with a family of gardeners, and he knew how to tend to Alpha's plants. He was not only able to keep all of the bushes and trees on the property well-trimmed, but he had advised Sr. Ignatius on how the boys might plant the gardens at the boys' home to be more productive. Magdalen served as interpreter, since Ignatius did not speak Spanish. In addition to tending the plants and the gardens, Mr. Lopez also cut the boys' hair, alternating each month between the Senior Home and the Junior Home.

One afternoon in early December, as I arrived home from St. George's, Q and O'Brien came charging at me all smiles and laughing. Both of them had shaved heads. They stopped abruptly right in front of me. "What's this?" I said, rubbing their heads, as they laughed.

"Mr. Lopez here to cut hair, sir. We told him we want bald this time," they said, slapping their hands together.

Since Mr. Lopez spoke neither English nor Jamaican, he and the boys had devised their own way to communicate. Mr. Lopez stood at one end of the verandah at Junior Home. One by one, the boys took a seat in a small metal chair in front of Mr. Lopez, facing away. With their thumb and forefinger they would show him how high they wanted their hair, or they would bring him a rough sketch of a design they wanted carved into their hair. If they wanted it all taken off, they would swipe their hands together quickly, as if to say, "All done!"

All around the yard boys were rubbing their heads, some now bald, most just getting the feel of their new look. Richard was still in line to get his hair cut. He smiled and slapped his hands together, showing me he too would soon be bald. I introduced myself to Mr. Lopez, and then went to open the game room. Nurse was in the refectory.

"Mr. Jay," she said. "Sister was looking for you earlier. A crate of books came today and she wanted you to take a look."

O'Brien, Q and I went off to find Magdalen, who usually spent the better part of the afternoon in the Senior Home kitchen, helping manage the meals. It took more than just Cook to cook. If you didn't manage supplies properly, including locking the storeroom every time you were going to step away, even for a minute, then you risked having a Senior Home boy steal supplies and sell them over the wall at the back of the compound.

"Jay," she said, all excited when we found her in the kitchen. "Have I got a job for you! Four barrels of books arrived from the States today. I am sure you can use some at Junior Home." Then she noticed the two boys. "My Goodness! What have you done," she said smiling and rubbing first O'Brien's head and then Q's. They both smirked and giggled.

"And Richard is about to join in them in the bald-man's club," I said. Her smile evaporated. "Richard Burns?" she asked.

"Yes," Q said proudly. "We all decided together to have it done."

"Cook! I'll be right back." She pushed by me and ran toward Junior Home. I had seen her move quickly before, but never at this pace. She was just short of a sprint. The boys and I followed.

"Is something wrong, Sister?" I asked.

"Richard Burns cannot shave his head," she said adamantly.

Sister had plenty of quirks and rules only she herself understood. I just shrugged and ran along. As soon as she could see the verandah, she started shouting, "Mr. Lopez! Mr. Lopez! Wait!" Richard was taking his seat as Magdalen darted up the stairs. "Richard," she said panting, "You may not shave your head. You can only trim his hair, Mr. Lopez. No shaving."

"But Sister," Richard pleaded. We are all going to look the same," he gestured at Q and O'Brien.

"I know you want to, Richard, but I love your hair," she said, pulling his head close to her. "Your hair makes me smile. Mr. Lopez can take some of it off, but you can't be bald." Then she spoke to Mr. Lopez in Spanish. His eyebrows raised and then nodded knowingly. Richard pouted, the scars next to his mouth puffing out his lower lip. "Richard, when you are done, go to the library and help Mr. Jay," Magdalen said, and he perked up immediately.

"Come, Jay," she said. "Let me show you where those books are."

As we walked to the library, Q and O'Brien walked a few paces behind us. Sister, still panting, pulled a handkerchief from the pocket in her dress and wiped her brow.

"All right, Sister. What was all that about?" I asked quietly so the boys wouldn't hear.

"You see Richard's face," she said softly. "Those scars by his lips? When Richard arrived at Alpha, his lower lip was torn almost completely off. It hung down like a flap. His mother was a mad-woman," she spoke with horror in her voice. "She used to beat him so badly. I pray for her every time I see him." We were talking as we walked and she was still catching her breath. "When boys first arrive here we always shave their heads because of lice. When we shaved Richard's head, it was heartbreaking. Every inch of that boy's scalp is covered in scars. His hair hides most of it. A wonderful American woman volunteered here for a while years ago. She paid for the surgery to fix his lips. But there is nothing we can do about the scars on his head. The boys can be cruel to each other. If they see his scars they will tease him about it and give him some awful nickname about them. More importantly, if he sees them himself, he will remember the pain. No boy should think of his mother as a beast. No one should know that the person who should love them most in the world is capable of doing that to them."

I thought of the Prayer of St. Francis:

> *Where there is injury, pardon.*
> *Where there is darkness, light.*

"How do you keep track of each boy's issues, Sister?"

"Ha! I wish I could. I just remember what I can and hope that someone else is there to catch the rest."

The door into the library led into a short hallway with storage rooms on either side. The hallway opened into the large room, more meeting hall than library. My room was off to the right. Off to the left were four large shipping drums. Each was about four feet high and three feet in diameter, composed of sturdy cardboard. The label on each drum read, "Food for the Poor, Florida," a charitable organization that funneled resources to agencies like Alpha all over the Caribbean.

"These arrived today, Jay. Food for the Poor dropped them off. They said they are books for the boys. Would you mind taking a look and organizing them for me?"

"Sure, Sister. We would be glad to."

"Q," I said, "Run over to the office and ask Mr. Herman for the toolkit so we can pry open these lids. O'Brien, help me roll these barrels over by the table. We tilted each drum and rolled it on its edge toward the row of tables in the center of the room.

Q walked in at the same time as Richard. "Well, aren't you looking sharp Mr. Burns, with that snazzy haircut of yours," I rubbed his head. He just smiled sheepishly. "Are you available this afternoon to help us?"

"Yes sir, Mr. Solomon."

We pried open the lids. Each drum brimmed with books that seemed to have been tossed in randomly. O'Brien grabbed the first book off the top, a small paperback, and immediately stepped back to inspect it. On the cover, a boy ran along a cliff Hardy Boys-style. The size of the book suggested it was well beyond O'Brien's ability, but he stared at the cover, taking in every element of the picture. Q sorted through the few books at the top layer, until he found one he liked, another paperback titled, The Boy Who Knew Too Much. From what I could see of the cover, it looked like science fiction. In the meantime, Richard just stared at the pile in the drum, like someone who knows they are in the presence of gold, but doesn't know how to spend it. He had the lowest reading level of the three boys.

"This is terrific, isn't it, Richard?" I said. He stared at the drum nodding. It took half an hour to unload all of the drums. It would take another hour to sort through the piles and stack duplicate copies. The boys worked quietly and diligently. Their days were so routine, that any variation, even if it smacked of work, was a welcome respite.

"Boys, let's try to sort these by difficulty level, so that we'll know which ones to take up to Junior Home and which to leave at Senior Home." Q was capable of figuring this out by himself, just by the length of the book and the size of the print. Richard was clueless. Every time he picked up a book he would check with me before putting it in one of the piles.

As I continued sorting, O'Brien couldn't contain himself any longer. He walked away from the table and sat down on the floor holding a large picture-book Bible. He was fascinated with the intricate colorful drawing on the cover and appeared to be in a trance as he lay it in front of him and opened to the first page.

When all the books were sorted, I brought two sodas out from my fridge, and poured each boy a cup of Coke. I handed Q and O'Brien two copies of an easy reader and told them to sit off to the side and read the book together. They sat next to each other on a nearby couch and opened to the first chapter of the book.

Q began, "Chapter One – The First Day of School." Then he read the first sentence and stopped. O'Brien immediately picked up with the second sentence. They automatically alternated, taking turns sentence by sentence. Because I always left early for St. George's, this was my first glimpse into how they must read in class. Their voices flowed in tandem, and they developed their own cadence as they read. Occasionally, O'Brien would struggle to pronounce a word. Q would soften his voice and pronounce the word in a near whisper. O'Brien would then read the sentence through without stopping, pronouncing a new word correctly. Somewhere along the way Q had learned how to help a friend, and protect the friend's ego at the same time.

"Richard, let's find a book for you." We had separated out the picture books from the paperbacks, and the variety of picture books was impressive – everything from small books printed on cardboard rather than paper, like <u>Pat the Bunny</u>, to atlas-sized books with small print and lots of details. "Why don't we do this," I offered. "Why don't we find a book that you like and practice it, and when Miss Irene comes later this week, you can impress her by reading it to her. How does that sound?" He was nodding in agreement before I even finished the thought. Although the idea of impressing someone with his reading skills may have been daunting to him on the inside, he somehow found the courage that men find when they want to impress the woman they love.

I suggested a few books, each of which he nixed when he saw the size of the print. And, if he couldn't pronounce the title of a particular book, we didn't even bother opening it. Finally, we found, <u>One Fish, Two Fish, Red Fish, Blue Fish.</u>

We sat on a couch across the room from O'Brien and Q and read through the first few pages. He struggled with the occasional word, but overall, did fine, and I knew he would do well for Irene.

"That was great, Richard. I'll ask you to read it to me tonight when I come up for bedtime stories, Okay?"

"Yes, Mr. Solomon. I can do that," he said, staring at the book with trepidation.

O'Brien and Q had finished a number of chapters by the time Richard and I closed his book, and it was getting late. "Boys, we need to wrap this up, so give me a hand here."

O'Brien said, "Mr. Solomon, I have to go to the bathroom."

"Okay, come with me." I took out my keys and unlocked the door of my room. From the doorway, I pointed out to him where the bathroom was. "It's right in there. Come right back out when you are done."

"Is dis where Desmond killed the rat, sir?" His smirk told me he wasn't inquiring out of concern, but to poke fun at me.

"Just get going, O'Brien. Never mind about any rats."

Q and Richard and I stored the books on the shelves that lined the room under the windows. We finished the job as O'Brien returned from the bathroom. Each boy took a book with him in payment for their afternoon of service.

I arrived for the story hour earlier than usual that evening so I could work with Richard on his book. The boys were still finishing their bathroom routine, washing their hands and brushing their teeth. As I arrived, Waldemar came running up to me.

"Mr. Solomon, can I come see all the new books tomorrow? Can I have one too?"

"We'll see about that Waldemar. I take it you got a chance to see the books that O'Brien and Q and Richard all have?"

"Yes sir. O'Brien is sick tonight, sir. Him throwing up in the bathroom, sir."

"Really! He seemed fine all afternoon."

"Well it's not that surprising," said Sister Magdalen, as she came out of the boys' bathroom. "He brushed his teeth with this," she handed me a tube of acne cream. "I don't know where he got his hands on it," she said.

"I do. It's mine. He used my bathroom this afternoon when we were sorting books."

"Well, then," she shrugged, "served him right, the little thief. You really shouldn't have them go in your personal room though, Jay. When they see your things, your radio and such, it just tempts them to steal."

"Poor kid." Just then O'Brien came out of the bathroom, looking sheepish.

"O'Brien," I said softly. He raised his head, but not his eyes. "Do you feel all right?" He shook his head slowly. "Well, what you used to brush your teeth isn't tooth paste, but it won't kill you either. Any lesson learned?"

"Yes sir," he said. "I should read things carefully before I steal them."

It wasn't quite the lesson I had in mind.

Nov. 14, 1986

My Very Dear Jay,

This is a rather hurried note – just like me! I'm always in a hurry. But I fear I'm going to be late for your birthday. Still it is never too late to wish you many happy returns of the day.

I'm sure your parents and the rest of the family will make it a nice day for you. Do have a good time. I could charter a plane and come with all my boys for the big day – but then I hear it is already very cold up there- so we have to abandon that idea!

Sr. Ignatius & Sr. Regine join me in sending you the very best wishes & greetings for the 19th. Incidentally, Sister Ignatius' is on the 18th. She is so glad you are a Scorpio!! She said that's why you are nice! Poor me! I'm a Pisces! She believes in the Stars and loves horoscopes!

Mr. Melvin, the Old Boy, came for another visit and has finally left. I spent 14 days driving him all over creation! I have enough trouble with my 96 boys – I didn't need another big baby to care for. Next time he comes I will go for a retreat at the other end of the island!

Well, dear, this is it for the present. You will hear again from me when I have time. I hope!

Yours in a hurry!

Sr. Magdalen

18
BEACHED

Many Jamaicans don't swim. Those in Kingston that do, and don't want to drive all the way to Negril in the west, or Boston Beach in the east, head to Black Beach, a dark-sand beach just west of Kingston Harbor. It takes about forty minutes to reach Black Beach by car from the center of Kingston, and considerably longer by bus. Irene and her five housemates had decided to make it a Saturday day-trip.

Kingston's central square, close to the harbor, bustled with vendors. Car and bus traffic whizzed around its perimeter while pedestrian traffic crisscrossed the square. Although the designers clearly envisioned a green and shaded park-like setting for the square, in the 1980's it was a dry and dusty two acre lot, with a non-working fountain in the middle, makeshift booths selling fresh produce, and dozens of small boys running around selling peanuts and trinkets. On the south side of the square, bus conductors jockeyed for position, trying to attract passengers, yelling "Black Beach! Black Beach!" Or, "Mandeville!" Or, "Harbourtown!"

Karen led the group across the square taking in the energy, the commerce, and the squalor.

A Black Beach conductor spotted the group headed his way, with towels under their arms and their Ray Ban sunglasses already deployed. Standing tall, with a foot in the open doorway of his bus, he caught Karen's eye over the heads of the crowd and was waving her over. But as he jumped down from the doorway, a large Jamaican woman handed him her bags and huffed as she started to haul herself up into his minibus.

The conductor suddenly found himself torn. "Come now lady," he pleaded with the woman who was already half in his van, "hurry now!" He used his shoulder to lean on the woman's large rear end to push her into the bus, which caused her to turn her head and swat at him. His haste backfired, as it drew the attention of another conductor who then spotted Karen and the group. The second conductor made a mad dash across the street.

"Come now, pretty lady. We are ready to leave right away," he said as he half-led, half-dragged Karen toward his waiting bus. He already had three passengers, and Karen's group would allow him to head out on his first trip of the day. Irene, Melissa and Doug piled into the back row, where a woman with a large mesh bag of fresh vegetables sat against the window. Brian, who had played football for BC, was significantly taller and broader than the other men and could not have fit in the back row. Instead, he filled out the row directly behind the driver. Karen and Peter squeezed into the front seat.

The bus quickly pulled out of the marketplace. The front seat was tight and Karen was wedged in between Peter and the stick shift. Peter did his best to lean as much of his weight as he could against the door, but the bus was old and he wasn't confident the door would hold him in.

In the back row, Irene put her head down on the beach bag in her lap and tried to sleep. The woman with the groceries just stared out the window and didn't say a word. Brian was soon deep in conversation with an older couple in his row. The man had graduated from St. George's and was very interested in an update on the school. He had cousins who lived in Boston, which dragged Doug into the conversation from the back seat. During a brief lull in the conversation, Doug looked out the window at the fields of sugar cane, which the bus had been passing for twenty minutes.

"Aren't the fields beautiful," Karen said, to no one in particular.

"Yeah," Doug offered from the back. Then asked in all seriousness, "But who eats all that corn anyway?"

He didn't understand why everyone on the bus, the woman in the back included, burst into laughter.

Peter and Karen in the front had tried a half-dozen positions to get comfortable in the tight front seat, none of which worked for more than a few minutes, when Karen finally decided to just perch in Peter's lap. The bus had a low ceiling and Karen had to bend her head over uncomfortably to fit. The back of her neck bounced on the roof of the van whenever they hit a bump in the road.

The last two miles to the beach were on a rough, rutted stretch, more path in the sand dunes than paved road. Bump after bump sent Karen's head into the roof of the van, and with each hit she either laughed or winced depending on how hard she hit. Peter's reaction was the same as Karen slammed down on his lap with each bump. Brian and the driver laughed as they watched the two of them endure the ride.

After one particularly tough rut in the road, Peter said, "Driver, one more bump like that and I'm never going to have any children!"

The driver laughed and swerved to avoid the next big hole in the road.

"Peter," Karen said, "one more bump like that and *I'm* gonna have your children!"

As the driver and the rest of the bus exploded in laughter, a goat walked into the road and the driver turned the wheel hard to miss it, running into the bushes. The bus stayed upright, but was leaning significantly in the sand. The group piled out. The beach was just up over the next small hill and the group would be fine making it on foot. But the driver and conductor needed help pushing the bus back onto the road. Irene was the only one of the three BC women who knew how to drive a stick shift, so she got behind the wheel. The three BC men got in front of the van, alongside the older gentleman. The conductor pushed from the open sliding door of the van, and the driver pushed from his open door window. In just a few minutes, they had the van back on the road.

The group walked the remaining short distance down the sand and dirt road to the clearing in the scrub where a half-dozen cars were parked around a few shacks selling food and drinks. The shacks were clustered around a concrete platform that was covered with a thatched roof, where a few families sat at the picnic tables enjoying an early lunch.

Irene and Karen selected a spot in the sand where the thinly-leaved trees provided spotty shade. Once they got settled, the men headed into the water while the women put on sunscreen and stretched out on their towels and talked about their plans for the Christmas holiday.

Melissa mentioned how her large, extended family would be gathering at her grandmother's home in Marblehead.

Irene said, "I'm thinking of bringing three of the boys from Alpha home with me for Christmas." She was thinking specifically about O'Brien, Richard and Q.

"Home to Mrs. Creighton's, or home to Long Island?" Karen asked with a surprised voice.

"Why, home to Long Island of course. Why would I bring them to Mrs. Creighton's?"

"I don't know. I thought maybe you wanted them to spend some time in a real house," Karen answered.

"No. I want them to spend time in a real family. My parents would just die over them."

"I don't know, Irene. Bringing them home is one thing," Melissa said. "But then you have to bring them back. What are you hoping to accomplish?"

"I don't know," she said defensively. "I'm still trying to sort out if it's the right thing to do. My parents would help me with the tickets, and I'm sure would be open to having the boys for a few weeks. But like you said, why would I do it? Would it even be fair to them?" She was silent for a while. "You know....I don't care," she said with great determination. "I would be doing it for the right reasons, to give them a different experience, show them a different part of the world, really show them how a family acts. It could only be good."

"I'm all in favor of that," Karen said. "I agree with you. It could only be good."

Melissa interrupted, choosing her words carefully so she wouldn't offend. "But the reality is, unless you are going to keep them, after their great experience, you are going to bring them back to live in a Third World orphanage. What would they be taking away from the whole experience? Both the trip, and the aftermath?"

"I know it would be difficult! I know! But I can't help but feel that it would be a good thing to do."

"Have you even looked into how difficult it would be to get them passports?" Melissa asked?

"I would be glad to help you with that," Karen offered.

Irene said, "I'm sure the logistics alone would be a nightmare and would probably make the whole thing impossible. But I still want to."

"Can't you just see the look on their faces when they have their first plane ride? Their first look at New York City? Their first Christmas tree in a real home? It would be amazing," Karen said, already caught up in the idea. "It might be the first time they received a toy that belonged just to them. It would be so nice to just spoil someone for a while. We all deserve to be spoiled every once in a while."

"I'm just playing Devil's Advocate here," Melissa cautioned, "But what happens to those toys when they return to Alpha? Are they going to have to fight every day just to hold onto whatever you give them? And does it cause too much strife with the other boys? Do they become the target of jealousy? I don't know...It just seems like a Pandora's box to me."

"Look, I know it would be difficult to pull off, let alone difficult to justify. But every once in a while, I like to dream, o.k. Just let me have my little fantasy, o.k."

"No problem," Melissa said in her best Jamaican accent, as she and the other women lay back down on their towels.

The group spent the afternoon in and out of the water and back and forth to the snack shacks, enjoying a plate of ackie and saltfish and cornbread bammy. And, of course, Red Stripe. It was December and the sun was hotter than any of them had experienced at Crane's Beach north of Boston or anywhere on Cape Cod or the Jersey Shore, even in late August. At some point in the afternoon, they were each sound asleep on their towels, except for Melissa, who worked diligently to correct the many folders of school papers she had brought with her.

The ride home was less of an adventure in a less crowded minibus,. Most of the group slept a good part of the way. Irene stared out the window wondering, "Why not bring them home?"

19
THE GAME ROOM

Q, hands folded neatly in front of him, stared across a chessboard at Orlando. Orlando's left hand clutched one of Q's bishops, while the fingers of his right drummed the table.

O'Brien, sitting to Q's right, leaned over and tapped him on the shoulder and said softly, "It's your turn." Q turned toward O'Brien and glanced quickly at the checkerboard between them. He reached over, captured two of O'Brien's men, and turned his attention back to his chess game. O'Brien sighed and then stared intently trying to figure out his next move. Q had few worthy chess opponents in Junior Home, but Orlando was forcing him to think at least a few moves ahead. Many of the boys had played chess before coming to Alpha. Q was a home-grown player.

Q had been brought to Alpha as a four year old by his grandfather, who came somewhere from "country." His grandfather was frail and spoke slowly and with dignity.

"'Im mother died of da fever, Sista" he had told Sister Magdalen. "'Im a good boy. 'Im very sweet. Him not give you no trouble, Sista. Mi a cannot care fi im. But him a good boy." Magdalen had taken down as much information as the old man could provide. "Mi daughter was a sweet girl. She was kind to de boy. 'Im very sweet."

He had turned to Q in the office doorway, rubbed the boy's cheek, and said, "You be good for the sisters, now Alfred. You be good now, ya 'ear, me." He turned and pulled out a handkerchief, and blew his nose and wiped his tears as he walked down the driveway and out the gate. Q stood with his small hand in sister's and watched his grandfather walk away. He did not cry. His large eyes stared blankly at his grandfather's back, the last he would ever see of family.

That was four years ago. Q was the youngest boy at Alpha. The Sisters would usually send boys that young to St. John Bosco Home in Mandeville, in the mountains.

"He was just too easy," Sister Magdalen said. "He had a calm about him that made you want to keep him. He was too young to leave around the other boys. They would have picked on him," she had told me. "I used to let him follow me around all day. It was like having a puppy. He's never been an angry child like some of the others. His grandfather must have been right that his mother was gentle with him."

I turned from watching Q, to Richard, who was sitting with me building a jigsaw puzzle. Although Richard was nine, he liked working on the puzzles intended for kids about six.

"Mi a get this one fast sir," he said, flicking his wrist and letting his index finger and pointer snap together in a clacking sound, a Jamaican finger snap. Teenage boys in particular, elevated the finger snap into an art form, and occasionally converted it into a talent, holding contests to see who could snap their fingers the fastest, sounding like a pair of castanets.

I wandered to the other table where other boys were playing Chutes & Ladders. Morris Mathers stood nearby, watching.

"Morris, why don't you sit down and play?" I asked. He just shook his head. "Would you like to play a card game with me?"

He shrugged.

"How was your day today?" I asked, while I laid out the cards for a game of Concentration.

"Fine," he replied, staring at me, expressionless.

"Are you in Mr. Estig's class?" He nodded. I was used to tough conversations with some of the boys until they felt comfortable, but usually their tone was cautious. Morris was more reserved and diffident than shy.

"Come. Sit down," I said, as I finished laying out the cards, all face-down, spread across the table in rows. I went first, explaining the rules. I had turned over one queen and one ace, saying the names of the cards as I turned them over. As I turned them back face down, Morris took his turn, announcing each card as he turned it over. Within five turns he had gathered almost a dozen pairs. When there were only a few pairs left and he knew he would win, he stood and, lightning fast, turned over the last few pairs. As he turned over the last card, the left corner of his mouth turned up ever so slightly. It was the closest I would ever see of a smile on his face. But even that trace evaporated quickly as he sat back down.

"So now we're done?" he asked.

"Unless you'd like to play again," I offered.

"Yes," he announced flatly.

I shuffled the cards and handed the deck to him, "You lay out the cards while I check on the other boys."

"You'll come back?" he asked hesitantly.

"Yes, Morris. I'll come right back after I check on the others."

I roamed from table to table and returned just as he was straightening the last few cards. He played even more confidently the second time through, and once a card had been turned over once, he never forgot its location. His hands moved so quickly on his turn that other boys started to gather around and watch. He won decisively, and on the last card said simply, "Again."

"We have time for one more game, Morris."

As Morris laid out the cards, Jomo asked if he could join us. Morris' hand stopped in mid-air, poised to halt the game altogether.

"Jomo, let me and Morris play this one last game. Here's another deck. You and the other boys can start your own game."

Jomo willingly took the deck, and Morris laid out the rest of the cards.

Morris and I finished just as two Senior Home boys arrived with dinner. "All right, boys. Time to pack up the games." As I stood up, I turned to Morris, "It was a pleasure playing with you today, Morris."

"Yes, sir," he shrugged as he turned and walked out the door of the refectory.

Lord, make me a channel of your peace.
Teach me how to reach a child.
Teach me how to listen to his silence.

* * *

Later that evening, after I had finished dinner, I sat on Junior Home verandah with silent Malcolm. I leaned forward, looking at a National Geographic map of Europe that O'Brien had spread out on the tile floor. Four other boys were crowded around it. We talked about how to read a map, with north always being at the top, and how to distinguish west from east, not always that easy to boys who easily confuse right and left. Then I quizzed them on particular countries and cities.

"Find Italy for me. It's shaped like a boot."

"Move now man!" Waldemar demanded as he leaned in over the map, effectively blocking the other boys' view with his head, and casting a shadow.

"Mi a find it first," O'Brien insisted, trying to view the map in spite of the Waldemar cloud that darkened most of the continent.

"It's right here," said Q, smiling at how quickly he had found it.

Waldemar sat back on his haunches with a huff. "Ask again, Mr. Solomon. Ask another."

O'Brien looked disgusted.

"All right, who can find Great Britain?"

The heads dove back over the map.

"Here's a hint. It's an island."

Immediately, Q put his finger directly on the star that represented London.

"Very good," I said, nodding at Q who was smiling broadly.

"Man 'im quick!" Waldemar said in amazement.

"How about Sweden? Can anyone find Sweden?"

"Oh! Oh! Oh! Mi know dis one! Mi know dis one!" Waldemar insisted as he snapped his fingers.

O'Brien was desperate to get an answer, and scanned the map over and over, like a hawk circling a doomed rodent on a meadow.

"I got it!" shouted Waldemar, as he put his finger on the "S" in Spain.

"Close Waldemar," I said. "They both begin with the same sound."

Q leaned forward on his knees, but glanced up at me before pointing right at Stockholm. I gave him a knowing look to say, "You and I both know you know, but let someone else have a turn." He smiled back and retreated.

"Sweden is at the top of the map. It's one of those countries that hangs down like bananas on a banana tree," I said.

"Man, im right. Look at the banana countries," cried Waldemar. "I found it! Sweden!"

O'Brien started to stand. "It's my map and I don't want to play anymore."

"Come on O'Brien. I'm sure you'll get one soon. They just got lucky on those first few. Stay just a while longer. Please."

O'Brien immediately sat down again.

"Let's try something harder. Let's try a city. See if you can find Berlin." They dove back in. While the other boys had their heads buried in the map, Q sat back, and looked over at me. I smiled and nodded a thank you.

Silent Malcolm, at my side the whole time, nudged me and put out his hand to thumb wrestle. I took his hand in mine, counted to three slowly, and then pretended to avoid his thumb. He just stared at me. Since he didn't move his thumb at all, or understand what he was supposed to do in the game, I eventually just said loudly, "You win!" and he smiled his peaceful smile and blinked.

I turned back to the boys and their search. "Would you like me to give you a hint?"

"Yessir," said O'Brien, sounding exasperated.

"What city are we looking for again?" asked Waldemar.

"You're looking for Berlin," I said. "Here's a clue. Remember we found Sweden a few seconds ago. Well directly south of Sweden is Germany, and Berlin is in Germany."

This time, their hands as well as their heads returned to the map, as they each tried to trace a straight line from Sweden to German.

"I found it," O'Brien shouted.

"Very good, O'Brien. Nice work. Now, let me tell you a little bit about Berlin. It's actually split into two cities," I began.

After a brief explanation, Richard asked, "So the whole city is surrounded by a wall?"

"Just like Alpha," Waldemar noted.

They showed interest in the Berlin Airlift and the accounts of people trying to cross the no-man's-land around the wall. But after only a few minutes of my explanation of communism and socialism, O'Brien interrupted

"Mr. Solomon, could you pick another city?"

"Sure. You're right. Too much grown-up talk. Why don't you find the river Tiber. It's in Rome, which is in the middle of Italy, remember – the boot."

They found Rome very quickly, and the Tiber just after that. I began to explain how the Vatican is a separate country inside a city, but it was getting dark and Benjamin, the Senior Home boy on duty that night called all the Junior Home boys to line up for the bathroom.

"You boys go on. O'Brien, why don't you stay here with me and I'll show you how to fold a map?"

"Okay Mr. Solomon," he said.

"I want to thank you for sharing your map with us. That was a lot of fun."

"Thank you sir. Mr. Estig gave it to me today, but he wants it back tomorrow."

"Okay. Well if you like geography, let me know and I will see if I can get you another map of your own sometime."

"Thank you, sir." O'Brien scrambled over to the line for the bathroom

As I looked across the courtyard at the boys in their lines, I thought of the few minutes we had just shared. There was no big moment. There were no great epiphanies. There was no breakthrough. There were just a few laughs; a smattering of learning; a calm non-event of an early evening. These boys, living in an orphanage, without any luxuries of any sort, had passed the last hour the way all kids should – calmly, securely, and each with minor victories for the day. I wanted to give them more, but wasn't sure what, or what more was needed.

Lord, let me not so much seek great things,
As to recognize the greatness in small moments.

20
HOLD TIGHT

Saturday mornings started a little slower than school days. Magdalen awoke at her normal time, but let the boys sleep in. Since they didn't have school they could take longer with their chores. The added quiet time allowed Magdalen a little breathing room as well. Magdalen joined Ignatius and Marie Therese upstairs in the convent for breakfast. The sisters made sure they committed time each day to support each other and just enjoy each other's company. It would have been too easy to let the relationships slip, since there was always more work to be done.

Magdalen was at the counter in the convent kitchen preparing toast, while Ignatius set the table. Ignatius was fully dressed since she had already made her first round of the Senior Home dormitory, and she would never leave the convent without her habit.

Marie Therese had adopted her own morning routine. Before she joined the other sisters for breakfast and their short morning prayers, she would lie in bed and thank the Lord for three things from the prior day - small events, perceived blessings, kind words spoken.

But lately she had been sleeping longer, and even when she woke, she found she was still tired. This morning, she could hear Magdalen and Ignatius preparing breakfast as she awoke. She didn't want to keep them waiting, and had been starting to feel bad that she wasn't as active as her sisters. Rather than take her few minutes to pray, she pushed back the covers and slid her feet over the side of the bed and stood up. She realized immediately that she had moved too quickly. The blood drained from her head, her eyes rolled back, and she passed out. As she tumbled forward, her head hit the corner of the side table, tearing a gash in the paper-thin skin on her forehead. Since she was only semi-conscious, she didn't brace herself for the fall. Her chin came crashing down on a small chair, causing her to bite through her lip. She landed in a heap on the floor.

Ignatius and Magdalen heard the fall. Together, they pushed the bedroom door open just enough to maneuver Marie Therese's shoulder so they could open the door fully and get into the small room.

Ignatius knelt next to Marie Therese. "Oh, Marie!" she said through her tears. "Oh, dear Lord, no. No. No. No." The blood from her forehead and lip had run down around her neck, making it impossible to see the severity of her injuries. It was already staining the her nightgown collar black.

Magdalen ran to the sink and wet two clean dishtowels. By the time she returned to the bedroom, Ignatius was cradling Marie Therese's head in her lap, and Marie Therese had started to come around. Ignatius gently wiped the blood from Marie Therese's face and neck, while her sister was moaning in pain. Magdalen rushed out to call for help. She and Ignatius would not be able to move Marie Therese on their own. She ran to the top of the stairs and saw a Senior Home boy sneaking a drink from the pipe under the grape arbor. "You there," she yelled.

The boy thought he was in trouble and froze as he looked up at her.

"Quickly, run to Junior Home! Get Plunkett for me! And make it quick!"

The boy, grateful to not be yelled at, said, "Yes sista," and ran to Junior Home. Plunkett was the fastest moving of the office boys, and the one the sisters trusted most.

Magdalen returned to Ignatius who was still cradling Marie Therese, but now Marie Therese, still whimpering, was mumbling, "What happened? What happened?"

Magdalen brought two new damp towels to Ignatius, who traded the bloody towel for the fresh one, keeping the pressure on Marie Therese's forehead to stem the blood flow, which has slowed but was steady. A large bump was already forming. Desmond Plunkett arrived at the top of the stairs, and called out to Magdalen from the gate, knowing not to enter without permission. Magdalen called him in. He knew from her voice it must be serious. Ignatius threw a thin robe over Marie Therese before Plunkett walked into her room. He didn't speak, but his eyes showed how surprised and scared he felt.

Magdalen said, "Ignatius, Plunkett and I will lift her. You just hold the towel on her head." Marie Therese was able to prop herself up on her elbow to assist in the move, and Magdalen and Plunkett lifted her from under the arms and slid her into her chair. She was still moaning and seemed disoriented.

"We're going to take you to the hospital, Marie," Ignatius said slowly while she still held the towel on her forehead. With her free hand, she reached a housedress, hung on a hook on the back of the bedroom door. She couldn't have Marie Therese leave the convent in only her nightgown.

"Run and get Mr. Sullivan, Plunkett," Magdalen said She didn't have to add, "And make it quick." Plunkett took every task with urgency.

I had not been in the sisters living quarters before, and, like Plunkett, hesitated at the top of the stairs. But Magdalen was beckoning.

"Jay. We're in here. Please come in."

Marie Therese was still sitting in the chair in her room. Ignatius and Magdalen, had managed to get her into the housedress. She was holding a cold compress to her own head while Ignatius held another to her mouth. She looked like she had aged ten years in a single morning.

"Jay, we need your help to get sister down the stairs," Ignatius said calmly.

"I will go bring the car around," Magdalen said. "Plunkett, run up to Junior Home and tell Benjamin to start the morning routine without me. He will know what to do."

I knelt down next to Marie Therese. Her face looked drawn and there were tears in her eyes. "Do you think you're ready to move yet, sister?" I asked. She nodded, so I put her left arm around my shoulder, and put my right arm behind her to support her. I started to lift her, only to realize that I wouldn't be able to stand up straight since she was about a foot shorter than I. Stooped over and trying to support as much of her weight as possible, I maneuvered through the door of her room and down the narrow hall. Fortunately, the door to the porch was wider and we walked through easily. By the time we were making our way slowly around the porch, Magdalen was already pulling the car into position in front of the office.

Marie Therese was leaning heavily on me for balance and shaking continuously. Ignatius walked behind us with her hand on Marie Therese's back, saying, "Careful, Mr. Jay. Not too fast, you know."

We made slow but steady progress across the porch, with Marie Therese breathing heavily and occasionally groaning. She was supporting enough of her own weight that she couldn't have broken any bones, but was limping and was clearly in pain. When we reached the top of the long flight of concrete steps she gasped and blurted out, "I can't take those stairs!" and turned to head back into the convent. Ignatius was determined that Marie Therese get to the hospital to be x-rayed, but the stairs were only wide enough for one person at a time.

"Sister, I will walk right in front of you," I said. "I will hold your arm and you will lean on my shoulder and we will make it just fine."

But still she protested, and her fear was turning to panic.

"Then Mr. Jay will carry you, sister," Ignatius declared.

I looked at her with surprise, since Marie Therese looked steady enough on her feet to handle the stairs, and since I wasn't as confident of my own strength as Ignatius was.

"Well, that will work I suppose," Marie Therese said immediately.

"You'll have to carry her, Mr. Jay," Ignatius insisted. "Marie, put your arm around his neck."

My look of surprise didn't seem to register with Ignatius, but at the bottom of the stairs Magdalen rolled her eyes. Marie Therese dutifully put her arm around my neck, "O.K. I'm ready," she said, as if all systems were go.

"Well, all right sister, if this is the only way. Just let me get through the gate and onto the top landing." I stepped through the gate while Ignatius supported Marie Therese. Marie Therese then put her arm around my neck again. As I lifted her in my arms, she winced, just loud enough to cover the sound of my own grunt.

Lord, give me strength. Give me balance.

Instead of resting her head on my shoulder, Marie Therese tucked her head in the crook of my arm, instinctively inward for protection. At the time, it struck me as odd. I didn't recognize her movement until many years later when my sleeping four-year old daughter, Teresa Marie, made the same movement in my arms as I carried her to bed. The last man to hold Marie Therese in his arms had probably been her father, when she was a child. Now, in my arms, she returned to that secure pose. An old neighbor of mine who had been a medic in World War II once told me that, on the battlefield, all injured soldiers, no matter how old or how tough, call out for their mothers. I wondered if, in times of distress, when feeling threatened, all women instinctively yearn for the secure arms of their fathers.

I had to lean back significantly to balance sister's weight. It had rained the night before and the steps glistened with small puddles that formed in the uneven concrete. With Marie Therese in my arms, I turned slowly from the porch to the long flight of stairs. As I turned, my left foot slipped – not enough to cause me to lose my balance, but enough to cause my entire body to tense. Marie Therese's body didn't flinch, but the occasional gasp of breath told me she was still in pain. As we descended the steps slowly and carefully, I debated with myself whether I should have taken off my flip-flops and done this barefoot, or if that would have been even worse on the wet slippery surface. At the bottom of the stairs, Magdalen and Plunkett waited nervously. Magdalen kept encouraging me. "You're doing fine, Jay. You're doing fine." Then she leaned over to Plunkett and whispered from the side of her mouth, "If he starts to fall, just get out of the way."

Step after step I imagined the worst possible scenarios. Most likely, I would slip and fall backward on the stairs. Not a complete disaster. My body would cushion the blow to Marie Therese, but her weight on top of me would shatter both my elbows when they pounded into the concrete steps. I could live with that. Second possibility, I pitch forward and topple head-over-nun down the long stairs with both of us landing at the bottom, dead, in a mangled heap. I would die the death of a clumsy fool. By the middle of the staircase I realized the ultimate horror. We both fall down the flight of stairs - she dies and I live. My whole life would be defined by one slip. I would be responsible for the death of a saint.

By the time we made it to the bottom step, Marie Therese was breathing normally and looked up from the crook of my arm. As I lowered her feet to the ground she turned and hugged me. With Magdalen on one side, me on the other, and Ignatius running back and forth between the waiting car and us, we made our way to the Volvo.

"Jay, can you help at Junior Home while I bring them to the hospital?" Magdalen asked. "Plunkett, come with me in case I need you."

"Yes sister," Plunkett and I said in unison.

"Oh, I don't want to be a bother to anyone," Marie Therese said, and then whimpered as her lip started to bleed again.

The three nuns and Plunkett got in the car and I watched them pull out the gate and turn right, up South Camp Road for the short drive to St. Catherine's Hospital.

It was the first time I was at Alpha without any of the sisters present. I was in charge. As it turned out, everyone knew the routine, and the routine worked, so I answered whatever questions arose, and gave direction when needed. Craig and Q were my best sources of information on how things should work. This time, the twenty-something supposed hero was relying on the three-foot tall eight-year olds for guidance.

Magdalen was back a few hours later. The look of concern on her face was not encouraging.

"How's she doing?" I asked.

Magdalen looked over at me, "Physically, she'll be fine. She needed a few stitches on both her head and her lip. Those are painful, of course. But she will recover. It's just harder at our age, Jay, to recover emotionally from these things." She sighed heavily. "Marie Therese had a nervous breakdown a few years ago. She over-reacts sometimes. And Ignatius plays into it." Her tone softened. "Marie Therese entered the convent about eight years before Ignatius. They have worked together ever since Ignatius joined. Ignatius wouldn't know what to do without Marie Therese to take care of." She was quiet for a few moments. "Marie Therese was already slowing physically, and now this." She shook her head.

She took a deep breath. "It's a good thing you were there to carry her down the stairs. She'll be telling that story for years now," she laughed.

"I was just glad I didn't drop her," I said, relieved.

"How were things here?" she asked.

"Fine. No issues. You've created a well-oiled machine."

"And you've been running it for the last few hours," she observed.

And she was right. I was apparently now qualified to run a large orphanage, assuming of course, that nothing happens while I'm in charge. It was the first time at Alpha that I had had a role that could be defined. All the strategizing and reflection on my role so far had produced nothing, and yet, in an instant, I was asked to step up. I was a help instead of a hindrance, a support instead of an aside. And yet, the only thing I had done while Magdalen was gone was to be present. I wondered if that would have to be enough this year.

Plunkett walked up and handed Magdalen a set of keys, which she slipped in the pocket of her white dress. "I think Plunkett and I were both worried that if you fell, we would have to pick you both up and carry you to the car." She and Plunkett, both laughed. "My goodness, Plunkett! You haven't eaten yet. You must be starving."

Plunkett smiled. "I'm okay, Sista," he replied, just as his stomach rumbled. Like most teenagers, Plunkett wanted badly to be considered an adult, and he knew from watching the sisters and staff that self-sacrifice without complaint was a sign of maturity. If he wanted the opportunity to be part of the team, he needed to act like the sisters, not like the other boys.

Magdalen turned to me, "Jay, you seem to have everything under control here. Come Plunkett, I think breakfast is still on the table at the convent. I will get you something." I watched the two of them head toward the convent, Magdalen's gait a little slower, and Plunkett standing a little taller.

21
THE SOCIAL CONTRACT

The last Saturday before school ended for the Christmas break, Melissa and Karen awoke for their morning jog. In white t-shirts and BC running shorts, they moved quietly through the house so that they wouldn't wake anyone. We had all been out late at a bar in Half-Way Tree the night before, and it was still early. The roosters were crowing, but in Kingston, the roosters seemed to crow all night long. Melissa undid the padlock on the iron grillwork that served as a front door, and locked it again behind them, tucking the key into a small pocket in her shorts. Even in Liguanea, which was a relatively safe neighborhood, you never left your door unlocked.

They stretched in the driveway before opening the garden gate and heading out to the street. They jogged down Mrs. Creighton's street and then turned left down Old Hope Road, heading toward Crossroads. It was a route they had run a dozen times before.

They started out quiet, just settling into a comfortable pace, but soon started talking They would both be heading home the following weekend, Melissa to New Hampshire, and Karen to New Jersey. Melissa had struggled to adapt throughout the year, often homesick and uncomfortable with the pressure of teaching. The heat also bothered her more than it did some of the others. Karen, on the other hand, had never had a down day in Kingston. She was thrilled with the newness of everything, inspired by the resilience of the kids she worked with, enamored of the openness of the Jamaican culture, and upbeat with just about everything.

Kingston had no discernible zoning laws, so groups of shacks where people lived were wedged in between small factories. High-rise apartment buildings sat next to empty lots that looked like no one planned to develop anything on them any time soon.

The women were about a mile into their run, chatting about how they would spend their holidays. The only other life they had seen so far was one taxi that passed them on its way to Crossroads, and two goats, foraging in a vacant lot.

It was Melissa who first heard the footstep behind her. She turned only in time to see the fist coming toward her head. The force of the blow into her temple knocked her sideways into Karen, who stumbled and fell. It happened so quickly, neither woman had time to scream. The first man leaned over her and clamped his hand over her mouth, threw his arm around her waist and lifted her off the street. She kicked so wildly her left shoe flew off, but he was probably eight inches taller and a hundred pounds heavier than she was. He was holding her so tightly around the waist she could barely breathe, and her body went into full panic as he slipped his hand under her t-shirt. She could smell his sweat and feel his breath on her neck.

The other man was less delicate with Karen. He too covered her mouth, but he simply grabbed her around the chest and dragged her in the same direction, to the abandoned lot on the side of the road. When he threw her to the ground her head hit the dirt hard, but she didn't lose consciousness. As the man carrying Melissa got closer to the side of the road, he loosened his grip slightly to adjust his hold. Her body jerked wildly and her head smashed back hard into his face. He dropped her and grabbed his nose. She landed on her side, but quickly scrambled to her feet. She ran a few steps away, panting heavily, trying to regain her breath and some much needed oxygen. The man was holding his hands to his face, cursing, and Melissa could see blood starting to run between his fingers. She suddenly realized she was frozen, standing silently. She started to scream for help as loud as she could.

The other man, standing over Karen, was opening his pants. When he heard Melissa, he started to move toward her. Melissa kept screaming full throttle, but there was only the vacant lot and a row of closed up stores, and no one to hear. Even the goats had moved further away. Melissa was now twenty feet from her attacker, and at least thirty feet from the other man. Karen was on her back on the ground trying to inch away on her elbows. Melissa wanted desperately to run, but couldn't leave Karen. As the first man wiped the blood from his nose and regained his intent, cursing at her in words she couldn't decipher, he started toward her. Although she kept screaming as she backed away, it was the cab that appeared in the distant that scared him off. The other man kicked at Karen on the ground and then the two men walked quickly but nonchalantly across the street and down an alley.

Melissa ran to Karen and then the two ran into the street still calling for help, looking over their shoulders to see if their attackers were coming back.

The cab pulled to a stop in front of them. The driver had seen the two men walk away, but this was not his neighborhood, and he was not going to pursue the attackers down the alley. The women fumbled with the door as they frantically climbed in. They both burst into tears and were shaking so violently, they forgot to tell the cab driver their address.

When the cab dropped them at Mrs. Creighton's, Melissa couldn't find her key. They had to bang on the front grill, both still in tears, waking everyone in the house just to get in.

As Doug paid the cab fare, the driver kept saying, "I'm so sorry dis happened to your friends. Dis shouldn't happen. But it's not safe for them to be out alone so early in the morning." Doug nodded quietly and returned to the house.

Karen and Melissa sat shivering in the living room, telling the others about what had happened through their tears. Irene brought them wet towels to wipe their scrapes and Doug brought them bandages.

"We should have known this would happen. But after the first few times we went, it just seemed safe." Melissa sobbed.

Karen asked for ice to dull the growing bump on the back of her head. "I can't believe this happened. Don't they know we're here to help them? How could this happen? To us!" After only a few minutes, they both wanted showers and some privacy. Each went into a separate bathroom to shower and change. Irene went back and forth between the two rooms a number of times to check on them and see if they needed anything. After long showers, both of them climbed into their beds and slept the rest of the morning.

The whole house had planned to spend the day out at Lime Key, a small island just outside of Kingston Harbor. Instead, they all just sat stunned around the dining room table.

"I can't believe this happened," Peter said.

"What part can't you believe?" Brian asked, quietly.

"Why do you say that?" Irene asked.

Brian looked up from his coffee cup, "How many times did we mention to them that it wasn't a good idea to run when the streets are empty?" he asked softly, looking around to make sure neither of them had come into the room.

"Don't start blaming them for this," Irene said flatly. She was trying to defend the women's actions, but her tone was only half-hearted.

"Really," Brian asked, "then how come you have never gone running with them?"

In our many nights talking over beers, we had discussed what it meant to be "culturally sensitive." To some, it meant eating local food, riding on the minibuses instead of taking cabs, and not complaining about the heat. To others, it meant more. Some of us curtailed our lifestyle to be in line with our surroundings.

"Have you *ever* seen Jamaican women out running by themselves, *ever*?" Brian asked. "Let alone in the dark? They don't do that here. This isn't a jog around the reservoir at BC at night when eight thousand other people are out running. We're in *Kingston*, for God's sake! We stand out like a sore thumb just waiting for the bus in the morning. How do you think they look in running shorts and t-shirts at six in the morning down a dark street?" His voice was getting louder and more emphatic.

"Lower your voice, Brian," Irene said. "They need support right now, and hearing you blame them, even in part, isn't going to help."

"I'm just glad they weren't hurt worse," Peter said. "This could have been really horrible for them both."

"It could have been horrible for all of us," Brian said.

Brian pointed out that BC wanted the program to be successful, in part, because it was a fulfillment of the school's mission to create graduates dedicated to helping others, and, in part, because it reflected well on the school itself. If two participants in the program had been raped or killed, the school would have seriously had to consider shutting down the program. "We would all be heading home next week, and we wouldn't be coming back after Christmas."

"You're probably right," Doug responded.

"The first time they went running, we all told them we didn't think it was a good idea," Doug continued. "When nothing bad happened, it only made them bolder. Think about it…those two guys may have been watching them for weeks now. They made themselves targets."

"That seems a bit strong, Brian," Irene said. "You're blaming the victims."

Brian said, "Look, the two men are guilty of attacking them. The girls are just guilty of making it easy for them." He continued, "It's the social contract. We talk about acclimating to the culture here, but we don't walk the talk. The minute the culture becomes inconvenient for us, we ignore it and do things our way. And it's not just curbing our freedoms, like not going running. We've all noticed that everyone here dresses up for church, right. And yet we still wear jeans and t-shirts, as if we were back at BC. To us, it's too hot to dress up, so we do whatever works for us, even if it's disrespectful to the rest of the congregation.

"But we do act differently here," Irene interjected. "Would you *ever* talk about religion at home with people the way we do here? It's totally different. Here everyone talks about it all the time. Back home, we'd be considered freaks if we wore God on our sleeve the way we do here. They'd think we were nuts. And *we've all* changed in the way we talk about race. I'm so used to being called "whitey" on the street, that I'll have to watch myself back home, because I can't talk about race the same way there without sounding bigoted. We came here because we wanted to experience another culture, and I think we're trying our best."

Brian continued, "I'm just saying we're not really experiencing it unless we give up the freedoms the people here have to give up."

Peter interrupted, "Hey, do you think we should call the police?"

"Let's let them make that decision when they get up," Irene said.

Our connection with the program coordinators back at BC was so tenuous that it never occurred to anyone to share the information with the school, and it seemed a personal event, inappropriate to share with our employers in Kingston. The reaction from the BC teachers who had arrived in the country a year earlier was one of surprise - that nothing had happened sooner. There was sympathy for Melissa and Karen, coupled with disbelief at their naiveté.

I was bewildered more than anything else. I tend to follow the rules, whether they are in writing or just implied. When someone more experienced cautions me about a course of action, I tend to follow his or her advice. Whether that's humble and respectful, or timid and spineless, or all of the above, I'm not sure. There's an old saying, that after the age of 30, most wounds are self-inflicted. Although none of us in Kingston that year were even close to thirty, that wouldn't keep us from making our own mistakes, whether from bucking the rules, or following them.

22
GOING HOME AGAIN

Two weeks before the Christmas holiday, midterm exams had started at St. George's. Determined to avoid my mistakes of the previous year, this time, instead of devising hard, multiple choice tests, I posed questions that had to be answered in essays, which gave me a fairer assessment of each boy's skills, and made it impossible for anyone to cheat. It also made grading the papers more difficult and time consuming. Most of the St. George's boys would experience Christmas as an extra-long church service, a single gift from their family, and an opportunity for two weeks without a long commute to school. Some would visit relatives in the U.S. or U.K., and others would have relatives visit. Those who went to the U.S. would return to school with the newest gadgets and clothes. I would spend the first two weeks of class in January confiscating Gameboys from my First Form students.

Ignatius directed the boys as they hung a few decorations in the refectories at Senior Home. Magdalen would show the Junior Home boys a few Christmas movies, *The Little Drummer Boy*, *A Christmas Carol*, others with religious themes, rather than Santa story-lines. The choir had been practicing Christmas hymns for weeks. The focus would be on Mass on Christmas Eve and Christmas Day, and dinner would include more meat than usual, and dessert, which was rare.

Some of the Alpha boys who had family would visit them, coming back a few weeks later. Those without families would stay put, except for Q. He was going to spend Christmas with Miss Donegan, a friend of Sr. Ignatius. Miss Donegan was in her late thirties and had never had children. She had offered to take in a boy for the holidays. Q was excited but nervous. He had been at Alpha for four years now, and in that time, had never slept anywhere but on his cot at the end of the sixth row, with 95 other boys in the room. He sat in his Sunday clothes on the bench by the office, waiting for Miss Donegan. He sat perfectly still from the waist up, but his feet were fidgeting nervously, mostly I assume because he wasn't used to wearing shoes. The small suitcase next to him, barely bigger than a large purse, contained two changes of clothes, a bar of soap, a toothbrush and a few books that he liked.

I headed up to Junior Home to say goodbye to the boys before Mr. Johnson, the van driver, took me to the airport. I said a quick goodbye to Q, told him to behave for Miss Donegan, and went to pack. By the time I returned to the office, Miss Donegan had come and gone. I took my knapsack, said my last goodbyes, and jumped in the van with Mr. Johnson for the ride to the airport.

In New York, I spent a few days helping my parents set up the tree and wrap countless gifts, with my mother reviewing lists for each of us, worrying if she had enough under the tree to make everyone feel special. It would have been easy to be put off by or indignant at the differences between the energy and focus at home versus Alpha, but it didn't bother me that much. The world isn't fair, and some people have more than others. One person's excess is another's necessity. My family's indulgence wasn't excessive by our neighborhood's standard, and my mother's stress about gift-giving was borne of the same love for her children that Ignatius put into decorating the dining hall.

After two hectic days, I headed up to BC to pick up my sister, now in the middle of her senior year. I stopped in at the BC bookstore, where Mr. Fitzpatrick, the manager, proudly showed me the pictures of the Alpha boys in BC t-shirts on the bulletin board in his office. I didn't even need to ask this time as he loaded my arms with dozens of out-of-style t-shirts and shorts for the boys. He kept trying to push the XL and XXL sizes, but even the mediums would hang like tents on the boys' narrow frames. Better to leave the larger sizes for him to donate to someone else.

Christmas with my family was as wonderful as ever. I took full advantage of the hot showers and good food. But by the end of the second week, I had embarrassed my family by stopping by a number of stores in town and asking for donations for Alpha. It's amazing how you aren't ashamed to beg when you know the faces of those you're begging for.

Irene and I were on the same flight back to Kingston and were able to catch up on the plane. Her sister and brothers were all home from college and work. Her sister Kate had gone shopping with her to buy gifts for Magdalen and a few of the boys. One of her brothers, who worked in a TV production studio, made bootleg copies of an entire season of Sesame Street. The videotapes filled an enormous canvas bag, which still didn't compare to the gigantic suitcases that other passengers piled onto carts in the customs area of Norman Manley Airport. Irene had decided not to bring any of the boys home with her for the holidays. Magdalen had not supported the idea, which made moot all of the hurdles of getting passports and visas, and the tough transitions for the boys from Kingston to Long Island and back again.

I had traveled home with one small knapsack with a single change of clothes, knowing my winter clothes were waiting for me. I returned with two enormous duffle bags of t-shirts and socks, deflated soccer balls, coloring books and candy-canes. The customs agent unloaded most of the goods on the table and started arguing that this much merchandise was clearly not for my use and that I was intending to sell it. That would require paying a tariff. I insisted politely that I wasn't intending to sell anything but she persisted, and the holdup was causing a ruckus. I started to get nervous until she called over her supervisor.

"Mr. Sullivan, good to see you again, sir," said Mr. Jarrett, the father of one of my St. George's students.

"Mr. Jarrett. Merry Christmas and Happy New Year, to you, sir. How is Barry?"

"He's good, sir. He was doing a lot of the reading you assigned him for the holidays."

"Well, I look forward to seeing him back at George's in a few days."

"Miss Jenkins," he said to his co-worker, "This is all o.k. Whatever he has is o.k. Mr. Sullivan, you are good to go now." Miss Jenkins looked none too pleased at having been overruled, but stamped the proper documents and waved me on.

Before Mr. Jarrett turned to leave, I introduced to him to Irene. He greeted her warmly, and waved her through as well.

Mr. Johnson was waiting as Irene and I emerged from customs. Magdalen had sent Richard and O'Brien along for the ride, and it was an extra special treat for them to ride with Irene. We loaded the bags in the back, and the boys piled into the middle seat. Standing next to the open door, I helped Irene up, figuring the two of us would take the back row. "Make room in the middle, boys," she said as she wedged herself between the two of them. They giggled as she put her arms around them and crossed her legs, "Now, tell me all about your Christmas!"

I smiled weakly, closed the van door, and climbed up into the front passenger seat, and away we went.

Things were different for the entire BC group after Christmas. Melissa returned with a new attitude, her weeks with her family helping her rejuvenate. She was determined to be a stronger teacher, and to be flexible enough to truly enjoy being in Kingston. It would be a tough road, and especially hard since Karen didn't return at all. Karen had been so vocal in her love of the place and the experience, that she had been blind to the realities of living in a tough city in a poor country, where not everyone welcomed her. The reasons for her decision not to return were fodder for dinner discussion on and off for months.

The day after we returned from New York, Irene and I were up at Junior Home running the game room when Q walked in, returning from Miss Donegan's, and grinning broadly.

"Well, look who's back! Welcome home, Q!"

"Hello, sir," he said, still clutching his suitcase. "Hello, Miss Irene."

He walked over to Irene who hugged him close and laughed, "Look at you all dressed up." Irene had never been at Alpha on a Sunday and only saw the boys in in their shorts and t-shirts. He sat down next to her on a bench, never letting go of his suitcase.

"So, tell us about Miss Donegan's. Did you have a nice time?" I asked.

"Yes, sir," he said smiling, but looking over at the other tables.

"What did you do? Anything special?"

"Yes, sir," he said again, now looking at the nearby chess game two of the boys were playing.

"Why don't you go put your things away, Q, and then come back and join us," I suggested, sensing he wasn't ready to talk yet.

"Yes, sir," he said as he got up and headed to the dormitory.

Within a few minutes, Q reappeared dressed in his usual shorts and t-shirts, and lacking shoes. The only difference was a new plastic digital watch on his wrist.

"Whoa, Q! Fancy watch you got there," I said. The boys at the other tables came over to see his Christmas gift from Miss Donegan. He showed off the features proudly. Eventually, he sat down to a game of checkers and everything started to feel normal again.

Irene stayed later than usual. She had missed the boys, but admitted she was glad she hadn't take any home. "It would have been the wrong thing to do," she said. "I had forgotten how intense Christmas is at home. It's all about 'Too much.' Too much food. Too many presents. Too many people. Too much activity. I think it would have been overwhelming for them. Q looks startled just coming back from someone's home nearby. Can you imagine coming back here after two weeks on Long Island?"

We talked about the awkward moments we experienced as we had left our families, inadvertently saying, "Well, it's time to get back home now," referring to another country. Having come from similar backgrounds though, we both felt the backing of our parents, their acknowledgment of our new communities, and our personal focus at this point in our lives. More than anything else, more than age or race or nationality or education or economic reality, it was the support and love of our families that distinguished our lives from the boys'.

The next day, in the gameroom, I sat down next to Q as he put away the pieces of a puzzle he finished. "Q, I thought it would be a good idea for you to write a 'Thank You' note to Miss Donegan. What do you think?"

"Yes, sir. I would like that."

"Okay. Have you ever written a 'thank you' note before?"

"No sir."

"Well, it's pretty easy. Before you write it, think of all the nice things you were able to do at Miss Donegan's. Then just write a few lines to thank her for making your holiday special, and mention of few of the things you liked most." I gave him two pieces of paper and a pencil. "Write a rough draft on this page, and then I'll take a look. Then you can write a nice version on this piece of paper."

I left him with his thoughts and went off to work with the other kids. When I returned a few minutes later, he was staring at the first sheet. In very neat handwriting, he had printed a beautiful note saying how much he appreciated staying with her. He had mentioned how much he had enjoyed sleeping in a comfortable bed, and eating the wonderful chicken dinner she had made, and served to him off a real plate. He enjoyed most sitting next to her on the couch in the evenings while she read stories to him. He ended by writing, "Thank you for all of your kindness."

"Q, this is terrific. You don't even need to re-write a thing. You did a wonderful job. Now just sign your name and you're done."

He continued to stare at the page. He had written the letter so quickly, he had clearly been thinking of all of these things ever since getting back. Now he was stuck.

"Q, is there something else you want to write?"

He stared at the page and his shoulders heaved as he drew deep breaths. I could see his tiny hand tighten on the pencil. "Is there something else, Q?" This time he nodded quickly but still didn't raise his eyes from the page. Again I asked, "What do you want to write?"

He didn't speak. His hand started to quiver. "Is everything all right, Q?"

Again he nodded, but he was stuck. "Then just sign your name and we're done, Q."

He hung his head further, now looking at his feet under the table instead of at the paper. It was a look of utter defeat. But still he didn't sign his name. Then I recognized the look of defeat, and it clicked. There comes a time in every man's life when he goes out on a limb to tell a woman he loves her, without knowing for sure if the sentiment will be returned. We feel sick at the potential of being rejected, and sicker still at the thought of not taking the chance.

"Q, do you want to write, 'I love you.'?"

He nodded quickly, raising his head only far enough to stare at the paper, still unable to make eye contact with me. There was too much at risk if I were to say, "no."

"I think that's a very nice idea, Q. Why don't you do that."

In precise print, pressed a little too hard into the paper, Q wrote words he had never uttered to anyone in his short life. Then he signed his name slowly and with care. His shoulders relaxed as he looked up and pushed the paper toward me, his eyes filled with trepidation and hope.

I was honored and humbled to be present for Q at that moment in his life. I was proud of him for taking that important step. And I was sad and furious as well. A man should face that moment as a man, not as a boy. He should face that moment before a potential lover, not before a substitute mother. We all need to hear the words, "I love you," often in life. But just as much, we need to *say* those words. A child should not be paralyzed by the thought of saying, "I love you," to someone, scared to the bone that the feeling might not be returned. It was the great injustice of their lives, these wonderful boys, that they were not sure they were entitled to love someone, and afraid of the consequences of asking for that love in return.

"Well done, Q. Well done. Enough of the game room for today. Go play outside now."

I folded the letter carefully, and brought it to the office. Mr. Herman was sending out invoices for the print shop and the carpentry shop, and paying an assortment of bills. I asked him for an envelope, a stamp, and Miss Donegan's address. When I left the office, Q's brave little letter was sitting in Mr. Herman's outbox with other debts being paid and requests for things owed.

23
THE STRIKE

For weeks, the lunchroom discussion among the teachers at St. George's had been about the impending increase in fuel prices. Only a few of George's teachers could afford cars; most took public transportation. But either way, the fuel increase would affect them substantially. Gas had always been expensive on the island, but the latest increase was coupled with a government announcement that they would not allow the minibuses to increase fares. Most minibuses stopped frequently to take on a few gallons of fuel at a time, since the drivers couldn't afford to fill the tank. They ran on rather thin margins, so the newest fuel increase would cripple them. The minibus drivers were threatening to strike.

That morning, in mid-January, on my short walk from Alpha to St. George's, fewer cars zipped up and down South Camp Road. The gaggles of schoolgirls at the front of Alpha Academy and the primary school were missing. The street vendors that usually crowded the intersection of South Camp and North Streets had not bothered to set up their booths, and the few people who were on the street seemed agitated and hurried. The headline on The Daily Gleaner read, *Minibuses to Strike at Noon*. Anyone commuting to work knew there was a good chance they would have difficulty getting home that evening.

At school, the boys alternated between nervous and oblivious. Classes started and the morning ran smoothly, even though it seemed about a third of the boys were absent. For most of the morning I taught in the First Form block, the highest point on the property. As I wrapped up the lesson and prepared to send the class to lunch, one of the boys yelled, "Smoke! Something's on fire!"

The other boys flew from their seats. A column of smoke was rising a few blocks south of the school's main gate.

"Boys, back to your seats!" I ordered, but one of the boys shouted, "More smoke!" and pointed out the windows on the north side of the building. We could see three columns of smoke rising from different parts of the city. All of the boys rushed to the windows. While they guessed at what parts of town were on fire, I concentrated on the column of smoke off to the right, at what would be near the front gate of Alpha.

"That other one looks like it's right outside the school wall!" said another pointing at the thickest smoke plume, on the left.

"All right, boys. I'm sure everything will be just fine by the time school gets out," I lied. "Let's get back to our seats."

Just then, the bell rang for lunch and the boys started to scramble to go eat. "Whoa, boys! Just a minute. Let me find out what's going on here before you all head out in different directions." Just then, Father Tom Brodley, the Vice Principal, appeared in the doorway. He was a slight man and always struck me as an odd choice to be the chief disciplinarian, since he had an awkward demeanor, a timid presence, a high-pitched squeaky voice, and didn't appear to have a collar-bone; his shoulders just sloped away from his neck until his arms appeared out of his sides. He motioned for the boys to sit. They immediately became silent. He gestured with his head to beckon me to step out of the room onto the verandah. In a near whisper, he said, "We're going to dismiss the boys now and close school for the day. There are cars overturned and burning at most of the major intersections in the city."

"Shouldn't we keep them here where they're safe?"

"We can't keep 1,200 boys here on the compound. We have no way to feed them and nowhere for them to sleep. There is no public transportation and it will take many of them all day to walk home. They have to get started now so that they get home by nightfall."

"How dangerous is it out there?"

"Well, we haven't heard any gunfire, yet. The boys aren't usually targets since they don't have any money. Many parents have already called and those that have cars are trying to drive down here, but many roads are blocked. The tough part will be the next few days. If the roads are shut down for a number of days, the stores will run out of food pretty quickly and then who knows what will happen."

"What do you need me to do?"

"Nothing right now. I will make the announcement and then once all of the boys are gone, you can head home."

Fr. Brodley came into the classroom, "All right boys. I know you've seen the smoke from the fires. Let's just settle down. We're closing school early today." Normally, at an announcement that school was closing early the boys would burst into shouts of joy. But given the circumstances, the boys stayed quiet, looking around at each other to judge how to react. Some were smiling, but most appeared anxious. "If you usually get dropped off at school, go to the principal's office to call home. If you take the bus to school, you are going to want to start walking home now. If you all gather down by the front gate, we're trying to organize things so that if there are older boys who live in your neighborhood, you can all walk together."

Some of the boys immediately started waving their hands to ask questions. "I don't have time for questions right now. I have to talk to the other teachers and classes. Gather your belongings and head toward the main gate." He turned to me. "Please make sure all of your boys make it to the front gate. The janitor will be locking all of the classrooms shortly." Fr. Brodley walked out the door and a few steps down the verandah to the next class.

"All right boys. You heard Father. Let's pack up and head down toward the Sixth Form block." The boys all scrambled to pack up their books and papers. Some immediately bolted for the door and ran toward the front gate.

As I packed up my own papers, a small voice said, "Mr. Sullivan?" I looked up to see Joshua Motley, one of the quietest kids in class. His voice was controlled but his eyes screamed panic. His hands were quaking.

"Yes, Joshua," I said, putting a hand on his arm.

"Mr. Sullivan, no one from school lives near me. I live out toward Spanishtown. I can't walk home. I don't know how, and it takes me more than an hour to get here by bus. I don't know what to do." Tears were already welling in his eyes. Sometimes when boys got upset about things at school, their fears were divided between the cause of their concern and the thought of crying in front of their classmates. For Joshua, appearances weren't the issue. He was holding it in more out of habit than out of pride.

"Well, Joshua, do your parents work in Kingston? Maybe someone could come pick you up."

"My mother lives in country, sir. I live with my grandmother. She cleans houses for people in Spanishtown."

"Let's walk down to the office, Joshua, and try to call your grandmother."

"We don't have a phone sir," he said, sensing he was in real trouble if I didn't understand the nature of his situation. The shivering in his hands started to extend to his forearms..

"Joshua, everything is going to be fine," I said. "Let's go down by the front gate and see what arrangements we can make."

He nodded and stared at the ground, "Yessir." He pulled his book bag up on his shoulder, and we headed for the front gate.

Hundreds of boys were gathered at the school entrance, sitting on the verandah along the Fourth Form block and along the low wall separating the main road through campus from the football field. Some were kicking around a football, waiting to be told what to do. Others were playing cards or just talking to one another. Many were pointing anxiously to the column of smoke that was clearly coming from just a few blocks east of the school, down North Street. There was an odd mix of excitement, dread, panic and playfulness in the crowd. Groups of boys who didn't live far away, set off immediately. Every few minutes, the guard would open the front gate for a parent who had been able to navigate the streets to get to the school. Fr. Hosie, the principal, and Fr. Brodley, knew most of the parents. As cars arrived and the drivers shared what they knew of the situation outside the wall, it became clear that there were no buses running anywhere in the city. There were cars overturned and burning at many intersections, but many roads were still passable, and there wasn't a sense of anarchy, yet. The two priests quickly filled each car with boys from the respective neighborhoods and the drivers left as soon as possible. In between arriving cars, Fr. Brodley, a master at logistics, grouped the boys by their neighborhood. He was encouraging all who could conceivably walk home to start out now. The situation would deteriorate quickly once it turned dark.

"Father, are any of these boys heading to Spanishtown?" I asked, with Joshua standing by my side.

"What?" he asked over his shoulder as he herded one group into a waiting van.

"Spanishtown. Joshua here lives with his grandmother there."

"No. No. We only have a few boys from that far away and, as far as I can tell, none of them made it in today. Given the news, they probably felt it was safer to just stay home." He turned his attention back to the van. "All right, that's everyone for this van. Thank you, Mr. Daly," he said to the man behind the wheel. He slid the door shut, and pounded twice on the roof, "Drive, driver." Mr. Daly made his way slowly down the driveway honking a few times to clear groups of boys from the road. As he approached the main gate, the security guard swung his arm to clear boys out of the way, lifted the latch and pulled open the tall gate.

I trailed behind Fr. Brodley as he moved from group to group.

"Well, Father. What can we do to help Joshua?"

"I don't know right now, Mr. Sullivan. You will have to give me a minute. You boys," he called to another group of a half dozen boys kicking a ball around on the field. "Where are you headed?"

"Up by Immaculate, Fadda."

"Well, how are you planning to get there?" he called.

"My father's driver is coming, Fadda," one of the boys said nonchalantly.

"All right," Father said, mostly to himself, as he turned to another group sitting on the wall. "And you boys?"

"My mother always picks me up after she gets off work. These two boys come with us. And him is joining us today," he said, pointing at another boy who nodded.

"All right, good," Fr. Brodley again mumbled.

I looked at Joshua, whose grip on the strap of his knapsack tightened, a reflection I was sure of the knot that must be forming in his stomach. "And Joshua, Father?"

"Again, Mr. Sullivan, you need to give me a few minutes. Please." He was sharp and shrill. Then he turned to walk off, but caught Joshua's eye. He looked down, put his hand on Joshua's shoulder, and changed his tone. "Don't worry, son. We'll think of something." Then he walked away quickly toward another group. "You boys over there...."

I looked down at Joshua. "Let me go pack up my stuff for the day. Do you want to come to the teacher's office with me, or sit with the other boys," I said gesturing toward other First Form boys sitting on the verandah playing cards.

"I'll stay here, sir," he said hesitantly. "You won't forget though, will you?"

"No, Joshua, I won't forget. I'll come back to check on you in a bit."

As I turned to head back to the teachers' offices, loud popping noises came from the wall dividing St. George's from North Street. I'd been in Kingston long enough to know the sound of gunfire. All of the playing on the field and the chatter from the driveway stopped. The security guard quickly opened the gate and about fifty boys who had been waiting on the street in front of the school came rushing into the property. I saw Fr. Brodley walking quickly toward the gate, and then calmly shepherd all of the boys further up the driveway. Some were clearly frightened, while others made guns with their hands and fired at each other, laughing.

"I'm sure it was nothing," Fr. Brodley said unconvincingly. "Probably just a car backfiring." Then he disappeared in the office to call more parents.

I looked over at the verandah where Joshua was sitting. He was staring at me wide eyed and hesitant, as if he didn't know if he should now come with me or wait with his friends. I motioned for him to stay put and nodded slowly as if to say everything would be all right. I was surprised by how good I had become with meaningless platitudes, both in speech and gesture. And equally surprised at how well they seemed to work.

In the teacher's office, I filled my knapsack with papers to be corrected. Some of the other teachers were organizing rides home among themselves. I got tied up in their conversation and suddenly realized that I needed to check on Joshua.

As I headed to the Fourth Form block with my knapsack on my shoulder, I wondered if Joshua could stay here at St. George's. They had stopped having boarders at the school many years ago, and they didn't have the staff to provide a dormitory. I could certainly find a bed for him at Alpha, but I didn't like the idea of mixing those two worlds. The boys at Alpha might not take kindly to having a George's Boy in their midst and might decide to pick on him. And taking a boy who had a home and was used to the care of his grandmother, and plopping him in an institution for a night might be quite a shock to his system and psyche.

The crowd of boys on the verandah had thinned considerably. The group Joshua had been sitting with was gone entirely. I walked further down the driveway to the field. There were only a handful of boys sitting on the wall, and none on the field. I couldn't see Joshua anywhere. In the office, Fr. Brodley was on the phone and sounded like he would be talking for a while. I ran up to the First Form block, thinking Joshua might have headed back there. The lower form blocks were largely deserted, and the janitor was locking each classroom as he finished sweeping each room.

By the time I got back to the office, even fewer boys were left on the property. After only a minute, Fr. Brodley hung up the phone, and then sighed deeply and rested his head in his hand.

"Well, this has been quite a day," he said, pulling out a handkerchief and wiping the sweat from his forehead.

"Father, have you seen Joshua?"

"Who?"

"Joshua, Father. The First Former who needed to get to Spanishtown. I've been looking all over for him and can't find him."

"Motley, you mean?"

"Yes, Father, Joshua Motley. Have you seen him?"

"Yes. Mr. Howe who runs the cafeteria is taking him home. After you left, I realized that Mr. Howe lived out in Spanishtown. He will drop Motley at his grandmother's. They left fifteen minutes ago."

"Well, that's a relief," I sighed.

"I told you it would all work out, Mr. Sullivan. It's probably time you headed home soon yourself."

"I'm on my way, Father. See you tomorrow."

"Don't count on it," he said. "Listen to the radio for school closings. If the buses aren't running tomorrow, no one will be here."

As I exited through the main gate I could smell the acrid smoke from burning rubber. I rounded the wall in front of the school. Just ahead of me, smoke and flames burst from what looked like an overturned car in the first intersection outside the school gate. The heat was causing the paint to peel on the front of the small snack shop where I sometimes bought lunch. As I rushed by, I saw that the smoke rose not from an overturned car, but from a pile of debris. Tires and some zinc sheets were piled atop a wooden cart. Through the smoke, I could see the red hibiscus flowers on the side of Mr. Shipman's cart. He would not be selling coconuts again anytime soon outside of St. George's. Without his cart, he would have no way of getting the coconuts from the market down by the main square up to North Street. In a few days, most of the reminders of the strike would be gone, but to Mr. Shipman, today would be a turning point in his life – the day he lost his income. Someone else's notion of how to protest a gasoline price increase just ruined the livelihood of a man who didn't use gas.

As I hurried down the street, close to the high concrete wall that separated St. George's football field from North Street, gunshots rang out a few blocks into the neighborhood south of the campus. I looked down the side street which headed directly toward Kingston Harbor, about two miles to the south. I had never ventured down that street. It was a notoriously rough neighborhood. It had been from this side-street that two teens had emerged one beautiful and quiet Sunday afternoon, held a knife to my side and changed my view of the city and taught me what it meant to be a victim.

I had only been in the country for two weeks. I was still living at St. George's while some of the other volunteers and I looked for a house. We had gone to the beach for the day. When we got back to Kingston, the girls took a minibus back to Liguanea. Michael, another BC teacher, and I took a bus up South Camp Road and got off at North Street. We walked past the cathedral and, as we approached St. George's, at the very spot I was standing now, two boys, probably about fifteen or sixteen, emerged from one of the side streets and started to follow us on the deserted street. As we approached St. George's gate, the two boys walked faster toward us.

"This doesn't look good, Jay. Run," Michael said as he broke into a sprint for the gate and the security of St. George's compound. I was more naïve and didn't think the boys looked dangerous. Michael made it around the corner of the St. George's wall and up to the gate, where he slipped through. I made it to the corner when the two boys caught up to me, blocking me from the gate. Even when they both pulled out knives they didn't look threatening. They seemed too young. But there they stood poking my side with a six inch blade. One quickly put his hand in my pockets, pulling out the money I had left from the day trip. Only five Jamaican dollars, a bad haul for the trouble.

Michael was standing inside the gate, yelling, "Help! Help! Robbery!"

But the Jesuit residence was too far back on the property for anyone there to hear, and the area by the front gate was empty on a Sunday.

Then the kid who had rifled my pockets noticed the gold chain on my neck, a St. Christopher's medal that had been owned by my grandfather and that my father had given me just before I came to Kingston; something to keep me safe.

The thief grabbed the chain, "Gimme da chain," he said, holding the knife to my cheek.

"All right! All right!" I said quickly. "You can have it." I lifted the chain over my head.

The other thief grabbed my sunglasses. I had just paid a fortune for them not a month before and didn't want to lose them.

"Hey! You can't have those!" I said, as if this was a garage sale and they had reached for a family heirloom. "They're prescription. They're no good to you."

The kid tried them on and realized he wouldn't be able to wear them, so he nonchalantly handed them back to me.

He still held the knife against my side and I could feel the point in my flesh. Then, without a word, they turned and walked away. They didn't run...just walked, as if we had just had pleasant conversation and they had said their "goodbyes."

I turned and ran to the gate, where Michael stood, looking panicked.

"Are you all right?" he asked.

"I guess so," I said, still more dazed than frightened. It wouldn't hit me until later than night, and in the many sleepless nights for weeks afterward, how close I had come to being casually cut or stabbed, an incident that would surely have shortened my experience in Jamaica from two years to two weeks. And now I walked past the same intersection on a day when the city was in more turmoil and in more danger than I had been. In retrospect, getting mugged so early in my time in Jamaica helped me deal with the other difficulties of the experience. It gave me perspective. I knew my existence was defined by how others saw me, whether as "Fadda," or "Sir," or as a help, a hindrance, or a victim. Getting mugged helped give me perspective.

On the next block on North Street sat KC, Kingston College, another boys' high school. The grounds of KC looked nothing like St. George's. There was no large grass field; no colonial style buildings; only a large stucco rectangle of a school, three floors high. Many of the classrooms had broken windows. The school yard, visible through the high gates, was empty. Since most of the boys at KC were from local neighborhoods, they would have all fled for home as soon as the strike had started.

At the intersection of North Street and South Camp Road a minivan was on its side. Flames were shooting out of the front. The back end smoldered, with black smoke pouring out. At this time of day, mid-afternoon, this intersection was usually crowded with cars and pedestrians. There was always a crowd of adults and school kids waiting at the bus stop, and a line of cars and buses waiting to pull into the gas station. Today, the healthy bustle was instead nervous chaos. I turned left and hustled up South Camp Road. As I passed the entrance to Alpha Academy, the girls' school, I noticed that the driveway was empty. Sr. Bernadette, the Principal, had dismissed school as soon as possible. Many would have just as far to travel as some of the George's boys, and the sisters wanted them home before dark. The streets of Kingston could be tough on a young boy walking alone at night, but they were treacherous for a young girl.

Not a single vehicle passed me on the ten minute walk back to Alpha. As I neared Alpha's gate, I could see another car burning in the intersection about a quarter mile past the school entrance, just in front of *You Must Come In*. I wondered if the bartender, Elizabeth, was all right. Usually, during the day, Alpha's gate was closed but unlocked, manned by a Senior Home boy who would let in anyone who approached. Today the gate was locked and one of the groundskeepers, Mr. Stapleton, stood nearby. He opened the gate as I approached.

"How is everyting out dere, sir?"

"There are some cars burning, and the streets are deserted, but no big crowds," I replied.

I found Sr. Magdalen in the storeroom, helping Cook get ready for supper.

"Oh, Jay! You made it home safe. I was worried. How are you?" She turned to two Senior Home boys standing at the door of the storeroom. "Here now, you two. Bring these bags of potatoes to Cook."

"I'm fine, Sister. What's gone on here?"

"Nothing, really," she swiped her hand at a cat perched on the top of a sack of rice. The cat jumped down and darted out the door. "That one's a good mouser, but it's always underfoot." She pulled open the door of the walk-in freezer and stepped inside. "Help me with this bag." She reached for an enormous plastic bag of frozen chicken backs. I pulled it off the shelf for her. "Just hand it to the boys. They'll know what to do with it."

She closed the freezer door firmly and looked at the temperature gauge on the side. She tapped the dial with her finger a few times, more out of habit than anything else. "This old freezer has been giving us problems for months now. Sister Marie Therese just got word last week that the government of Denmark is giving us a new one. The wife of the ambassador will be coming here herself when they deliver it. It will be quite an event." It was typical Magdalen to be talking about nothing in particular while there were cars burning in the street. But in fact, she took all strife in stride. She dealt with the world the way it was presented to her, day in and day out.

As we stepped out of the storeroom, she pulled a large ring of keys out of the right pocket of her dress. "Because of the strike, we had to send the teachers home early, and Nurse didn't make it in, so Mr. Estig will stay later than usual."

"How can I help today, Sister?"

"You can help me organize supper." She turned to the two boys. "Here now, you two, what are you waiting for? I told you to bring the bags to cook!" By the edge in her voice, I could tell she was more affected by the day's events than she wanted to let on.

"What do we need to be worried about?" I asked.

"I'm not sure. I don't give to worrying too much," she said as she hurried over to the kitchen.

I was used to seeing the kitchen only in the evening, when dinner was over and the activity was in the refectory where the clean-up took place. What had always struck me was how barren the kitchen felt. The large black stove stood against the back wall, next to a rack of metal shelves filled with huge pots and pans. When you are cooking for more than 250 people every day, you don't need any small skillets or medium sized saucepans. Empty metal tables formed an island in the center of the room.

Next to the rack of pots and pans other racks sat empty. There were no shelves teeming with spices or food; no rows of cookbooks or kitchen appliances. Not even rows of utensils hanging from hooks; just an empty room of empty shelves. But I learned that in a poor country, if you don't protect what's yours, you can't blame hungry people for sneaking some for themselves. All of the staff at Alpha ate lunch and dinner at the school, but they had people back home to feed as well, and you wouldn't blame them if they snuck a few things from the kitchen to help feed their families. And, if the boys knew things were left out on shelves, they would be tempted to break into the kitchen to steal. So every night, everything from the kitchen was moved into the storeroom for safe keeping.

But today, the kitchen was bustling. Cook had three boys from Senior Home helping her. They were noticeably thicker than the other boys at Alpha. The shelves next to the stove were filled with large containers of spices and ingredients. The tables were covered with vegetables being diced by one of the helpers.

The boys who carried in the bag of frozen chicken backs were ripping open the bag on another table and spreading out the frozen pieces, none of which looked like they had much meat left on them. One teen with a large knife at the vegetable table moved over toward the meat table. As he did so, one of the boys who had carried in the chicken reached over to grab a carrot. The boy with the knife made a menacing gesture, and brought the knife down on the table near the other boy's hand. Although I was startled, sister didn't flinch, and the boy with the knife smiled and tossed the carrot to the other boy. The boys who helped in the kitchen knew they had it good and weren't going to jeopardize their roles by getting into trouble.

"Sister, when I came in through the gate, I noticed that the van wasn't out in front of the office. Is someone out on the road today?"

"No. No. It's too dangerous to go out today. We don't know how violent or desperate people might get. We left the van parked behind the dormitory so no one on the street would see it. You know. 'Out of sight. Out of mind.'"

Off in the corner, Francis knelt next to a small stool, which sat next to a large metal tub of colored water. Two other boys poured buckets of water into the dark red mixture, which had the grainy texture Jello when you first mix in the package.

"Come," Magdalen said. "I'm making suck-suck for the boys."

She sat on the stool and the boy on her left handed her a small plastic bag. The other boy handed her a ladle, as Francis stirred. Magdalen scooped a ladle-full of the mixture from the tub into the bag and handed the bag to the boy on her right. He twisted the bag around tight, wrapped a twist-tie around it, and put the bag on a tray on a nearby table, while Magdalen filled another bag. It took her about half an hour to fill three hundred bags. Once the trays were filled, I moved them on to shelves in the freezer.

"It's a hot afternoon," Magdalen said. I wondered how she was distinguishing this hot afternoon from any of the countless other hot afternoons in Kingston. "Grab that bucket for me, Jay."

I dragged a large bucket off the bottom shelf of the freezer, and took it outside the storeroom. It was filled with bags of the frozen juice, Magdalen's homemade version of freezer pops. As Magdalen fumbled with the padlock in the doorway a cat raced into the storeroom. "Come now, boys. Pull the door shut for me." She unlocked the padlock from the clasp. She had had too many padlocks stolen over the years to leave one open and dangling on a hook by an open door, even for a few minutes. As soon as the boys pushed the large wooden door shut, she reattached the clasp and relocked the lock.

The two boys carried the bucket up to the Junior Home verandah. The Junior Home boys lined up and Magdalen handed out the suck-suck. Each boy bit a small hole in the corner of the bag, and sucked out the juice. I stood on the edge of the soccer field, watching the boys mill around, taking a break from playing soccer to enjoy their treat. With the chaos on the streets and the threat of danger in the neighborhood, it seemed like an odd day for Magdalen to be making suck-suck for the boys. But the lack of staff meant the boys' day was already out of whack. She wanted to create more of a sense of normalcy. Besides, the alternative was to hunker down and wait for something to happen, while praying that nothing would, not an easy thing to do with a dormitory full of energetic boys.

Q, Richard and O'Brien scampered over, looking eager to talk, but not wanting to stop eating their treat.

"And how was your day, boys?"

"Fine sir," each one said, only long enough to make sure they didn't miss a drop of the juice.

Winston approached. He had been at Alpha for a few weeks now and was starting to feel more comfortable. Given that he had grown up on the streets, this may have been the first time he was holding a chunk of ice, and he seemed to be enjoying every drop.

"Hello, Winston," I said, looking around. "And where is Morris Mathers? I wanted to tell him something."

"Him run away today," Craig blurted out, waving his hand toward the front gate.

"Really? Why did he do that?"

"Mr. Estig yelled at him in class today, so he cursed at him and him run out of the room."

"Well, I'm sure he's around here somewhere," I said.

"No, sir. Him left Alpha, sir," Q said. "Sister said she saw him walking up the street."

"Well, that's a shame." I looked out toward the road, wondering how a boy as small as Morris could feel more comfortable there than at a place like Alpha.

"Mr. Solomon," Winston tugged at my shirt. "Mr. Solomon, you read to us again tonight, sir?"

"Yes, Winston. I'll read again tonight. Make sure you think about what kind of book you want to hear. Why don't you boys go and sit in the shade so your treat doesn't melt all over the place before you can enjoy it."

"Yes, sir," they replied as they wandered off to the verandah.

Later that evening, as I walked up to Junior Home to read to the boys, I passed Magdalen on her way to the convent. "So what's the news on the strike, Sister?"

"I don't know. With Nurse out I haven't had a chance to stop for two minutes today. Although, I have to say, with the roads being dangerous, Marie Therese told me not to run any errands today, so I haven't had to take the car out. That's been nice."

"I heard on the radio earlier that they expect the strike to hamper any travel for a few days. Is that going to be a problem for us?"

"We should be fine. We just got a bread delivery yesterday, so we should have enough for a few days. We grow our own vegetables. The freezer is as full as it ever gets. But if roads aren't open after a few days, the neighborhood will start lining up outside the gate looking for help."

"And then?"

"We'll help them as much as we can. Our first duty is to the boys, but we can't let people go away hungry."

"Sister, I heard Morris Mathers ran away today."

"Yes. Poor boy. This wasn't the right place for him."

"But he had a roof over his head. More to eat than I'm sure he's used to. And opportunity to just be a boy and not have to fend for himself. What's hard to get used to?"

"You and I can't understand it, Jay. What's obviously important to us, isn't necessarily important to him."

"Well. I'm sure he'll come back," I smiled weakly.

"No. He won't be back," she said softly. "He's been on the streets for too long. He can't take the structure of a place like this." She looked up at the boys lined up on the verandah, waiting to head to the dormitory for the night. "Keep him in your prayers." Then she turned her attention to the immediate. "I need to bring these keys to Sister Ignatius. I'll see you tomorrow, Jay."

"Good night, Sister. If St. George's is closed tomorrow, I'll be around all day if you need anything."

"Good. The boys will enjoy having you around," she said over her shoulder as she walked down the path to the convent.

I watched her walk away, and then turned toward South Camp Road. Not a single car was in sight on the usually bustling street. I looked out at the eerie emptiness, and thought of Morris' tiny frame making his way around Crossroads or Half Way Tree or Liguanea. It occurred to me that Morris was the fourth boy to have left in the last few months. There had been the boy with the cleft pallet who liked to play checkers, the boy with the orange tint to his hair, a result of a vitamin deficiency, and the exceedingly thin very dark skinned boy with the yellow eyes and the missing two front teeth. I had known each of them and their names at some point, and now I was struggling to remember more than the most cursory impression of who they were and what they looked like. I had been, on some small level, responsible for those boys for the brief time they were here, and now I couldn't even remember their names. And I thought of Morris Mathers. I prayed to God that I wouldn't forget him the way I had forgotten the others, and I prayed that he would come back safely.

September 28, 1986

My dear Jay,

Thanks for your lovely letter of September 3 and for your telephone call. We have had a lot of celebrations because of Sr. Marie Teresa' diamond Jubilee. The dinner was lovely and the boys did all the entertaining – band, choir, etc. Dwight Richards won everybody's heart by his singing. He is really great. We hope to be able to help him develop it.

Sister Susan now occupies your room when she visits Kingston. We are now amalgamated with St. John Bosco – we are one! I can only say that we are enjoying lovely pork chops, ham, bacon etc. from Bosco – free of charge – because it is part of our school. Soon, how soon I don't know, the Junior Home will be the place of frozen pigs! I often tell some of my children that they are pigs, but I prefer them to the four footed ones. Some boys, the youngest ones, will be going to Bosco & the others squeezed into the Senior Home dorm.

Sr. Regine is very nice. She has already taken some of my driving burden – it is safer on the road now! Maybe I will take your offer to teach driving up there – but Rome will suit me better – everybody drives their own way there.

I still make suck-suck. I made over 300 before we came to the north. It is an easy occupation & as you know, the roads will be safer while I'm sitting down by the store room. So hurrah for suck-suck!

You must be tired of reading this awful scribbling & I must not keep you too long from your studies. It will all soon pass away & you will be some famous lawyer in no time. Then I will say, "remember that great lawyer? He used to live at Alpha at one time!"

Do give my love to your dear Mom & Dad & all your sweet sisters. Do not work too hard pushing too many buttons!

Lots of love –

Sr. M. Magdalen, RSM

24
COMMUNITY

The strike continued into the next day. St. George's and all schools in Kingston were closed since most of the students and faculty couldn't get to the campus. Since Alpha's teachers couldn't travel to the school either, I ran the game room for most of the day and did my best to help occupy the boys. The busier we kept them, the better chance they would stay out of trouble. For the first time, I also worked with the boys at the Senior Home, although for them, it was mostly just showing movies, and doling out decks of cards and comic books.

By the morning of the second day, water in Kingston had been turned off, as happened sporadically. There was a rumor that a dead body had been found floating in the city's reservoir and that the government was testing the water to see if it was safe to drink. Since Alpha had its own well, as long as there was electricity, there was water. And if the electricity went off, the sisters had the generator.

Around mid-morning on the second day a young woman with two small boys appeared at the front gate. She carried a large tin can with her, and each of the boys had a small water jug by his side. She asked to fill her can at the pipe in the small yard between the front gate and the office, just a few yards inside the compound. The guard looked around cautiously, and then let them in and fill their jugs. The woman thanked him as she and the boys snuck out quietly, without anyone seeing. As he closed the gate, he worried what would happen next. Ten minutes later, Ignatius saw the guard arguing through the fence with a small group of woman, all holding buckets, and all with small kids. As she hustled to the gate, she could hear the guard say, "I can't let you all in. I just can't do it! Now please, go away!"

Ignatius thanked the guard for his diligence, and then told him to allow the women in. He was surprised, but immediately complied. Ignatius knew what the results would be. Within half an hour an orderly line snaked from the street to the pipe. The guard did his best to keep the bulk of the growing crowd outside the fence, allowing in only enough to form a straight line to the pipe. Alpha had always been *in,* but not *a part of,* the community. But now, we had become a vital neighbor. People waited for up to an hour to fill their jugs. Then, with their buckets perched precariously on their heads, they walked slowly out the gate and across South Camp Road to the small neighborhood just behind the businesses that lined the street.

I had the game room running smoothly in the Junior Home refectory and Stars Wars playing for the Senior Home boys, and like everyone else, I wanted news on the strike. When I walked by the office, Ignatius was leaning forward across Mr. Herman's desk, listening intently to the radio.

"Any news, Sister?"

"Well, yes. Yes, there is. They say that the gas stations will open tomorrow and be able to sell gas at a lower price. The van drivers have agreed to drive again."

Magdalen walked in, "But it will take a day or two for the stores to have their food again, and for things to get back to normal, whatever normal is. In the meantime, I need some help. Come."

I followed her around to the kitchen. Two Senior Home boys were opening bags of bread and laying the slices out in a long line, while another boy peeled slices from one of the longest blocks of bright orange cheese I had ever seen. "We get this government cheese from the U.S.," Magdalen said. "I love the United States. Always helpful."

"Is this supper for tonight?" I asked.

"No. No. We need to feed these people waiting in line for water. I'm certain some haven't eaten for days. It's a very poor community across the street there."

"Do we have enough for the boys if we use all this bread?" I asked.

"The boys will be fine. They will have the same thing for supper tonight."

"What if we don't get the bread delivery tomorrow, Sister? Then what?"

"I mentioned to Marie Therese that we have only enough for tomorrow, and then we are out ourselves. She said it's still only right to feed those who show up. God will provide for us all tomorrow." Her tone told me she was not so sure. "We always have the gardens, and hopefully Cook can make it in tomorrow and will be able to prepare vegetables for the boys."

"What do you need me to do, Sister?"

"Supervise this while I go deal with some things up at Junior Home." She turned to the boys, "Remember, one slice of cheese on each sandwich. Two sandwiches and one package of biscuits in each bag." She reached into a large cardboard box and pulled out a small bag of Lorna Doones, another donation someone had sent for the boys. She turned to me, speaking quickly, with an adamant tone. "Keep making sandwiches until the bread runs out. Save three hundred sandwiches for us. Whatever is left, hand out to the people. Give one bag to each adult and child. They will all ask you for a second bag for someone back home. Tell them that's who the second sandwich in the bag is for. Don't bring more than a dozen bags with you at any one time, or they will mob you for them. You will run out of bags before you run out of people, so just know that you will have to turn people away by the end."

Suddenly and silently a man appeared in the doorway. He was tall, about thirty years old, filthy and dressed in tattered clothes. Although his sudden appearance was startling, he himself wasn't menacing. Regardless, I recoiled at his decrepit state and turned to chase him away. Magdalen addressed him first, "Here now. What you doing back here?"

she asked firmly.

"Sista, I beg you some food, please. I'm hungry." As he stepped forward, his smell reached us before his outstretched hands.

"You cannot be back here." She gently put her hand on his shoulder and turned him around. "Please go wait up by the gate." My instincts were otherwise. Eighteen months in the country and I was still taken aback by the sight and smell of extreme poverty. I would have shooed him away, and avoided touching him at all cost. Magdalen's instincts were different. The way she spoke and touched him said everything - to her, he was Jesus. To her, he needed to be treated with ultimate dignity and respect. I was ashamed at my own revulsion.

Lord, let me learn from my own blindness.

As she walked him toward the gate, Magdalen looked over her shoulder at me. "The boys can manage the sandwiches, Jay. I need you up front now," she said. "The crowd will listen to you better than they will to the boys." Her eyes added, "It's begun. We're going to have a hell of a day."

Magdalen led the man around front, and then reminded the security guard to keep an eye on the line, to make sure people didn't wander off around the grounds. Her ultimate duty was to protect the boys, and unusual circumstances were the perfect opportunity for things to go wrong.

The kitchen boys made the sandwiches and assembled the bags. After leaving enough sandwiches for the boys, they had enough for about one hundred and fifty bags. They loaded a dozen bags each into two cardboard boxes and carried them around to the front of the compound where more than a hundred people stood in line, each holding empty jugs.

Each time I handed someone a bag, they replied, "Tank you, Fadda. Tank you. Can mi get one for mi children at home?" I had lived in the country long enough to get used to being called "Fadda." The only white men poor Jamaicans were used to coming into contact with were priests.

"I'm sorry, but we don't have enough. There are two sandwiches in each bag. That will have to do." It's hard to feel that you're helping when you know your efforts are inadequate, but that too is a feeling you get used to.

Magdalen stayed busy with other issues. Without Nurse, Cook and Mr. Estig monitoring things at Junior Home, she knew she couldn't blink or the discipline could quickly crumble. She believed firmly that discipline and structure kept the boys safe. When the boys knew someone was always watching, the place ran smoothly. But when they sensed a chance to misbehave, some of them would take it, and that would leave others vulnerable. She spent the rest of the day roaming from the soccer fields to the dormitory, to the gardens, to the office and back again to the fields, making sure the boys saw her frequently. Each time she stopped at the fields, she would shout out to the boys the furthest away to get away from the walls, or to play over this way or that. Her directions didn't have any rhyme or reason. She just wanted them to hear her voice and feel her presence. When she checked the dormitory, where the children were not allowed during the day, she found three boys going through the treasures under other boys' mattresses. She hurried them all out and locked the screen door for the second time that afternoon. She must have clocked five miles that day in her many laps around the compound. Ignatius traveled much further covering the Senior Home property, which was much more extensive. The Senior Home boys were known to steal food from the gardens, scale the back wall of the compound, and sell the produce for pennies, to anyone passing by. The loss of food to Alpha wasn't the issue. The real concern was the potential for trouble the boys might get into if they got off the property, or brought someone else in.

Once we ran out of the bags of sandwiches, the tension in the front of the property died down, but the line of people seeking water continued for hours. I followed Magdalen's lead, making laps around the property, just being a presence and doing nothing in particular. As I would walk out of the gameroom onto the verandah and see Magdalen on her way up, she would spot me, turn and check the gardens instead.

The city seemed to be calming down by evening, and then nightly news on the radio confirmed that the buses would be running and that schools would open the next day. Nevertheless, the lack of traffic on the street and the occasional sound of gunfire suggested that the police still had their hands full.

Dinner of cheese sandwiches, Lorna Doones and water was easy to supervise, and the story hour provided a sense of consistency to the evening, and a calm that belied the stress of the day. I'm not sure if the boys knew about the strike or noticed the added tension. If not, it just meant we had done our jobs well.

By the next day, the roads were open and traffic was running. The staff made it to work, and God provided, via Mr. Peters' bread truck. At St. George's, school was back in session. When I arrived at the campus, Joshua was sitting on the wall in front of Winchester Park playing cards with a few other boys. They all said, "Good morning, sir," but didn't stop their game, and Joshua didn't seem particularly moved to let me know about his trip home. His focus was not the teacher who had tried, but failed, to find a solution to his predicament. Later, I asked and he said he caught a ride with Mr. Howe. In fact, Mr. Howe told him he could always have a ride home, which was going to make Joshua's life much easier now.

The other boys spent the first few minutes of each class telling their tales of adventure about how they had struggled to get home the day of the strike, and of the fires burning in their neighborhoods. No one spoke of any difficulty trying to get food for the intervening days. No one brags about not having enough.

25
GIFTS FROM THE FATHER

I always had mixed feelings about Ash Wednesday. I liked the outward sign of humility of wearing ashes. (Is there a greater contradiction than being proud of your humility?) But I didn't like the upcoming fasting of Lent. Catholics only fast on Ash Wednesday and Good Friday, not an enormous burden. But I'm so bad at self-sacrifice that I just get cranky for the whole forty days. Catholics always make a big deal of "giving something up" for Lent. One year in college, I gave up chocolate. I love chocolate. I lasted thirty-six hours before I snuck a Reese's peanut butter cup. So I adjusted my sacrifice – I gave up *buying* chocolate. That way, if someone offered me a cookie or a piece of candy, I was all in, and still true to my word. If being pathetic was one of the deadly sins, I was going straight to hell.

We had a special Ash Wednesday service first thing in the morning at St. George's, so by the time I got back to Alpha, what had been a distinct sign of the cross in black ashes on my forehead was now just a dark oily smudge. The sisters didn't require the boys to get ashes, and didn't have a way of holding Mass except on Sunday. The boys had seen Magdalen with ashes all day, but would never have asked her why her forehead was dirty. As I sat on the verandah in the afternoon, the boys crowded around. They never hesitated to ask me anything, so it didn't take more than a minute for Richard to say, "Your forehead want clean, sir."

Having been an English major, and now an English teacher, I loved the way Jamaicans ascribed human desires to inanimate objects. "You're forehead *wants* clean, sir. Your bag *wants* closed, sir. Your hair *likes* the wind, sir. Your skin *not like* the sun, sir." It added to the cadence of their speech.

"My forehead is happy the way it is, Richard. But thank you for noticing." When they asked about the ashes, I explained the best I could. "And then the priest makes the sign of the cross on your forehead." Francis, the giggler, was standing next to me. He could barely contain his fidgeting as I made the sign of the cross with my thumb on his forehead. "And he says, 'From dust thou did come, and to dust thou shall return.'" I did my best to explain the symbolism.

"I don't understand," Q said. "Sister always says we look just like God. God didn't come from dust. Father Williams keeps telling us Jesus died for our sins. Why would Jesus die for dust?"

"That's a great point, Q. It's really one of the toughest things to understand about being Christian. *God…God Himself*, sent his only son, just to redeem *you*." I poked him in the chest. "And just for *you*," I poked Francis, who giggled again. "And just for you, and you, and you. The whole world was put here just for each one of us. And yet, we only really get to enjoy it properly if we realize we aren't worthy. That means we have to spend our lives trying to be worthy, or at least being grateful."

It was one of the many conversations were I thought, "I am talking to ten year olds and I'm already in way over my head! Some Catholic theologian somewhere is rolling over in his grave at the way I am botching church dogma."

The boys looked at me with a mix of confusion and boredom, which put them in the same place as most adult Catholics. St. Francis is quoted as having said, "Preach the Gospel every day. If necessary, use words." That's how I felt most days at Alpha. To whatever extent I was trying to teach the boys a lesson, I think it came through much more powerfully through my actions than when I opened my mouth.

Over the last few months, the boys had asked many questions, usually when we were sitting on the verandah by ourselves. Richard had wanted to know why his mother had hurt him so terribly. Q had asked why some kids get to live with their families and others not. O'Brien wondered why God would take away Silent Malcolm's voice. And I had sought from God how Morris Mathers would rather stay out on the street than live under the protection of Alpha, enjoying the benefits of living here. Good, legitimate questions all. I had nothing to offer but the occasional platitude. And God still hasn't helped me understand Morris. I guess when we ask, "Why?" of God, we ask too much.

"What if *I* ask *you* some questions?" I asked the boys. "I'll keep them easy, such as 'Where's the book you borrowed yesterday, Richard?" He smirked and then said, "I give to you tonight at storytime, sir."

"Great. Then how about a question for you, O'Brien?" He suddenly looked anxious.

"What's the capital of Jamaica?'"

"Kingston!" he shouted.

"What's 4 times 4, Richard?"

"Sixteen," he yelled.

"And, 'Why do you all ask Mr. Solomon so many tough questions?'" I said to Q.

"Because it's fun!" O'Brien blurted out.

"I think if we stick to the questions we can answer we're better off. We need to ponder the big questions, but we can't expect the big answers." They were all nodding, but I think their nod was less, "Yes, we agree," and more, "Are we done yet, because we really want to get back to playing checkers."

"So tell me, what does *ponder* mean?" I asked.

"It's a big pond," O'Brien said proudly, stretching out his arms as wide as they could go. "That other one is a little pond, but this one is even ponder!"

I hung my head laughing and thought about Sister Magdalen and Pontius Pilate. Some causes are hopeless.

* * *

Early in the morning on the first Saturday in Lent, O'Brien walked slowly and carefully behind Richard and in front of Q as they processed through the rows in the garden, balancing buckets of water on their heads. After emptying their contents on a row of new sprouts of calaloo, they turned to head back toward the pipe. As the three boys neared the pipe in the garden, Plunkett called from the plaza in front of Junior Home.

"O'Brien. 'Dere you are. Sista looking for you. She want you at de office." Plunkett turned and headed back toward the convent, and to Magdalen's next errand.

O'Brien handed his bucket to Richard and scampered toward the office. He couldn't think of anything he had done wrong. He caught up with Plunkett as fast as he could. "What sista want?"

"Mi not know," Plunkett said dismissively. "I tink someone is here for you."

O'Brien picked up the pace, excited at the prospect of seeing his mother, the only person who could possibly have come to see him. It had been many months since she had been able to make the trip from St. Andrew Parish. His feet couldn't keep up with the pace of his heartbeat. He tore around the corner of the office and then came to an abrupt stop. On the other side of the open office door stood a slender man who appeared to be in his mid-thirties. His workman's pants and boots were crusted with the red clay of the bauxite mines that scarred the inner part of the island. In his left hand he held his hat, and with his right, he wiped his brow with a dark blue bandana.

"O'Brien?" the man asked, nodding toward a boy he didn't know.

O'Brien nodded back.

"Do you know who I am?" the man asked.

O'Brien paused only briefly, and took a deep breath. "You my fadda?" He asked not because he could see any resemblance, or because of even the faintest memory of the man. He asked because it was the question on his lips every time he met any adult male. It was the question he had wanted to ask every day, to every stranger, but dared not. The constant rejection would be too much, and the reminder of his isolation too painful. But now, this stranger had invited the question, and O'Brien asked it without thinking.

"Yes. Mi your fadda," Mr. Stewart paused. "I come to see how you gettin' on."

Sister Ignatius stepped out of the office onto the verandah. "So, I see you two have met," she said. Why don't you sit down over here on the bench for a while. "Mr. Stewart, can I get you something to drink?"

"Tank you, Sista. Dat would be very nice," Mr. Stewart said, half bowing to Ignatius, as she turned her back and called for Plunkett to bring Mr. Stewart some lemonade.

Mr. Stewart kept his eyes on O'Brien as he backed up two steps to the bench on the verandah and sat. O'Brien walked carefully over and sat on the far end of the bench. He studied his father's face. The whites of his eyes were yellowed and bloodshot. His patchy facial hair was more than a lack of shaving, but less than a true beard or mustache. His skin color was just the slightest bit darker than O'Brien's. To O'Brien, he seemed a handsome man.

"You keeping well?" Mr. Stewart asked.

"Yes sir," O'Brien answered, staring at the man's knees. Mr. Stewart's hands were together in this lap, holding onto his hat. His hands were thin but muscular, and appeared to be those of a manual laborer, one who ate, but never quite got enough. A thousand questions swirled through O'Brien's head, but he couldn't think fast enough to ask any of them.

"You mudda sent me," Mr. Stewart started. "I saw her last month in St. Andrew. When I told her I was coming to Kingston to visit family, she told me you were 'ere and dat I should come see you."

The whirlwind of questions was starting to sort itself out, but O'Brien still wasn't ready to speak.

"You look good," Mr. Stewart continued. He was sizing up his son, while his son was evaluating him, but without the questions. He was there to check in, to see that everything was all right, whatever that meant, and to move on again. Unlike O'Brien, Mr. Stewart didn't hold much hope that the two would truly get to know each other. This wasn't a reunion, and it wasn't the start of something long-lasting. It was merely the best he could do to establish a connection. "Do dey treat you well here?"

"Yessir," O'Brien responded, raising his eyes to his father's. "The questions started to spill from his brain, but couldn't find their way to his lips. *"Why are you here? Where have you been? What are you like? Do you love me? Do you like me? Are you here to take me home?"* His brain was screaming, and his voice was silent.

"How you do in school?" his father asked.

"Fine sir," he paused. "I can read and write." He thought hard, trying to find something to tell his father who he was. "Mr. Estig says I'm good at Maths too." The beginning of a conversation seemed to loosen his tongue. "Is my mother all right?" He was concerned his father's appearance meant bad news from home.

"She's fine," his father said, gesturing as if to say everything is ok. He could hear the concern in his son's voice and wanted to be the calming parent he knew was buried in him. "She said it's been too long dat me not know mi own son."

Plunkett came around the corner of the office, carrying a small tray with two glasses of lemonade, and with a white towel draped over his arm. He offered a glass to Mr. Stewart, and the other to O'Brien, who had never been waited on before and felt even more awkward, if that were possible. Plunkett left without saying a word.

For thirty minutes O'Brien and his father talked about whatever came to mind, from who Mr. Stewart was visiting in Kingston, to his other children, to what instrument O'Brien would like to play in the band, if he gets in, to the quality of food at Alpha. Their talk was punctuated by awkward pauses, during which Mr. Stewart would stare at his shoes.

After one rather long silence, Mr. Stewart said, "Well, I should be going now."

But O'Brien hadn't minded the silences. They were a chance to study and simply be with the man whose only gift to his son so far had been his name. O'Brien started to panic. This unexpected opportunity to know his father, to know himself, was ending too soon.

"You can't stay?" he asked, not sure whether he meant *for a few more minutes*, or *in my life.*

"No," his father said, really to both questions. "But I brought you something." He lifted the basket by his side and placed it carefully on the bench. And in that unexpected meeting, on an unexpectedly exciting morning for O'Brien, O'Brien received a second, and very unexpected gift from his father.

* * *

I spent Saturday morning grading papers, and hadn't decided what to do with the afternoon. The boys had chores and a very structured day, and it wasn't helpful when I interfered with the schedule. I kept my involvement with them limited to their free time.

I had cashed my paycheck from St. George's the day before, so I needed to find Magdalen and pay my rent. Because the sisters provided me with food and a room, I insisted on paying rent, which I set at the same amount I had paid the previous year when I had lived with the other volunteers. At first the sisters objected, and for the first few months, Sister Magdalen didn't want to accept the money. Eventually, her protests became looks of puzzlement, then amusement, and by mid-year, handing her the money was a non-event.

Wilbert and Plunkett were sitting on the bench in front of the office. "Hello Mr. Sullivan," Plunkett said carefully. He had been working on pronouncing my name correctly.

"Hello, Plunkett. Hello, Wilbert. What's with the suitcases?" I asked, gesturing toward the two good-sized pieces of luggage next to the bench.

"Sister Ignatius sent them down from the convent, sir," Plunkett said, pulling each suitcase closer to the side of the bench.

"They're for Michael Winters and Anthony Gayle, sir," Wilbert offered.

Two weeks earlier, Sisters Ignatius and Marie Teresa met with Michael and Anthony and told them of "the possibility" that they might be going on a trip. Even just a few weeks out, they didn't want the boys' hopes to be built up, only to be dashed. But once the organization running the trip had purchased the tickets, it seemed only right to let the boys prepare mentally for what could be the biggest adventure of their lives. Within a day, the entire school had learned all about Lourdes from Michael, and all about nervousness from Anthony. I walked by Plunkett, shaking my head and thinking how absurd an idea it was for two Alpha boys to be taking a European vacation.

As I walked the verandah around the Senior Home dormitory, I stepped over Rags, the ten year old mangy orange ugly mutt that guarded Senior Home. During the day, she slept or wandered slowly around. The only time she showed any energy at all was when a car would arrive at the front gate. I found Sister Magdalen around by the laundry area, a covered area behind the senior home dormitory with a row of sinks where the senior boys scrubbed their clothes. Off to the side was a small room where the seamstress, Miss Madge, usually referred to as Mrs. Laundry, either sat at her sewing machine repairing holes in some bed sheets, or sat in the doorway mending some of the boys' clothes. Miss Madge, like so many of the women who worked at Alpha, wore a simple housedress over her narrow frame. Her thin arms and gaunt face made her seem older than she probably was. She and Magdalen were standing in front of two large oil drums, one filled with a deep blue liquid, another, with deep red. A Senior Home boy slowly and laboriously stirred each drum.

"What are you up to today, Sister?" I asked.

"Oh, hello, Jay!" she said over her shoulder. She routinely greeted me with a sense of surprise, as if she didn't realize that I was around.

"We're dying shirts today," she said, turning back to her work. "We always end up with white t-shirts for the boys, either because that's what people donate, or because that's all we can afford. But they look so dirty so quickly that we dye them." She turned back to Miss Madge. "Leave these in for another fifteen minutes and then drape them on the line. Then put in the next dozen."

"Yes, sista," Miss Madge replied, nodding.

Magdalen slipped her apron off over her head and handed it to Miss Madge. Turning she said to me, "Come. I'll show you."

I followed her around the back of the laundry building into a walled yard about twenty feet square, bordered on one side by the back of the laundry area, on another by the back of the bathroom and shower facilities for Senior Home, and on the other two sides by a wall separating the space from the expansive Senior Home garden. Heavy duty wires were strung taut across the top of the wall, forming a lattice, on which the Senior Home boys hung their wash. The first two batches of dyed t-shirts hung from clothes pins. Beneath each shirt the dripping dye created a puddle of dark blue or red in the dust. "We have about two hundred shirts to do today," she said. "It takes a while to dye each set so we can't do too many in a day. The boys go through so many clothes! It's good we get donations. I don't know how Marie Therese keeps things coming in the way she does."

After her fall, Marie Therese had stayed in the hospital for a few days, and then returned to Alpha. Although she was desperate to get back to work, the fall had taken away some of her energy, and she now limited her activity to what she could do at her desk in the convent. She came downstairs only a few times a week.

"I don't know how you keep up with it all, Sister."

"Ah. It keeps me young," she said, laughing, as she patted me on the arm and we turned to head out. She motioned at the high cinderblock walls around the laundry yard. "We built this area for the laundry to dry so that when the wind blows it doesn't blow all of the dust from the garden onto the clean clothes."

"Good thinking," I said, doubting that anything stayed clean long on a windy day in Kingston.

As we walked by the side of the garage, she asked, "Did you hear about our big news? We're getting a new van. Sister has some benefactor in the States. I don't know who, but he really likes us."

"That's amazing, sister."

"We have had that old van for ten years. It runs o.k. most of the time, but it breaks down too frequently, so you never really trust it. It also doesn't hold the entire band, so Mr. Johnson has to make three trips, two for the boys and one for the instruments every time they go on an engagement. It will be nice to get them all in the same van."

"I've never seen you use the garage before."

"We keep my car out all the time, and the van we park back here out of sight. We only put the van in the garage on the weekends because, really, who would steal our old van? "

"When will the new van arrive?"

"Late next month. We're very excited."

As we walked back toward the office, I remembered about the suitcases. "Sister, I see Michael and Anthony are getting ready for their trip."

"They leave next week," she replied, shaking her head. "I don't know. I wish my faith was that strong."

"You don't believe in miracles, Sister?" I asked.

"Believe in them? I count on them! I've been here twenty years and I haven't killed one of my darling Junior Home brats yet. That's a miracle, don't you think?" she smiled. "I just don't think God will make Michael walk straight or Anthony's hand better, just because they pray at Lourdes. Then again, maybe there are other miracles they need in their lives, and this trip might be one of those."

"Well, it will be a great experience for them, whether they are cured or not."

"Michael needs to be cured of thinking of himself as special. I'm not sure this will accomplish that."

Michael's turned leg gave him an awkward gait, and every step he took looked painful. Magdalen thought Michael used his illness as a way of getting special treatment; it was more a result of her no-nonsense attitude than anything Michael did or said. Because he was limited physically, Michael read more than the other boys, and took on a more intellectual air. He was, in fact, smarter than most of the other boys. But I had a hard time picturing any of the boys at Alpha as spoiled. And we all need to feel special about something about ourselves.

Anthony was another matter. His withered right arm and twisted left leg slowed him down a bit, and made it all but impossible for him to participate in the soccer games and other activities on the field with the other Senior Home boys. That lack of mobility contributed to the fact that he was chunkier than most of the boys at Alpha, who were typically somewhere between skinny and gaunt. But Anthony's physical limitations didn't seem to impact his spirit. He smiled warmly at everyone. He lacked any trace of guile, and approached the world with an innocence unusual for a fifteen-year-old. In addition, he didn't have a strong sense of personal space, so when he walked up to you, he would bump into you, which in turn, led him to throw his good arm around you for a hug. Anthony was a big St. Bernard of a kid, clumsy and drooling and warm and endearing.

As I handed her my rent, I asked, "Sister, any word on Morris Mathers? Any sign of him at all?"

"Mathers?" she asked, as she headed up the stairs to the convent.

"The one who ran away the day of the minibus strike. I was wondering if you heard anything about him."

"Oh, no. I'm afraid not. Don't keep a vigil for that one, Jay. He won't be back."

I nodded as if I understood, but I didn't. I didn't understand how Morris could choose the streets. I didn't understand how he wouldn't realize his mistake and come running back as soon as he got hungry. I didn't understand how Magdalen could be so sure.

"All right Sister," I said, trying to refocus on the needs of the moment. "I'll be up at Junior Home. Do you mind if I set up the TV in one of the classrooms and show one of the Sesame Street tapes to the boys this afternoon?"

She tossed me the keys from the top step. "Send them back with Plunkett."

I grabbed a few Sesame Street videos from my room. As I headed up to Junior Home, I looked out a South Camp Road and said a quick prayer for Morris to be safe.

With the help of the Senior Home boy on duty, I wheeled the TV on its stand into the classroom adjacent to the Junior Home dormitory. As soon as the boys saw something out of the ordinary going on, they started to gather. Once I explained what the video was about, some lost interest, but at least two dozen boys stayed. We set up chairs in front of the TV. At Francis' request, I stayed and watched the beginning of the first tape. Once Francis and the others were engrossed in the show, I slipped out to check on the other boys. I walked around the outside of the classroom and looked across the playing field. With at least a quarter of the boys off the playing field watching TV, those who spent every possible moment playing football had a better chance of getting at the ball.

Richard, O'Brien and Q came up to me. O'Brien was in the center cradling something small in his hands, wrapped in a small towel. It wasn't until they were right in front of me that O'Brien looked up with a huge smile, and opened his hands.

"Look Mr. Solomon," he beamed.

"O'Brien! A puppy!" I reached out to pet its head. It was thin and frail looking, mostly white with some light brown patches starting to appear in its fur. Its eyes were closed and you could see the skin stretch tight over its ribcage as it breathed. It looked too young to be away from its mother. "Where did you get a puppy from, O'Brien?"

"My fadda, sir," he said, still beaming, as he lowered his head. "He came to see me this morning. He brought me this puppy."

"Well, that's very special, O'Brien. Did you get a chance to visit with him for long?"

"No, sir." He shook his head. "He just came to say hello. I haven't seen him in a long time." His face brightened again. "He came to bring me a gift." Just then another boy joined us. "Look. My fadda bring me a gift," O'Brien said to him proudly. "Careful!" he said, pulling back as more boys reached over to see the puppy.

"Have you named him yet?" I asked.

"I tink I will call him 'Lucky', sir."

"That's a nice name, O'Brien. Have you fed him yet?"

"Yes, sir. Sister give me a ting to feed him with." The puppy started to stir and its mouth started to move. "I tink I should feed him again sir."

We headed off to the Junior Home kitchen, where O'Brien had left milk for the puppy. Sister Magdalen had taken a quart-sized plastic bag and snipped off the corner. She stuffed a cloth in the bag and added enough milk to soak the cloth. Lucky was able to latch onto the tip of the cloth protruding through the corner and suck out the milk. O'Brien sat on the bench on the verandah and let the dog lie across his lap. He wiggled to position himself properly, while Richard stood at the ready with the milk. "O.K., Richard," he said extending his hand. Richard had been holding the bag with the open tip raised so as not to lose any milk. He handed the bag carefully to O'Brien.

"Where did you boys learn how to do this?" I asked.

"Sista showed us this morning," Richard said.

O'Brien stroked the puppy gently, "Here, Lucky. Here's your dinner," he said in a soft, soothing tone.

While they fed the puppy, I went to check on the video. Most of the boys were still sitting in their chairs attentively watching Big Bird and Cookie Monster. A few had drifted to the back of the classroom and appeared to be getting into some of the supplies.

"Boys, let's leave all that stuff alone. Sister won't let us use this room if you are going to be getting into things. If you don't want to watch the TV, play outside please."

"Yes sir," they replied as they returned to their seats.

After Lucky had had his fill, O'Brien handed the milk to Richard, who carefully carried it back to the kitchen. Some other boys had gathered around again. Lucky had fallen asleep. Q spread the towel out on the bench next to O'Brien, and O'Brien stood to lay Lucky on the towel.

"Whoa! Look at him!" One of the boys pointed at O'Brien. "Him pants all wet!" The boy pointed to a wet spot on O'Brien's shorts where Lucky had peed. The other boys laughed at him.

O'Brien gritted his teeth, angry and embarrassed.

I put my hand on his shoulder. "It's all right, O'Brien. It's bound to happen and it's not a big deal. I will wrap up the puppy. You go and wash out your shorts. In this heat they will dry very quickly." He lay Lucky gingerly on the towel and walked away, throwing an angry look at the boys.

I turned to the other boys. "That's not very helpful boys. O'Brien did very well feeding Lucky. Cleaning up is just part of taking care of another creature." They wandered off smirking and laughing.

Richard and Q stood guard over Lucky, petting him until O'Brien came back.

O'Brien scooped up Lucky and held him gingerly, speaking softly, "Hello, Lucky. You're a pretty puppy, you are. I'm going to take care of you. But don't you pee on me anymore, O.K.?"

Q and Richard ran off to play. "O'Brien, are you going to be O.K. sitting here by yourself while the other boys play?"

"Yes sir. I want to stay here with Lucky." Just then another boy came up to see the dog. "This is Lucky. He was a gift from my fadda."

26
DANCING WITH THE STARS

That evening about a dozen BC teachers were going out in New Kingston. In Crossroads, where I changed buses, many young boys milled about, selling peanuts or begging, or both. I pictured Morris Mathews doing the same here, or in the central market, or at Half-Way Tree, another large and hectic square in the city. I wondered if he had joined with other boys, or perhaps fallen in with a group of thieves, or had been taken in by an experienced criminal, like Fagin took in Oliver Twist. I stood in Crossroads for a few moments, wondering if I should wander around the square and look for Morris. He had asked me why I was in Kingston, at Alpha, and I wondered if the answer was to keep him from harm, to save Morris from himself. It would certainly have been a more powerful cause that to read bedtime stories; a more tangible result that playing checkers; a more noble accomplishment than taking kids to the zoo. But as the buses of Crossroads belched their smoke, and the theatre goers at the Carib came and went, and the scores of other children scurried about, I knew I would not search for Morris. Sister had said we weren't the right place for him. I don't know if I didn't have the nerve, the drive or guts to go on such a search, or if I just knew that it wasn't the best use of my time. Was I weak, or just practical? Did I lack conviction, or possess perspective? I had plenty of quiet, reflective time at Alpha to ponder the big questions in life, but when it came to the big questions about myself, I often abandoned the internal debate too readily, afraid I might not like the answer.

At The Lemon Tree, the newest restaurant in town, I met up with the others, and with some Peace Corps volunteers we knew. To create a bar the restaurant built a wall around half of the parking lot, and arranged tables and chairs around the perimeter, leaving lots of room for dancing. The bar itself was off to one side, with a half-dozen stools in front of a bamboo structure with a thatched roof. The speakers pounded out a heavy bass beat that bounced off the concrete block wall, echoing back on itself. We could carry on a conversation, but I knew by the end of the night my teeth would ache and my head would be pounding.

David and I each carried four Red Stripes over to the table. Irene and Kathy were deep in conversation about school. Kristin and Claire were comparing tans from their day at the beach. Mary and Peter were on the dance floor. We were half of the crowd at the bar so we had plenty of space.

"I ran into two of my students when I was shopping today," Kristin said, finishing off her first beer. "I was holding up a new bathing suit in front of the mirror, when I hear, 'Hi, Miss Olson.' I turned around and there were two of the biggest pains in the butt in my Fourth Form class. They were smiling when I saw them, but I know I'm gonna get to school on Monday and everyone is gonna ask me if I bought the bikini. I swear I have no privacy in this place."

We talked about school and then travel plans for the upcoming Easter break.

"Speaking of traveling," I said, turning to Irene, "Guess where Anthony Gayle and Michael Winters are going this week?"

"Spanishtown?" she guessed.

In my best Don Adams voice I said, "Would you believe, Lourdes?"

I explained the situation. "It seems so ironic, and almost unfair," I said, "taking them on a trip like that and then bringing them back to Alpha. How will anything compare to this trip?

"Are you saying they shouldn't take him because his whole life won't live up to this trip?" Kathy asked.

"No, of course not," I said. "I just think it's ironic. *Think* about it. Anthony uses the Senior Home lavatory - an outhouse. The first time in his life that he will use a flush toilet will be at 30,000 feet in an Air Jamaica flight to Miami. I think that's incredibly ironic."

"I think it's absurd," David commented, throwing back another swig of beer. "What a waste of money. What someone is spending on that trip could feed a family here for an entire year.."

"Well, sometimes you have to feed their spirit, too," Irene offered.

"That's nice in principle," David said. "But in reality it's a shame to spend that time, energy and money on a silly trip to a tourist trap. Those boys will come home just as crippled as they are now, loaded down with cheap rosaries and crosses 'blessed' by the 'holy waters of Lourdes.' Then they'll spend the rest of their lives waiting for the next big adventure to happen to them."

"Wow. When did you turn into a cranky, middle-aged, life-has-let me-down, broken man?" Claire asked laughing.

"Yeah," Irene said. "Where's your sense of idealism? Of hope?"

"Of hope that they'll be 'cured'?" David asked.

"Not necessarily. But what if they come back renewed? What if they spend the rest of their lives grateful for the truly wonderful opportunity they have been given? What if...," now she was on a roll. Her voice was more determined and she started pointing at him, "What if they come back with deeper faith and with a commitment to wonder and awe and a desire to do good in the world? Wouldn't that justify the time and the trouble?"

"What if we didn't worry about *justifying* it at all," Mary asked quietly. "I bet the people who sponsor this trip don't think at all about justifying it. They just know it's the right thing to do, so they do it. That's what faith is all about."

David shrugged. "Look, it's not my money, so I don't care. I have just never understood how people choose to spend their money on something where they can't show a return. And don't tell me, 'You'll see the return in the look on his face when he comes home.' That's a lot of bull."

"The most interesting part of this whole thing to me is that the guy who runs this group is Jewish," I said. "He's Jewish and he takes kids who aren't any particular faith to a Catholic shrine to pray for a miracle."

"That's how faith works," Mary said. "He's obviously a very pious man who feels this is a legitimate way to help people connect with God. He's not even getting all caught up in the details of whose faith he's connected to. He doesn't care. He just believes and that's enough."

The conversation segued into the value of pilgrimages in general, then to the similarities between most of the world's great faiths, and trying to figure out what purpose we serve in the world, and finally to the nature of sacrifice for one's beliefs, as a bunch of twenty-somethings tried to make sense of the many seemingly senseless events we experienced each day. The conversation didn't break up until the DJ started blaring *Buffalo Soldier* and we all got up to dance. Philosophical discussions can tug at corners of the brain, but a reggae pulse can pull you right out of your seat.

As I lay in bed that night, I wondered about Mary's comment about justifying ourselves and our actions. I had spent all year trying to define my role at Alpha as a way of justifying being there. Would that energy and self-absorption have been better spent just being present to those around me – my students, the boys at Alpha, the other BC teachers? It was the times when I forgot about myself, forgot about my role, and just did what was needed that I seemed to have contributed the most. It was a simple concept, but it had taken me the better part of a year to figure it out. But I still wanted more.

27
FINDING PURPOSE

The next morning I woke at the usual time to join the boys for Mass. By the time I walked around to the area between the Senior Home dormitory and the refectory, they were already in neat lines, more or less in pairs. For most, it was the only day of the week they would wear shoes. Only the newest boys, who hadn't yet been assigned a pair, or who had grown so fast that they no longer fit the pair they had been given, would go barefoot. For most of the boys, going barefoot to church was embarrassing.

"Good morning, boys," I announced to the whole group.

"Morning, Mr. Solomon," some replied.

Francis waved excitedly.

"Good morning, Francis. That's quite a fine shirt you're wearing this morning."

He beamed, and ran his hands down the faded pink plaid shirt, tucked neatly in his navy blue and gray striped pants.

"And Jomo. Your hair is growing in again. It looks sharp."

Q was at the head of the line, holding up his hand and wiggling his fingers in his signature wave. He was usually paired with O'Brien, but today, he stood next to Richard.

"Morning Richard, Q. Where's O'Brien this morning?"

"Him get in trouble last night sir. Him back in the dormitory," Craig Fraser offered.

"Why is he in trouble?" I asked.

"Dat stupid puppy," Craig said. "It cried *all night long*. The boy in charge, him yell at O'Brien to shut dat puppy up!" Craig said while wagging his finger.

Q said, "Poor O'Brien had to sit up with the puppy outside on the verandah for most of the night, sir."

Craig laughed, "Him so tired this morning he couldn't stand. He was stumbling all over." Craig staggered in a circle, imitating O'Brien.

"The other boys started laughing at him," Richard said. "So he got in a fight."

"Then the puppy pooped on da floor and Sista made O'Brien clean it up. Him was *so* angry," Craig said.

Just then I saw Sister Magdalen hurrying down from Junior Home. "Jay, would you please escort the boys to the church? I have to run up to the convent."

"Certainly, sister. Let's go boys." We walked in silence down the long row of bougainvillea bushes to the chapel at the girls' high school.

After Mass, I waited outside the chapel with the boys, ready for our walk back to Junior Home. Sister Thaddeus approached me and asked me if I would join the sisters at the convent for brunch. I had never met most of the other sisters who lived at the main convent at the girls' school "Go ahead," said Magdalen, who had hurried in just before Mass started. "I'll bring the boys back myself. We'll see you later."

I had been invited to join the sisters for breakfast after mass on a number of occasions, but had always been eager to get on the road with the boys and head for the park. I knew if I didn't join them now, I probably never would. In addition, if I didn't accept, breakfast would be toast on the grill with guava jelly yet again.

The main convent was a hodgepodge structure, having grown organically over time to meet various needs. In the center was an open courtyard with a beautifully tended garden. It was bordered on one side by the administrative building of the school, on another by the chapel, on a third by the convent residence and on a fourth by a wall with lattice brickwork that allowed some view of an open field beyond. The ground floor of the convent residence was the sisters' dining hall. The entire side of the hall that faced the courtyard was a series of double doors, which opened onto a covered verandah, so that when all of the doors were open, as they were for breakfast, you felt as though you were eating in the garden. The nuns' meals were simpler than meals I had shared with the Jesuits, and the conversation livelier. In fact, the sisters chatted up a storm. They all knew that I was the American living at Boys School, but I had never spoken with most of them. As I listened to the conversations, I couldn't figure out why all of these women who lived together and worked together still had so much to tell each other. One conversation after another didn't seem to add anything new that they wouldn't all already know. At first, I thought they might be sharing these stories and events for my benefit. But since I couldn't follow along – not knowing most of the people they were discussing - it was clearly for each other's benefit, not mine that they were talking.

I sat between Sister Thaddeus and Sister Philomena, whose legs were swollen with elephantitis. I always thought she must be in such pain, and yet she was as cheerful as could be. She was the librarian at the Academy, I think in part so that she wouldn't have to walk far from the convent.

"How are you enjoying your stay at Boys School, Jay?" Sister Thaddeus asked.

"It's been quite an experience," I answered vaguely. "I feel like I learn so much from the boys."

"It's so good for them to have you as a role model," Sister Philomena offered, as she poured herself a cup of tea. I detected a faded Boston accent in her voice.

"I don't know about that, Sister. I just do what I can."

"You work mostly with Junior Home I understand," she said.

"When he isn't carrying Marie Therese down the stairs," Thaddeus said giggling into her napkin.

"Oh that's right. Marie Therese stayed here for a few weeks after her hospital stay. She must have told that story a dozen times," Philomena laughed heartily. "How long are you with us?"

"I'm here until June. Then I go home to get ready for law school."

"My older brother is a lawyer back in the states," Thaddeus said. "He lives in Cincinnati. If you need to talk to someone about the law, I'm sure you could write to him."

"What kind of law do you plan to study, Jay?" Philomena asked.

"I'm not sure yet, sister. I don't really know much about what I'm getting into."

"Neither do most of us when we start our careers," she said. "But if we are open to hearing God, we find the right path."

"Sister, I'm not sure I would say God is calling me to be a lawyer. I don't think it's the same thing as being called to the religious life."

"Don't be so sure, Jay," she warned. "There are many versions of a calling. The religious life is only one."

Since she opened the door to such a personal topic, I felt entitled to pry. "Do you ever look back on anything you might have missed by joining the convent, sister?" I asked.

"Every decision cuts off other decisions," Philomena said. "I chose the convent. So this became my life," she gestured at the room around us, smiling. "Then I chose the missions, so I left the cool ocean breezes of our convent near Boston and came to Kingston," she laughed, fanning herself to mock the heat. "Choices," Philomena said. "We always think it's about what we want *to get*. But it's really about what you are willing *to give up*. I have never regretted joining the convent, but I often have trouble with the heat." I could only imagine how oppressive the tropics must be for a woman her size. And that tight wimple on her head couldn't possibly help matters.

"I'm always amazed," Thaddeus offered, "when I hear some of you talk about how you chose the convent. I always thought the convent chose me. I was fifteen when I entered. My parents in Cincinnati sent me to a convent high school. I don't think they expected me to join the sisters, and I think they had mixed feelings when I did. But they supported me in the decision. At the time, I think they just thought, 'Well, at least she's safe and off the streets.'" They both laughed. "I too have never looked back, but I guess in my case, that just means the convent didn't reject me, since it chose me, not the other way around."

"Well, I think we've all found our home now," Philomena offered as she pushed back her chair. "Would you like another piece of coffee cake, Jay?" she asked as she rose with a great sigh and a slight grimace.

"No, thank you, Sister, but let me get it for you," I started to get up.

"Nonsense. Sit down. I'm old but I'm not crippled," she replied.

"You have been very good for the boys," Thaddeus said.

I paused for a moment, realizing that my time in Kingston and at Alpha was drawing to a close. "Well, they're so easy to be around. They make me laugh quite a bit. I don't think I'll be laughing as much next year in law school." The conversation veered into a discussion about the different stages in our lives.

"When I was your age, Jay," Thaddeus said, "and I would just be settling in at one school, Mother Superior would tell me I would be moving to another. It was hard, but I always thought, 'Well. It must be God's will.'" She stared at her napkin in her lap for a moment. "It doesn't mean I didn't cry sometimes."

"Thaddeus, you were always better at obedience than I was," Philomena said. "I always tried to negotiate. It never got me anywhere," she laughed. "But I tried."

"Did you ever feel that you made the wrong choice?" I asked.

"I'm not sure what 'wrong' would mean when you're in the convent," Philomena said. "Everywhere I have gone and in every job I have done, I know I have been serving the Lord. That means it had to be the right place for me to be."

"Of course, there was that one year that they made you the cook," Thaddeus smirked into her tea cup. "That was a bad choice for the rest of us." They both exploded in laughter.

Philomena's face turned deep purple as she laughed and I was afraid she was going to either choke on her biscuit, or drop dead of an aneurysm. "I'd forgotten about that," she laughed. "Do you remember that awful fruit cake I made?"

"Oh, Lord!" When Thaddeus stopped laughing, she turned to me, "She thought she could throw in anything, so she added JujyFruits and hard candy! It was so bad even the dogs didn't want it!"

"Everyone was so polite about it at the time, until someone found a piece of hard candy in the cake that still had the wrapper on it!" Philomena laughed at her own folly.

Later in the conversation I discovered that Philomena had made the cake thirty years earlier, and they were still talking about it. These women were a family like any other. They might live apart for years, work in different locations, and then find themselves colleagues again in a new school or agency. At times, one would supervise another in a job, and the next time they met, the roles might be reversed, and it didn't matter. There was no ego at play; only service. They just kept on going. They knew their purpose. They had it all figured out.

I tried to keep that thought in my head later that evening, when I was reading stories at Junior Home. Anansi the Spider was helping rescue a lost child by spinning a helpful message in her web. Many of the boys at my feet were paying rapt attention. Others, further back in the group were jostling each other as they sat cross-legged on the floor. I was only paying half attention to the story line. I kept looking to my left, down the long row of cots toward the screen door. There stood O'Brien, holding Lucky. He had been banished from the dorm until the puppy fell asleep so that the dog's whining wouldn't bother the boys. He cradled the puppy like a newborn baby, just like he had been shown. But the look on his face was not that of a new mother enrapt with the sight of her newborn. His scowl seemed so inconsistent with the way he gently stroked the puppy. Poor O'Brien didn't know how to feel. And I didn't know how to help him.

After I finished reading to the boys, I sent them to bed and made my rounds of thumb-wrestling. As I passed each row, I could see O'Brien moving along the windows, looking in from the verandah. Still stroking Lucky. Still sad-faced. When I had said my final good night, I went out on the verandah and sat down on one of the benches. "How are you doing, O'Brien?"

"Fine, sir," he said solemnly, looking down at Lucky.

"How's the puppy?" I asked, peering into his folded arms.

"He's fine, sir."

"O'Brien, since you couldn't join us tonight, I thought I would read to you out here this evening. Would that be all right?"

"Yes sir," he smiled weakly. "But read softly sir," he cautioned. Lucky just fell asleep and I don't want him to wake up again."

"Not a problem, O'Brien." I read two short books, and we talked some more.

"O'Brien, I am very proud of you. Do you know that?" He looked at me blankly. "It's a big responsibility to care for a puppy, and I think you're doing a great job. I know it isn't easy and you're getting very frustrated, but I think you're really learning a lot about yourself and about what it means to have responsibility."

"Yes sir," he sighed. He didn't look proud or pleased or complimented. Only tired. ""How do you feel about it?" I asked.

"I don't know, sir. I was very happy when my father gave me a puppy. But it's a lot of work and only seems to get me in trouble."

"Well, that's why I'm so proud of you. You're taking on a task and you're doing your best, even when it isn't easy. That's all anyone can ask of you." Lucky had now been asleep for quite a while, so I walked O'Brien back into the dorm. O'Brien sat down on his bed slowly so that the creaking springs wouldn't wake the puppy. He leaned over the side of his bed and lay Lucky in the box, covering him with an old dishtowel. As he lay his head on the pillow, I covered him with the thin sheet that lay crumbled at the foot of his bed. O'Brien draped his arm over the side of the bed, putting his hand on the small creature under the towel, and closed his eyes.

Lord, help me put these struggling boys
On the path to being gentle men.

28
A CATHARTIC CRY

The afternoons were getting hotter and on Tuesday there was almost no breeze at all. Jomo beat me at three games of checkers while a dozen other boys were playing cards and building puzzles. Richard was struggling through a chess game with Q. He couldn't always remember how the different pieces moved. I could hear Q stop him at every turn and show him the consequence of making the move and what it would allow him to do in response. Richard would get disgusted with himself for a minute, but he persisted, and Q was patient and had a knack for teaching.

Every few minutes one of the boys would ask, "Mr. Solomon, Miss Irene come today?" And each time, I would tell him I wasn't sure. We never knew what day Irene might show up, and that worked well on a number of levels. It gave us all something to look forward to. It taught us to take little disappointments in stride. And it reminded us, whether we knew it or not at the time, that the nature of life is to be filled with daily triumphs and let downs.

O'Brien was leaning over three other boys who were playing cards at the other table. After a few minutes, he put Lucky down on the end of the table and took a seat on the long bench. The boys dealt him a hand. I was relieved to see that he was able to play while still keeping a watchful eye on the dog. He had tied a thin rope around Lucky's neck and was holding his end of it to keep the dog from wandering off.

O'Brien's attempt at control reminded me of my own futile effort earlier in the day. At St. George's we had taken the students to the cathedral next door for a special mass. I wasn't sure what feast day we were celebrating, and it didn't matter much to the boys, most of whom weren't Catholic anyway. I spent most of the service walking up and down the side aisle next to my Fourth Form students, the fifteen-year-olds. While most of the other faculty sat at the back of the cathedral, I always opted to sit with my students. I felt I was better able to keep them in check that way. Besides, as the Form Supervisor, the de facto Dean of Discipline, I would end up with more work at the end of the service if someone got into trouble. I had learned that ninety percent of keeping discipline with the boys was just maintaining a presence with them. Like O'Brien, I kept my charges on a short leash.

I had been thinking about my breakfast with the sisters earlier that week; how they knew why they were where they were. They understand their role. And although their jobs changed often enough, their role on earth, their role for those they served, and the role they served for each other, was constant.

The days were ticking down for me in Kingston. I knew my role at George's, and it would be complete with final exams in another six weeks. My role there would end when the boys there ceased to need me to prepare them for their exams. But my haphazard role at Alpha had no clearly defined end-point. I would leave when I felt like leaving, or when leaving to start law school would become a necessity. My role would end when I was ready, not when the boys were ready. My commitment, if you could call it that, was completely self-serving. Sitting in the gameroom I was afraid that I had finally figured out my reason for being there – I was there to be happy and satisfied and I had made it all about me. It suddenly hit me that everything I was doing was selfish. While I had been trying to find meaning in my contribution, all I had done there to meet my own needs. A wave of disillusionment swept over me.

My navel-gazing and self-pity came to an abrupt halt when one of the boys at the next table yelled. "Stupid dog! Stupid, stupid dog!"

Everyone looked over at the table. The boys standing behind the benches had stepped back. Others were grabbing at the cards on the table trying to keep them out of the expanding puddle of dog urine. O'Brien was trying to get up from the bench when another player shoved him backward off the bench, yelling, "You and that stupid dog!" O'Brien fell backward and was barely able to brace himself as he hit the floor. He scrambled to his feet and grabbed Lucky, and holding him close, ran out to the verandah, bursting into tears as he got to the door.

I jumped up and had one boy get some towels, told another to throw out the cards that were soiled. "Richard and Q, go check on O'Brien for me."

As I scolded the bully for pushing O'Brien, Richard yelled from the doorway,

"Mr. Solomon! Mr. Solomon! Him killing the puppy! Him killing the puppy!"

I ran outside. O'Brien had his arms outstretched, holding Lucky by the throat. The puppy's tongue was bulging out and its legs were kicking. The tears were streaming down O'Brien's face. "O'Brien!" I yelled as I grabbed the puppy from his hands. He let go easily. I handed Lucky to Richard. "Get him some water."

"O'Brien. How could you?" And yet I knew how he could. The puppy's neck was so fragile that if he had really wanted to kill the dog, it would not have taken much. He wanted to love the dog and he wanted to be rid of the dog, and the conflict was too much. He stood with his arms by his side in complete resignation, sobbing uncontrollably. I couldn't be mad at him, and I didn't know how to help. I put my arms around him, and let him cry into my shirt. "Go back inside, boys," I told the others. "I'll be there in a minute to help clean up."

I don't know if O'Brien's frustration had been building for the entire week, or his entire ten years, but it took him a good long while to cry it all out. When the sobbing stopped, I said, "Why don't you have a seat here, O'Brien. I'll be back in a bit and we can talk." He sat on the bench and I went back to the refectory to finish cleaning the table so the boys could set up for dinner soon. I put more milk in the makeshift bottle that Magdalen had created for Lucky. I called for Richard to bring the puppy over. O'Brien and I sat in silence as I fed Lucky. When the puppy finished eating, I asked O'Brien if he was ready to hold the puppy again. He nodded softly and I lay the sleeping dog in O'Brien's arms.

Six months earlier I would have sat there stewing, angry at O'Brien's father for having put his son in such a tough spot, and angry at O'Brien for trying to kill his own puppy. But I had learned to slow my rush to judgment, and to accept the situation for what it was. I couldn't fix the injustices. I could only try to help O'Brien through the moment. We talked about how proud he had been when his father had given him Lucky, and how his father meant well, even though the gift had created a great deal of work for O'Brien. We talked about the real gift his father had given him – the sign that he cared about his son and had thought of him, and probably thought about him every day. As usual, I didn't know if I was helping or sending the right message. But I was trying. It wasn't until much later that I realized that, after that afternoon, I stopped wondering why I was there.

Lord, give me the wisdom to know what to say,
and the greater wisdom to know when to just be there for someone.

29
ACCEPTANCE & REJECTION

Toward the end of the school year, my responsibilities as the Form Supervisor were keeping me at St. George's later and later, while Irene seemed to be arriving at Alpha earlier, and more frequently. On a few occasions, she had opened and closed the gameroom before I even got home. On Wednesday in the third week of April, Irene arrived just before me, and was sitting on the verandah of Junior Home as I crossed the plaza. Richard was standing close by her side as always. Of all the boys, Richard's crush on Irene was the most obvious. As I approached, I could see that O'Brien was sitting next to Irene, leaning in over her lap.

"He's so cute," Irene gushed as she pet Lucky while she fed him.

"Keep him on the towel, Miss. He pees a lot," O'Brien warned.

"I've had a number of puppies over the years, O'Brien. I know they pee," she laughed. "And this bottle Magdalen made," Irene looked up at me, "That woman is so creative!"

"Do you think there's anything she hasn't had to figure out after all these years?" I offered.

"And why are you getting home so late, Mr. Sullivan?"

"I had a lot of paperwork today. And I didn't know *you* would be coming, Miss Irene. Richard spent most of the game room yesterday pestering me about whether you were coming, didn't you Richard?"

Richard turned away, blushing but smiling ear to ear. I marveled at the beauty of a smile even on a face as disfigured as Richard's. In addition to his scars, Richard's teeth were badly misshapen. I wasn't quite sure how he could chew properly. Dr. Check had been able to do some work to help straighten them, but Richard needed care well beyond what Dr. Check could offer in his clinic.

A line of boys was forming behind me, eager for me to open the game room. I left Irene with her entourage and went to the refectory. The boys had figured out the rules of the game room very quickly. All I had to do was open the cupboard, and turn around and stand silently. They would form a single line, and each would ask politely for whatever game or puzzle he wanted. The tone was civil and calm. Every time I opened the cupboard, I felt bad I didn't have something more educational for them - something to help them grow mentally. But I knew this was a good start, and I learned to be satisfied with less accomplishment – mine not theirs.

Once everyone was settled, I went out to the verandah. I knew from experience, that Richard, O'Brien and Q would not leave Irene's side. If she came into the game room, they would follow her. If she stayed outside, they would stay outside.

Just a step or two away from that little circle stood Silent Malcolm. Sister Magdalen told me early on that Malcolm had been raised by Rastafarians. "They served him ganja tea when he was a baby, to help quiet him. "Well it certainly worked. He's certainly quiet. He has nothing in his head now. I don't know what we will do with him when he turns 17." It was one of the few times I heard her talk of one of the boy's future. Magdalen remained in the present most of the time. She dealt with today's troubles and let God take care of tomorrow's.

Eventually, Irene moved into the game room, and her troop followed. O'Brien kept Lucky on the floor beside him, as he and Richard sat down to a game of Chutes & Ladders. Jomo challenged Q to a game of chess. We passed a pleasant afternoon, our odd little family, and eventually it was time to wrap things up. I walked Irene to the bus stop, which gave us enough time to catch up and make plans for the weekend.

As I headed to my room, Mr. Herman intercepted me. "Ah, Mr. Jay. I thought I saw you arrive home. This came for you today." He handed me a large manila envelope. Postmark – New York. Return address, Fordham University School of Law.

I thanked him, but couldn't take my eyes off the envelope. I stepped to the side and sat on one of the benches along the verandah outside the office. I didn't need to open the envelope since, by the size and weight, it was clearly good news. I just held it in my lap for a moment and looked out at the hibiscus bushes along the driveway, and watched one of the senior home boys kicking up clouds of dust as he swept the pavement around Magdalen's Volvo with a branch. In the distance, the sunset glinted off the brass faucet of the pipe in the yard where the local community had lined up for water during the national strike. The buses that brought and took Irene coughed their way up South Camp Road. I could hear Ignatius' footsteps upstairs as she walked along the porch and called for Plunkett.

After a minute of accepting this would all be over soon, I opened the envelope.

"Mr. Sullivan: We are pleased to inform you...."

I scanned the materials quickly, looking for what response the school needed and by when. I looked up just as Q was walking into the office.

"Hello, Mr. Solomon."

"Well hello, Q," I smiled, turning the materials upside down, as if I had been reading something inappropriate, and as if he could tell. "What brings you down here?"

"Sista asked me to bring these keys to Mr. Herman.".

Mr. Herman came out of the office and took the keys from Q. "Congratulations, Mr. Jay. I assume that such a big envelope carries good news."

"Yes, Mr. Herman. Thank you."

He returned to his office. Q stood still, staring at me. "What is the good news?" he asked, smiling.

It was good news. It was the fulfillment of my plan for myself. And yet I felt as if I was about to tell someone I had cancer. "I have been accepted to go to law school. Back in the states. Next year."

"Congratulations, sir." I don't think Q had ever used the word before, but he was a quick study and picked up on Mr. Herman's comment. "So that means you'll be leaving?" he asked, his eyes narrowing.

I could feel a salty taste rise in my throat and the need to breathe more deeply. "Not for a few more months, Q. But, yes. I will be leaving."

I wanted to be eloquent and reassuring, but I was caught off guard, and fumbled. Instead of carefully chosen words, Q got raw feelings. "I'm so sorry that I have to leave you, Q." I could feel my eyes start to water.

He blinked twice, shrugged and said, "It's okay, Mr. Solomon. Everyone leaves me." I looked in his eyes for sadness, but all I saw was truth.

Just then, O'Brien stuck his head around the corner of the building and called, "Q. Mr. Estig looking for you." Then he waved at me. "Hey, Mr. Solomon. You read to us tonight?"

I nodded but couldn't speak. Q smiled and waved as he turned to run off with O'Brien. I sat on the bench and stared out at the traffic again. I felt as if my heart had been torn from my chest. Q's reaction had not been an act of self-defense, trying to mask his true feelings. His version of our relationship and mine were completely different. The same was true of the other boys. I was one of many adults who had already and would continue to pass through their lives. But they would be the only orphans I would ever care for. They were defining people in my life. I was but a blip in theirs.

Lord, let me not so much seek to be loved, as to love.

I had prayed that line every night for almost a year now. Yet it wasn't until that moment that I understood what it meant, and how hard it was to accept.

* * *

While I sat on the verandah, feeling sorry for myself, Sister Magdalen and Plunkett tooled around New Kingston on errands for Marie Therese. As they drove, she pointed out landmarks to Plunkett who sat in the passenger seat. She almost always took him on her jaunts now, both enjoying the company and seeing it as a way to help him learn his own city. When Plunkett got in the car, he gently moved the packet of papers from his seat to the floor, where they would be out of sight. He was careful not to step on the packet with his shoes, which he was wearing regularly now that his trips in the car were more frequent. They stopped first at the British Embassy to drop off a thank you note for a donation to help pay for teachers' salaries. From there, they headed to the stationary store in Liguanea for school supplies. Magdalen was stopped at a red light at the intersection of Old Hope Road and Mountain View Road when a beggar started to cross the street. Plunkett glanced quickly at Magdalen's open window, and sat up straighter, his body tensing at the perceived threat. The frail-looking beggar had his eyes on the ground, rather than at the car. He had passed beyond the front of the car when the light turned green. Just as Magdalen slipped her foot off the brake, the man turned back into the intersection and started to bend over to pick up something off the road. The Volvo had neither power brakes nor power steering, and Magdalen gasped as she slammed her foot as hard as she could on the brake. The sound of Plunkett's hands hitting the dashboard was louder than the thud from the hood of the car when it hit the beggar, but the man's arms flew up in the air as he fell sideways onto the pavement. Magdalen jumped out, waving to the car behind her to come around her carefully.

"Sister," Plunkett implored, "you shouldn't get out. He might be a thief."

Magdalen ignored him as she stepped around the front of the car, and Plunkett was forced to join her if he was going to be any help.

The man was getting to his knees when Magdalen reached him. She helped him up, and saw his wrist and elbow were scraped. From the way he was supporting his weight as he got up, it didn't seem there were any broken bones.

"You hit me," he growled.

Magdalen helped him stand. "What you going back into the street for?" she admonished him. "You could have been killed."

"YOU could've killed me!" he yelled, as he made his way around to the curb, with Magdalen supporting him on one side and Plunkett on the other. Plunkett recoiled at the smell of the man, but he couldn't pick up any similar reaction from Magdalen. They sat him on the sidewalk. Magdalen pulled a handkerchief from her pocket and wiped the man's hand and elbow. Plunkett watched as she cradled the man's hand in hers.

"There now. You're barely hurt."

"You could've killed me," he repeated, softer this time.

"Nonsense. You're fine. What you go back in the street for anyway? What a foolish thing to do in traffic."

"I saw a coin on the street. I wanted to buy some food."

Plunkett walked to the front of the car and picked up the ten cent piece on the road and handed it to the man. It would not have bought the man anything. They sat with him for a moment until he regained his composure. Plunkett was not as worried about the man as he had been initially, but he was getting concerned about the number of cars trying to navigate around sister's Volvo. "Sista, we should be going now."

"Of course." She stood up from the curb and then extended a hand to the man on the sidewalk. "Come. Let's get something to eat."

Plunkett looked at her in disbelief. "Sista?"

"Help him into the car Plunkett." Since the man did not object, Plunkett guided the man into the back seat of the car. The man, surprised by the ride, forgot to hold the handkerchief to his wound, which had stopped bleeding anyway, and was clearly no more than a scrape.

Magdalen drove to a nearby ice cream shop in New Kingston. She ordered three dishes of ice cream, all different flavors, and joined Plunkett and the man at an outdoor table. When they finished their treat, she ordered two Jamaican meat patties, and left them with the man along with a few dollars from her pocket. "You'll be fine now," she said, as she patted him on the back. "Don't walk out into traffic again, ok?"

"Yes, sista," he replied.

Back in the car, Magdalen said only, "What a silly thing to do, walk out into traffic like that. How was your ice cream?"

"Very good, sista. Very good," Plunkett replied.

"So, I forget. Where were we going again?" she asked. Plunkett reminded her and they continued on their errands. She did not mention the incident again.

Plunkett shared the story with me and the other office boys that evening as we talked and listened to music on the verandah. He marveled at her response to the situation. He couldn't understand how she could have trusted anyone again after the attack from the man who tried to steal her money.

"I don't know that I can learn to trust people like Sista does," he commented.

"She does trust," I offered. "But I'm not sure it's in other people."

30
A MOST VERSATILE PRAYER

That Friday, the sun felt even hotter, and the air at Alpha carried a pungent odor. When Mr. Johnson wasn't driving Marie Therese or Ignatius on errands, he performed general maintenance around the property, and at least once each week, that meant burning the garbage.

As I passed the office on the way to Junior Home, I saw Michael Winters and Anthony Gayle standing in the office doorway. "Michael! Anthony! You're back! How was the trip?"

"Mr. Solomon! Oh, it was so wonderful!" Anthony started as he shuffled over and hugged me hello. He stuttered through his first few lines, grinning ear-to-ear as he always did when he was excited. He was a happy child, and, despite his disability, Anthony had the most positive outlook of any boy at Alpha. He talked about how it felt to be so far away; how he felt special being in such a holy place; how he could never forget all of the abandoned crutches and wheelchairs. His face glowed as he spoke of praying to be cured of his limitation. His spirit didn't seem the least bit deflated by the fact that he was sitting next to me, twisted leg and withered arm intact. I thought the trip had been a waste for him; not because he wasn't "cured," but rather, because Anthony did not suffer from anything that needed curing. He had been abandoned by his family, but found love and security at Alpha. He was physically limited and often picked on by the other boys, but his spirit was resilient. He would have been justified to feel like Job, plagued by torments. But like Job, his faith was strong. He finally stopped gushing about the trip not because he was done, but because he was exhausted.

"Now, Mr. Sullivan, let me tell you about everything we did," Michael began.   Sr. Thaddeus had given him a journal for the trip so he could record everything they had seen. He pulled it out of the small bag he carried, so that he could get the dates and place names correct. He started on day one, and ten minutes later, we hadn't even landed in France yet. Although Michael had looked on in dismay as Anthony had mangled most details, Anthony looked on in amazement as Michael retold the same adventure. Michael had clearly told his tale many times already, and his storytelling was gelling. Sister Magdalen had promised to develop his many rolls of film for him as soon as she could. He would hound her about it until she did so.

We spoke for so long that it became impractical to open up the gameroom that afternoon. I had planned to meet the other BC teachers that evening for dinner, so I wouldn't be reading stories that evening, either, so I headed to Junior Home to say a quick hello.

I sat on the verandah with Richard and Q. They told me what books they had read in class, and Richard bragged about finally understanding the six-times table. He recited if for me haltingly, but proudly. Q, to his credit, never corrected him, but looked at me each time, before Richard corrected his occasional mistakes. They showed me the checkerboard they made out of a piece of cardboard they had found, and how they had managed to play checkers using different colored pebbles from the yard, since I hadn't opened the gameroom. I was quietly pleased that they were bragging to me while rebuking me. "Well, then. It seems you didn't miss me at all," I said with mock indignation. "And by the way, where's O'Brien this afternoon?"

"Him around in the garden, sir," Q said. "Him very sad. De puppy died this morning."

"Oh, poor O'Brien."

I went around behind the Junior Home washroom and found O'Brien sitting with his back against the wall. He was throwing small pebbles at the ground., not slamming them in anger, as much as tossing them in boredom.

"Hey, buddy." I sat down beside him. He didn't respond. "I'm really sorry about Lucky." He sat quietly. "I think you did your best. He just wasn't strong enough. He probably needed to stay with his mother a bit longer." I thought, "And so did you, O'Brien. So did you."

"I didn't kill him, sir," he blurted out.

"Oh, O'Brien, I didn't think you had. He was a weak little puppy. Sweet...but weak."

"The other boys say I killed de puppy, but I didn't. I woke up this morning and he was dead in his box." He started to cry.

"O'Brien." I put my arm around him. "I know it must be tough. You just have to remember that you did the best job you could to care for him while you had him."

I looked around, "Where is he now?"

"Sister took him this morning when I went for morning chores."

"Well, would it help if we gave him a proper burial? You could say a few words. We could all say a few prayers and put him to rest. Would you like that?"

"Yes, sir. Dat would be nice."

"All right. I think the boys are lining up to wash for supper now. You go get in line, and I will check with Sister Magdalen."

As we walked around to the open plaza in front of Junior Home, Magdalen was coming up from the office. O'Brien and I met up with her as she reached the steps to the verandah. "How was your day, sister?"

"Busy, busy, busy. I spent the whole day at the Ministry of Transportation office getting license plates for the new van that comes next week. It's very exciting to get a new vehicle, but they make you work so hard for it. So much paperwork!"

"Sister, O'Brien and I would like to give Lucky a proper burial. Would that be all right?"

"Who?" She glanced at O'Brien. "Oh, the puppy. Yes, well. ..I don't know. I can't think of that right now. You," she pointed at O'Brien. "Run off and get ready for supper now." O'Brien turned immediately and ran off, seeming more energized since he would now get some closure on his puppy.

As soon as I turned back, Sr. Magdalen had started to walk away. "Sister. What did you do with the puppy?"

"You want to bury a puppy," she said more than asked, as she kept walking toward her office door, where Nurse and two boys were standing waiting. "I've never heard of such a thing except in some silly movies."

Even after a year at Alpha, I apparently thought I was just in a movie. Maybe I just didn't get it yet.

"I put the puppy in with the trash and Mr. Johnson burned the trash today. I'm afraid there's no puppy left to bury." She turned to Nurse who had an arm full of clothes, and handed her some keys. "You'll have to excuse me, Jay. I'll see you later." I heard her mumbling as she walked away, "Bury a puppy. You silly Americans." Apparently, sentiment for a pet is a luxury, like a big car, or too many choices of breakfast cereals.

I stood there for a moment. I had comforted O'Brien with the thought of a ceremony for his dog. Now I was going to be the cause of just one more disappointment in his life.

When I had promised O'Brien a burial for Lucky, I had immediately thought of using an empty shoe box I had in my room. I didn't have Lucky, but I still had the box. I took the box from on top of my wardrobe, wrapped a small piece of wood in a rag and put it in the box, surrounded by stuffing so it wouldn't shift around, and taped the box shut with duct tape, enough to dampen any request to open the box and view the body. O'Brien would never know.

By the time I got back up to Junior Home, dinner was over. O'Brien, Richard and Q came charging over, this time followed by a dozen other boys. O'Brien had spread the word that there was to be a service for his puppy.

With solemn ceremony, I handed the box to O'Brien, who tried to cradle the box as he had Lucky. We were going to bury the box down by past the Senior Home, near where the garbage was burned. I didn't want to bury the box in the Junior Home garden in case O'Brien, out of sadness, or morbid curiosity, decided to dig up the box at some point to see what the remains looked like. As our small band started our procession away from Junior Home, one boy on the sideline said, loud enough for all to hear, "Him kill his own puppy."

O'Brien's face filled with rage, but I put my hand on his shoulder and we kept walking.

Then Magdalen passed us, on her way to the convent for dinner. "Where are you all headed?" she asked, looking puzzled.

"We're going to bury Lucky," O'Brien said, holding up the box.

Sister's eyes widened, and she stared at O'Brien, then at me, then at the box, and again at O'Brien.

"We're going to bury a box," I paused, "with a puppy inside."

She shook her head slowly as she looked at me. I couldn't tell if she registered disapproval, dismay, or resignation. "O.K." she shrugged, and she kept on her way.

When we got to the right spot, I took a shovel, the same one I had used to remove a dead rat from my bathroom, and dug a small hole. O'Brien laid the box in the hole and I handed him the shovel. He pushed the small mound of dirt on top and tamped it down with his hands.

"Do you want to say a few words, O'Brien?"

He paused, but then said more at one time than I had ever heard him say. "Here lies Lucky. He was my puppy. He was from my father. I loved him and I think he loved me." O'Brien took a breath. "He liked milk, and he liked to lick my hand, and he liked to be petted."

There was a pause, then Q mumbled, "But he didn't like cards," and he and Richard giggled. O'Brien's face flashed anger, but only briefly, and then he too laughed.

I suggested we say a quick prayer. The Our Father was easiest and we said it in unison.

"Well, we should head back now," I said as I stooped to pick up the shovel. As I straightened up again, the boys, without prompting, all extended their right arm and held their hand out, palm down, over the little grave. In unison, they all began to sing softly,

May the Lord bless and keep you.

May His face shine upon you.

May the Lord bless and keep you all your days.

It was the prayer they sang at Mass to bless the Checks and other visitors. I hadn't realized until that moment what a versatile prayer it was.

Blessed be the Lord.

Magdalen worried that they hadn't learned, but they had.

Blessed be the Lord.

Their voices were clear and sincere.

Blessed be the Lord for all His good.

From their perspective, in that moment, the Lord had been good.

Blessed be the Lord.

Lucky had been a blessing.

Blessed be the Loooooooooord.

Not all blessings are easy.

Blessed be the Lord for all is His good.

Then, again without prompting, they made the sign of the cross, and started to move away.

"That was very nice, O'Brien."

"Thank you, sir. I think Lucky would have liked it."

Our work was done and the sun was setting as we headed back to Junior Home for the evening.

31
THE TRUTH AND THE CONSEQUENCES

By the time I arrived at the bar, everyone was already eating dinner. I walked up behind Irene and rubbed her shoulders as I said hello to everyone. Kathy shifted her chair over so I could join the table. The music had a heavy bass so the air seemed to pulsate, but the volume wasn't too loud to talk over.

"You're late," Irene leaned over and whispered, patting my knee under the table.

"Sorry. Had to bury a puppy."

"Oh. Poor O'Brien!"

"Yeah. It wasn't much fun. But we made a little ceremony out of it. I think it helped."

"Let me guess: shoe box, little mound of dirt, a little sign that reads 'Here lies Lucky. Best dog ever.'"

"Pretty much."

"How Mayberry of you."

"Except with one ironic Third World twist. We buried an empty box. The dog got thrown out in the trash earlier in the day."

"Why am I not surprised," she said.

David walked up to the table and handed me a Red Stripe.

"What did you do today?" David asked sitting across from me.

I recounted to them the afternoon events. "So basically, you lied to the kids to make them feel better," Kathy said.

"Yeah. I'm working on my parenting skills," I said.

"You have never lied to anyone to spare their feelings?" Irene asked.

"No. I don't think that's right. I think people need to deal honestly with each other."

"Just before we came over here tonight you told David you liked that shirt he's wearing," Irene said.

David looked down at his baggy faded tie dyed shirt. "Hey! What's wrong with my shirt?"

"That's different," Kathy defended herself. "I didn't say I liked it. I said he looked fine. It's not the same. Besides, I knew this place was dark and that I wouldn't see anyone I knew, so it was fine with me if he wanted to look like that."

"What's wrong with my shirt?"

"Nothing's wrong with it, David," she said, brushing him aside. "I just don't think you should lie to kids. That's all. It sends the wrong message."

"I was really just trying to soften the blow, that's all. I really don't see any harm in it."

"Those kids are going to have tough lives. You can't shelter them. They need to know that life is full of hard lessons."

"They live in an orphanage, Kathy! I think they already know about life's hard lessons," Irene said.

"I'm just saying. I think it's a slippery slope once you start lying."

"I can't believe you don't like this shirt. I love this shirt," David said, taking another drink.

"Oh for God's sake," she blurted out. "It's a hideous shirt. You look ridiculous. No one has worn tie dyed anything in fifteen years. I can't imagine where you found that shirt!"

He looked wounded. "Well. It was my uncle's. After he died in a car accident my senior year in high school, my mother kept a bunch of his stuff in our spare room. I took this with me here to remember him."

Kathy's mouth dropped open. "I'm so sorry, David. I didn't know."

"I know you didn't. It's okay. Does anyone want another beer?"

"I'll get it for you," Kathy said, jumping up. "I'm so sorry, David."

As Kathy walked to the bar, David leaned back in his chair, and put his hands behind his head, "And sometimes you can tell lies that make people feel bad instead of good," he smirked.

I laughed.

"That's rotten," Irene said, eating another French fry. "She was just trying to make a point. And I agree with her, to a certain extent."

"But that 'certain extent' is the slippery slope she was warning about," David said.

"I don't understand how we *can't* go there," I said. "We live there! Everything is on the slippery slope. Our job isn't to keep off the slope. It's to hold our ground as much as we can while we're sliding down."

"There you go taking the moral high ground again," he argued.

"I don't think I'm taking the high ground at all. I think I'm being a pragmatist, not an idealist," I said.

"I'm an idealist," Kathy said, returning with another round for everyone. "I think we have to start somewhere. And it might as well be as a purist. If you start in the middle, you just don't have far to go before you're in the tank."

"But what makes you compromise?" Irene asked. "Take the work I am doing with my class. I expect them all to do all the homework. Study hard for tests. Really buckle down. And I think if I demand that of them, they will rise to the challenge. I expect a lot, and yet day after day I allow their excuses. I compromise my own standard for them because, quite honestly, it's easier, and it makes me feel more human."

"But that's my point," Kathy interjected. "If you didn't start at the high end of the spectrum, you'd have nothing to offer them at all but weakness and moral wishy-washiness."

"Wishy-washiness? Is that a word? Talk about low standards," David teased. Kathy and David got into their own little battle.

We were all feeling the pressure the school year winding down and of figuring out what our time in Jamaica meant to each of us. After a long discussion of people's plans for the following year, David said, "I can't believe you are all so wrapped up in next year. I haven't figured out what to do next week. Anyone up for the beach tomorrow?"

"I'm not." I said. "I get too much sun just walking around Kingston. My Irish skin can't take the beach here. My face has peeled constantly since I got here two years ago," I said.

"I wanted to go out to St. Monica's tomorrow. Want to join me?" Irene asked the group.

"I wouldn't mind going with you," I said. "I haven't been in a year, and it would do me some good to get away from the kids for a bit."

"Why don't you come with us," Irene asked David.

"You know," he said. "I would, but I haven't been to the beach in months, and I need a break."

"O.K. Just wanted to offer."

"You know the real reason?" he said. "I think that if you go to a place like that, you have to commit your whole life to it. You can't just waltz in to talk to someone for the afternoon and then leave again so that you can feel good about yourself. Making a day trip like that seems absurd to me. Really, who is that for – them or you?"

"You may be right," I said. "I don't know if it really makes their lives any better for me to pop in for the afternoon and read with them, or pray with them, or just give them someone to talk to for the day. But it feels like the right thing to do."

"Besides," Irene said, "I think that's a cop-out on your part. If you want to go to the beach, I'm fine with that. I went last weekend myself. But to say you're not going to St. Monica's because you can't commit enough doesn't make any sense to me."

"And is it really any different than being at Alpha, or St. George's or Immaculate for a year?" Kathy said.

"You know, I gotta tell you. We are not a fun bunch! Every time we go out for dinner, we start with angst for an appetizer."

"I'll tell you what," Irene said. "If you can do the beach on Sunday instead of tomorrow, I'll go with you."

"That'll work," David said.

"Deal, then."

Later that night, as I lay in bed, I prayed as usual for Morris Mathers to be safe, and I thought about what it means to make a commitment. I had struggled all year to define my role at Alpha, as if my role only had value if I could put language around it. You can't measure your success at something if you can't define the "something," and success was important to me. I recalled a quote from Mother Teresa. "We aren't called to be successful. We are called to be faithful." It had struck me as a radical concept when I first heard it. How can we <u>not</u> be called to be successful? But here I was, after a year of bedtime stories, afternoons in the gameroom, and trips to the park, and I had not a single "success" to point to. Yet somehow, I felt at peace with trying.

We each have to figure out our role in life, and I had determined that mine wasn't here. My commitment to Alpha had been incomplete and inadequate. It would be the same level of commitment with which I would approach everything in life, until I married, and had my own children. My family would be my only complete commitment. Even Q understood this, at his gentle age. He knew without hesitation, that it was because he did not have family that "everyone leaves" him. And Magdalen knew it was important for the boys to hear and see that same message, that they might be better husbands and fathers. It's tough to teach the value of something by showing someone the effect of its absence, and a much harder way to learn the lesson. But it was the best we could do, and I was coming to terms with that.

Lord, let me not so much seek to seek,
as to be present to the moment.

March 3, 1991

Dear Jay,

This is just a hurried note. We are all well, thank God. I hope you, Mary, and all at home are well. Did I ever congratulate you & Mary for your engagement? I'm getting old & my memory plays tricks on me. I think I owe you a letter. Will write longer next time. Take good care of your sweet self. A big God bless you!

Sr. M. Magdalen

P.S. Thank God the war is over. I hope they get rid of Sadaam. Hell is too good for him.

32
A HOT NEW VAN

"Well, she a beauty, all right," Mr. Johnson said.

"I cannot believe it's finally here," Magdalen sighed.

"It is truly a lovely vehicle," Ignatius said. She was the only person who could call a "vehicle" *lovely* and sound completely sincere doing so.

They were standing in front of the new van, parked right in front of the office. Its white paint and light blue stripe along the side gleamed in the hot Jamaican sun. The old van, just across the drive and under the shade of the enormous mango tree, looked abandoned. Up until this moment, the old van had been a symbol of pride, a trusty work horse, an honored and highly productive member of the family. Now, in comparison with the shiny new vehicle, it seemed old and decaying. The rust on the fenders and around the wheel wells seemed more prominent. The dent in the back seemed like the van-equivalent of hip surgery scars: its permanently cloudy side windows its cataracts.

"Well, it certainly took enough paper work to get it here," Magdalen commented,. It was odd that she didn't seem more grateful. But then she ran most of her errands in her blue Volvo rather than the van. Ignatius used the van to transport the band to engagements, so she was overjoyed. Marie Therese looked down from up in the convent. "Ignatius, you must remind Father Williams to dedicate mass on Sunday to Mr. Mathers in the States for donating the van." Mr. Mathers was a wealthy Florida business man. His children attended a Sister of Mercy school in the U.S. He met Sister Marie Therese when she was visiting his daughter's school.

He was so moved by her devotion, he made Alpha his pet charity, and had become a significant sponsor over the years. He had not only bought the van in Miami, but paid to have the school's emblem painted on the side, and covered the transportation and import costs.

"Yes, sister," Ignatius replied. "Thank you for reminding me. I already told him twice, but one more time won't hurt."

Plunkett and Wilbert, the office boys, were walking around the van inspecting it, running their hands across the side.

"Please, boys," Ignatius warned them. "Don't go touching it just yet. It's nice and clean and I don't want it all marked up."

"Mr. Johnson, you will be parking it around back this afternoon, yes?"

"Around back," meant behind the Senior Home dormitory, where the classrooms and trade shops were clustered.

"Yes sista," Mr. Johnson nodded quickly. "I will put it away before I leave today."

"Please put both vans away now, Mr. Johnson. We have no more errands for the evening."

"But we don't usually lock up the old van, sista. Are you sure you want to? It won't be too much trouble to take out each time?" Of course, it was no trouble for Sister Ignatius. She didn't take the van out or put it away. It was more work for Mr. Johnson.

"No. We should use it for both vans," Sister replied. "Did you pick up the extra gasoline as well?" she asked him.

"Yes, sista. I fill up the two containers from the gas station."

"Good." She turned to us, "I don't know how much gasoline this new van takes, so we will keep some on hand for a while."

"Yes, sista," Mr. Johnson replied, and he started off toward the old van, keys in hand.

"Sister Magdalen, do you plan to drive the new van, or stick to your car?" Plunkett asked.

"Oh heavens! I couldn't drive that," she said, pointing that the new van. "I'm very comfortable with my car. We understand each other. I spend enough time on the road without having to drive everyone around in that thing." She said, waving her hand dismissively at the new van as she headed upstairs to the convent.

The double garage for the vans consisted of two parallel freestanding cinderblock walls about twenty feet apart, with wooden doors framed in on each end. The wooden peaked roof had corrugated zinc sheets on the outside to keep the rain and blazing sun off the wood. It was at least forty years old, and in a need of a paint job. The sisters rarely locked up the old van. They felt it was unlikely to be stolen since it was hidden behind the dormitory. Mr. Johnson parked both vans in the garage and padlocked the doors. A narrow alley separated the garage from the row of buildings that housed the shoe-making and woodworking shops.

In the carpentry shop, a dozen Senior Home boys were working on their projects, painting picture frames, spinning bowls on the lathe, gluing together strips of wood that would form cutting boards. Stacks of Blue Mahoe and Lignum Vitae wood lined the walls. The head carpenter sent his assistant to turn on the compressor in the small spraying room where they would put a final coat of varnish on a few chairs the boys had just completed.

Up at Junior Home, Irene had opened the game room in my absence, since I was working late at St. George's. The boys were playing well together, with nothing more than the typical disagreements. Irene sat on the verandah talking with Richard, Q, O'Brien and Waldemar. They talked about how the days were getting hotter as the summer neared, and about their lessons from the week, and who was the better football player. Richard compared himself to one of the much older boys and O'Brien laughed at the very idea. The verandah at Junior Home looked out across the plaza created by the u-shaped building, and then across a stand of trees and bushes separating it from the Senior Home dormitory, office and convent.

Around 3:00, Magdalen came down from the convent. "Plunkett, carry this for me." She pointed to two large bags by the office door.

"These have to go around back to Miss Laundry. Come. Walk with me." The laundry area was adjacent to the garage. As Magdalen and Plunkett arrived at the laundry building, they heard a loud bang from the direction of the trade shops. Almost immediately, they heard cries for help and saw smoke rise from the edges of the zinc sheets covering the roof of the woodworking shop. They ran to the front of the shop, where the head carpenter was helping his assistant who was limping badly.

"The compressor exploded!" the carpenter shouted. Sparks from the explosion ignited piles of sawdust on the floor. Flames were already wicking up the dry, wooden walls of the shop. "All of the boys got out!" he assured Magdalen.

Boys from the Senior Home poured out of their dormitory onto the parade ground. Magdalen quickly cleared the other trade shops. "Quickly! Buckets! Get water!"

Plunkett led two Senior Home boys to the stacks of buckets Miss Laundry kept on hand and quickly organized a bucket brigade from the laundry sink area to the side of the building, but even on the best of days, the water pressure at Alpha wasn't strong. Within minutes it was clear they wouldn't save the shop. Magdalen turned her attention to the roof of the building. Some of the Senior Home boys had grabbed the hoses used to water the Senior Home fields. They sprayed water on the roof of the adjacent shoe making shop. Since the two shops shared a wall, their efforts were futile, and as the fire spread, the smell of the chemicals from the carpentry shop mixed with the stench of burning leather. The smoke rose in thick black clouds, drawing Magdalen's gaze upward, into the tree branches above the shops. The leaves on many branches were curling in the heat, and a few had burst into flames already. As she watched cinders float upward, her gaze crossed over the alley to the Senior Home dorm. "Lord, please don't spread to the dormitory!" The Senior Home dormitory was connected to the convent, the office, the library, the kitchen and the Senior Home refectory. If the fire spread across the narrow gap to the dormitory, the entire Alpha Boys School compound except Junior Home would burn to the ground.

Ignatius came running from the office. "Ignatius, get help!" Magdalen called to her. Ignatius ran back toward the convent.

Because of the slight grade up to Junior Home, from the verandah you could almost see across the tops of the other buildings. With almost a hundred boys running around a soccer field, playing on the plaza, and competing in the gameroom, Irene didn't hear the first few cries for help. But the sudden rush of Senior Home boys off their playing field caught her eye, followed immediately by the shouts of, "Fire! Fire!" She and the boys on the verandah all saw the plume of black smoke rising from just beyond the Senior Home dormitory.

Irene pushed through the boys on the verandah and ran down the steps and across the plaza. As usual, Mr. Estig had his small metal chair stationed at the unofficial demarcation between the Junior Home and Senior Home territory. He was standing by the time Irene reached him, and a mad rush of all of the Junior Home boys was closing in behind her. On a typical day, the Junior Home boys knew not to venture past Mr. Estig's chair, but a fire on the grounds was too intriguing to resist, and the boys started to flock toward Senior Home. As they neared the alley between the Senior Home dorm and the kitchen they could already feel the heat of the fire. Irene's instincts kicked in and rather than rush to the flames, she held the Junior Home boys back, both for their protection and to keep them out of the way

The Senior Home boys kept the hoses trained on the trade rooms adjacent to the shoemaking shop. Meanwhile, a large tree branch above the carpentry shop was fully ablaze, and cinders fell onto the roof of the nearby garage. Although the zinc sheets on the wooden roof provided some protection, as branches started to drop on and around the garage, the building started to smolder.

Mr. Johnson, who had joined Magdalen at the head of the line in front of the carpentry shop, now ran to the garage and struggled with his keys to quickly open the garage doors. The back wall of the garage was already in flames. Johnson tried to enter, hoping to drive out the new van, but the fire was already spreading to the roof timbers in the back and the heat just inside the doorway was unbearable.

Magdalen grabbed coils of clothes line from the seamstress' room. She and Johnson leaned low inside the front of the garage doorway, positioned at either end of the front fender of the new van. She quickly ran the rope around the fender a few times. Johnson did the same on his end. Magdalen could feel the heat singeing the soft hair on her forearms. She and Johnson fell back to just outside the entrance. Johnson coiled line around his hands, and the largest Senior Home boy stepped up and gently pushed Magdalen aside, "Let me, sista," he said, as he followed Johnson example and wound the rope around his hands." "Help us boys!" Johnson shouted to the nearest Senior Home boys, many of whom were taller than him, and all of whom had tougher hands and feet. With a half-dozen boys on each line, Johnson shouted, "Together! Pull!" Their first attempt stretched the lines taut and tightened the line on the fender, but didn't budge the van. "Again! Pull!" he shouted.

The second time, the van resisted but slid a few feet. "They might actually be able to do this," Magdalen thought.

"Again! Pull!"

The third pull dragged the nose of the van just past the doorway. By the next two pulls the front door of the van was out of the garage. But by now a good part of the roof was in flames. Just as they were about to pull again, the rear window of the van shattered from the heat and the inside of the van filled with smoke.

"It's over!" Magdalen shouted. "Back away, everyone!" Johnson moved the boys back to the point where the heat was no longer searing. Magdalen's eyes stung from the smoke, and she shielded her face from the heat. Suddenly, the first piece of zinc from the roof fell into the garage behind the van and the roof started to cave in.

Magdalen headed around the back of the building to make sure the boys in the bucket brigade were away from the building. She didn't know about the two canisters of gasoline Johnson had put in the garage.

33
HELP IN MANY FORMS

When the first of the two gas canisters exploded, it blew two sheets of zinc off the roof toward the garden. A fireball - more black smoke than flame - blew up through the hole in the roof. Magdalen cried out from the back of the garage. As Plunkett ran around the side of the building, he saw her kneeling on the ground next to one of the Senior Home boys. The boy was lying on his back, his face covered in soot and his hair smoking. Magdalen was frantically patting out flames on his shirt. Parts of the tree overhead were now in flames and burning branches began falling around them. "Help me," Magdalen cried as she tried to lift the boy.

"I've got him, Sista!" Plunkett said. "Get going. Get back!" Plunkett lifted the other boy's shoulders off the ground and dragged him backward from the flaming building with Magdalen guiding him. Just then, the second gasoline canister exploded. What was left of the back wall of the garage blew out toward them, and they both slipped backward, more from surprise than from the force of the blast. They scrambled to their feet, lifted the injured boy a second time, and dragged him backward.

Just as they got him to a safe distance, the rest of the roof fell in on the vans. Two more explosions echoed against the dormitory wall, as the fire reached the gas tank in each van. The smoke was acrid from the burning tires and van upholstery. Magdalen kept backing up, and then started to lean against the cinderblock wall of the Senior Home dormitory, which was only about thirty feet from the garage. She was surprised by the intensity of the heat reflecting off the building.

Nurse from Junior Home had rushed down with a first aid kit and was tending to the Senior Home boy, who looked like he had second degree burns to his face and hands. He was conscious but clearly in pain. Mr. Herman from the office came around and said an ambulance was on its way.

Everything was moving in slow motion, until Magdalen yelled, "Come boys, quickly! Get those buckets filled again!"

"Sister, the building's gone," Plunkett said. "It's just going to burn out now."

"The garage is gone. We need to save the dormitory!" she said.

The boys looked up. There were a few burning embers landing on the rusting zinc sheets of the Senior Home dormitory.

With Magdalen supervising, the boys kept water flowing onto the dormitory roof for about twenty minutes. Others worked the bucket brigade again to throw water on the front doors of the garage, the only flammable part remaining. Magdalen knew she couldn't salvage the garage; she just wanted the fire out so the ordeal would be over.

The garage hadn't been used regularly, and no one had checked its stability. The wooden doors and ceiling were so eaten through by termites that they went up like kindling, and out just as quickly. Soon there was only a smoldering mess. Both vans were ruined. The tops of the walls had started to crumble where the roof supports had tied into the cinder blocks. Magdalen put the two oldest Senior Home boys in charge of the hoses while she went around front to make sure the Senior Home boy was cared for.

I arrived home from school to find Magdalen staring at the ruins, shaking her head. Once the flames died down, it became clear that the tree wasn't going to go up in flames and the dormitory was safe.

As Magdalen recounted the story, I asked, "Where was Ignatius?"

"She went for help," she said.

"They called the fire department?" I asked, looking around for signs of fire trucks.

"No. She and Marie Therese ran to the chapel and prayed." She added, "I wish my faith was that strong. I grabbed a bucket."

"Are you *kidding* me! They didn't call the fire department?"

"Mr. Herman had already done that. It didn't matter since the whole thing was over so quickly. Twenty minutes and we lost three buildings, two vans and thousands of dollars of woodworking equipment. It was over before the fire truck arrived. Besides, there are no fire hydrants this far back on the property, Jay." Magdalen said. "It's why we lost the dormitory last time," she referred to the fire almost twenty years earlier. "We called for the fire department last time and lost everything. Ignatius wasn't going to make the same mistake again. And it worked this time."

"I think *you* saved the day, Sister."

"It was arrogant to think I could put out the fire."

"Not acting would have been insanity, sister. You saved the whole place!"

"I've gotten used to my limitations, Jay. We all have our gifts from God. I just didn't get the faith they received. But I do try."

It was getting late, and we were standing in front of the smoldering wreckage of the garage.

She was exhausted. She was sixty-two and had done the work of a twenty-five year old New York City firefighter that afternoon. And she knew she still needed to feed ninety-six boys their dinner, lead them in their prayers, and get them to bed, making sure they each appreciated how lucky we had all been that day.

"Sister, I can supervise the clean up here. Why don't you go sit down for a bit?"

"I can't. It's time to get dinner ready for the boys."

"Irene is here. I'm sure she can help."

"Well, I could use the help this evening. I need to see if the Senior Home boy is all right. Mr. Johnson took him to the hospital in my car. Those looked like nasty burns on his arms."

"How about you, sister?" I asked.

"I'm fine." She paused, reaching up and touching her face gingerly.

"You know, your eyebrows are gone," I said.

She sighed. "They were too bushy anyway," she joked weakly. "O.K. I'm tired," she admitted, the smile draining from her face. "And also relieved, I have to say. This could have been so much worse."

"Were the vans insured?"

"Oh yes. They will be replaced. But it's just so embarrassing for Ignatius to have to write to the benefactor about the problem. It really is humiliating. We burned up his gift the first day it arrived! How tragic. I think she is just sick about it."

"Well, like you said, we really are lucky it wasn't worse."

"And now I have to stop saying that so I don't jinx myself!" She smiled. "Listen to me," she laughed. "First, my faith is weak, then I start talking superstition! A fine nun I am!"

"Well, sister. If you ever decide to stop being a nun, I'm sure any fire department would be glad to take you on."

"Jay, if I never see another fire as long as I live, that's fine with me."

"How is Sister Marie Therese?"

"She will blame herself for this. She told Ignatius to put the vans in the garage. The last time there was a fire, three boys died. She has never forgiven herself. If today's fire had reached the dormitory, I think it would have destroyed her. Anyway, Jay, we'll count our blessings this evening, won't we?" She turned and walked toward Junior Home.

I stayed at the garage until the last wisps of smoke stopped coming from under the pile of wood and ash. Then I showered and changed clothes and headed up to Junior Home. Irene and Mr. Estig had everything under control. Magdalen took a little longer to clean up, and emerged from her room with her forearms glistening with aloe to sooth the burns. Irene stayed until the boys finished their supper. It was starting to get dark as she left, and neither of us liked her traveling alone after dark. By then, things were already returning to normal.

That evening, instead of reading to the boys, we told each other stories. They told me what they remembered from their homes. Some had stories of fires, many of which had ended tragically. Others had pleasant memories of home, but even those stories had burnt edges, otherwise the boys wouldn't have been here. It was a longer evening than most since the boys were sharing instead of taking in. They did a great job just listening to each other, and our small band, sitting on the floor around the chair, ended with a short prayer of thanksgiving to God for containing the fire. As they walked to their beds, down the narrow aisles between the cots, I decided to include having them tell stories each evening, in addition to the ones that I would read. It would be good practice for them for some other day when they were the ones sitting in a chair, with their own children on the floor.

Alpha

June 23, 1988

Dearest Jay,

I got your sweet letter yesterday & to show you how much I appreciate hearing from you, I'm answering you immediately. That's a record!

First, the good news – we started building & hope it will be ready by September – but definitely before the year is over. We are building the woodworking shop in line with the classrooms & instead of the burnt up one we are building a Printery/Bindery/ 2 garages & an upstairs apartment for volunteers.

The sad news – our dear Sister Philomena passed away last month. She has been suffering for years but was in bed only a week before she died. She had a most peaceful death. We miss her very much, but we are glad for her – she must be enjoying her reward. Her funeral took place at the Cathedral – Alpha was not big enough. We had over 30 priests in the Sanctuary and the Cathedral was packed. The choir sang beautifully. It was something to remember. She was well loved.

My brother Louis, the architect, is finishing an apartment upstairs in the old junk room. I hope it will be ready when you come over.

Today I took him to the University Hospital. Like Ronald Reagan – he had some trouble in the colon – but the doctor (who happened to be Sr. Benedict's nephew) operated on him and assured us that it is not cancerous and that he is o.k. My other brother in Malta (2 years older than I) has only a few weeks to live. He is dying of cancer. Such is life – some good news & some bad!

Please take it easy.

Love to all at home – You have it always,

Magda.

34
WRAPPING UP

We spent the last week of class at St. George's preparing for the final exam, reviewing everything we had covered in the last half of the year. The exams themselves went smoothly, and the goodbyes were rushed, heartfelt, or non-existent, depending on the relationship I had developed with each student during the year. I was confident they had learned, or that I had at least given them the opportunity to do so. The ones I had gotten to know were, by and large, good kids. Some were well on their way to manhood. Others still struggled to stop being little boys. Student-teacher relationships are unique in our lives. They are the only relationships we enter into that have a pre-determined end-date. We know going in that we will be together for a clearly defined period, and for the last half of the year, students and teachers alike have that end date in mind as a goal. It's not a bad thing, just unusual.

As I said goodbye to some of my students, I was genuinely sad. I had grown by knowing them, and I hoped the same was true for them. I had become more competent at my craft, had honed my skills, had matured professionally. I was indebted to them and would miss them. Well, some of them.

I returned books I had borrowed to Fr. Doyle, turned in my grades to Mrs. Patchett in the office, left my keys to the faculty office in Fr. Brodley's mailbox. I had been given an opportunity to be part of this world of education, and like so many before me, and so many more to come, I had done my job and was moving on. It had been a privilege and an honor to work at St. George's and I would miss it tremendously. Leaving Alpha would be altogether different.

Since my role at Alpha was undefined, it didn't have an end date, like the last day of exams, or the final faculty meeting, or the final anything… or the final everything. There was just a date on an American Airlines ticket to JFK, and setting that date was up to me. I could stay at Alpha until the week before classes began at Fordham, or I could leave just after the end of exams at George's. But I had been away from home for two years. While I had worked and played with the boys at Alpha, my own younger brother had grown from a smart-aleck kid into a smart-ass teen. I missed him and my sisters, and my parents, and thought we should get to know each other again before I was consumed with law school. I also needed to make money, find a place to live in New York City, and mentally prepare to become a student again, sitting in the class rather than leading it. Adjustments take time.

The day after I handed in my last grades at George's, I took a minibus to New Kingston, where the two large American hotels, the bright pink Pegasus and the white Sheraton shared a parking lot, and cast shadows over a members-only cricket club where the accents were more British than Jamaican or American. Just outside the hotels' compound was a travel agency, where I picked up a ticket dated for one week later. I walked to a local ice cream stand, ordered a rum raisin, and sat on a bench in the shade just outside the cricket club. I had enjoyed many weekend evenings with Irene and the other BC teachers at restaurants and bars in this area, and I knew this was probably my last time to New Kingston. Many of the other teachers were leaving in the next few days. We tried to schedule a final dinner together, all two dozen of us, but couldn't make it work, so our goodbyes would be random, in smaller groups, or missed altogether. Irene was the only person from the BC class of 1985 who planned to return the following year. The new crop of teachers would take over Mrs. Creighton's house, and Irene decided she would rather live on her own than have to act as den mother to all the new recruits. She and I had already made plans to get together on Long Island later in the summer.

A few nights before I left, I asked Magdalen for permission to take the office boys out to dinner. I had never taken any of the boys off the property in the evening before, but Magdalen thought it a good idea, and Ignatius didn't object. Plunkett, Wilbert, Worldhead and Michael Winters and I took a minivan to a pizza parlor in Liguanea. The place was mostly empty, and fortunately, no one was waiting to order at the counter. I foolishly turned to the boys and asked, "So, what do you like on your pizza?" forgetting that they had never been to a restaurant before, even a pizza parlor. In fact, this would be their first pizza. Most importantly, these teenage boys had never had a choice of what to eat before. For their whole lives, they had eaten what was put in front of them, and done so eagerly. They stared at the list of toppings. Michael somehow knew what he didn't like. No mushrooms. No anchovies. No vegetables. Worldhead saw only the long list of meats he could have, and his eyes grew to the size of his head.

Wilbert stated emphatically, "I want an everything pizza, sir."

Plunkett was speechless. I read down the options. "What would you like, Plunkett?"

"I don't know, sir," he said softly. "What should I get?"

"Well, what do you like?"

"I don't know, sir."

I felt terrible having put him in that position, and more awkward at not having given him the opportunity sooner in the year to practice making decisions.

That night in Liguanea I thanked the boys for all they had done for me and told them how much I would miss them. We recounted stories that had happened during the year, and we just talked. That evening, sitting in a pizza parlor, they weren't orphans at an institution. They were just teenage boys enjoying a night out with friends.

The sisters had seen people come and go. They too were used to people passing through their lives, knowing that some paths cross again, and some are meant for a solitary encounter. A quick goodbye with Ignatius was punctuated with detached hug, with Marie Therese with a warmer embrace and a final recounting of how much she appreciated when, "you swooped me up in your arms and spirited me down the stairs," using a bit of artistic license with the verbs.

Packing my bags was easy. My clothes had been hand washed all year and were too worn and faded to be of any use back home. I doled out the shirts to the office boys, and left a few pairs of slacks for sister to give to the occasional beggars who would come by the front gate. Plunkett was thrilled when I offered him my extra pair of sneakers, even though holes had started to poke through at the toe.

The few articles I was taking with me fit in my knapsack, along with a mostly empty journal. I had promised myself I would be disciplined and write each day, but when you're writing you aren't living, and there had been far too much living to do in the few months I had been privileged to call Alpha my home.

Magdalen stopped by my room as I finished packing. "Just wanted to make sure you remembered everything," she said. "Just leave all the sheets and towels in a pile on your bed. After Mrs. Laundry cleans them she will put them in storage until next month."

"What happens next month?" I asked.

"Oh, we just heard from some lawyer named Dermott Something-or-other. He is a District Attorney in New York, whatever that means. He is coming to live with us for a year or two. He is arriving in July. This room seems to have worked well for you. I think he'll like it too."

"Well, sister," I said, looking around. "I think that's everything. Are you coming to the airport?" I asked, as I slung my knapsack on my shoulder. I wanted to put off a goodbye with her as long as possible.

"No. Mr. Johnson will take you. I have some things I need to do."

She could tell I was a little hurt she didn't have the time for the trip.

"O.K. I'll be honest. I have nothing else to do. I just hate goodbyes."

She started to sniffle and pulled crumpled tissue from her housedress pocket. As she blew her nose, the tears welled around her eyes. I wasn't as dignified and wept openly as we hugged goodbye. "Come now," she said after a minute. "Mr. Johnson is waiting."

A handful of boys from Junior Home were lined up on the verandah outside the office as we walked out to the car. I shook hands with each, telling them how proud I was of each and smiling broadly to force my face from crumbling.

Plunkett was last in line, standing tall in one of my faded shirts and wearing my worn sneakers. Gradually over the year, his hesitant tone had given way to one of confidence. His hurried gait transformed into a man's stride. He was respectful of, but not afraid of, Sister Ignatius. He reached out to shake my hand, but seemed grateful when I embraced him and told him for the hundredth time that year how proud I was of him and how confident I was he would grow to be a strong and confident and good man. I turned to hug Magdalen one more time, but her embrace was short and her voice firm this time, "You have to go now. It's time," she said, pulling back and gesturing toward the car.

Mr. Johnson was waiting by the car door. It was a step down for him, having to drive Magdalen's car instead of the now burnt-out van. He stood by the open back door. He wasn't used to sharing the front of the vehicle with anyone. I slid in the back and rolled down the windows. Magdalen stood behind the boys, blowing her nose. Richard, Q, O'Brien, Waldemar and the office boys all waved as we pulled out the gate. I realized then I was just another Alpha boy being pushed out the door, being told it was time to grow up and get on with life.

Dec. 20, 1996

My very dear Jay,

I received your most welcome letter four days ago. I was so thrilled with the lovely family picture. You see, I consider myself one of your family. Naturally I just love little Magdalen. That was sweet of you to give me all those compliments. I really do not have those qualities, but I do hope that your Magda will have them.

This year I had some ordeals to face. In July, I got Mastectomy. I had cancer in my left breast. Thank God that is over and according to the doctor, they got rid of all my badness. God was really good to me. I was back to work at Boys school after three weeks. I feel all right, in fact I feel much better than before my operation. Then, on the 20th Nov. I had a cataract operation, and although it was very successful, I still cannot see well as I have no glasses yet. I thought that it was easier to write you by the computer, but I can hardly see the printing. On Monday I shall have my glasses, so do please excuse me if I make mistakes. It is a poor excuse because I always make mistakes – glasses or no glasses!!!

Do give my love to Mary. I think she is great. I can imagine how the children keep you on your toes, but in no time they will grow up and be a great help. It is just nice to have 2 boys and 2 girls. The dear Lord has blessed you!

My computer is mad – just like me. It wasted a lot of paper at the heading and it could not finish the letter, so I finish in long hand. It must be my fault somewhere – I must get more lessons! When I can see!!

God love you,

Magda.

35
THE NEXT CHAPTER

Three days after I left the island, Irene found an apartment for the next year. She arranged with Mrs. Creighton to leave her belongings in her room over the summer, and planned to pick them up in September. After turning in her final grades at Immaculate and planning for the following year, she headed to Alpha. She arrived just after dusk and headed to Junior Home. The moon rose over Long Mountain in the distance, bright enough that she could make out the difference between the blue-black of the sky, and the dark green of the hillside. The night insects chirped louder at this time of year. The occasional breeze rustled the leaves of the banana trees and the bougainvillea bushes. As she approached the steps of the verandah, Patches, the uglier of the two dogs, lifted an eye lid, but not her head. Apparently after a year of visiting the dormitory, Irene was no longer a stranger worthy of setting off Patches' alarm.

The screen door had its familiar squeak as it swung open. Magdalen was at the convent and the Senior Home boy on duty nodded a hello from his perch by the door. He tapped on his leg with the long thin dowel in his hand, his threatening gesture to keep the boys in bed and in line. Heads raised from the bunks as Irene walked the length of the dorm. Little voices whispered, "Good evening, Miss Irene."

"Good evening, boys," she said softly back. As she walked toward the Adirondack chair, she spotted a new face. "Well, hello there," she said.

"Hello, Miss," a soft voice answered, and the young boy leaned up from his cot on one elbow.

"What's your name?" she asked.

"Pennington, Miss," he said, dropping his eyes.

"He's new, Miss," the boy in the next cot offered. Pennington hung his head.

"Well, welcome to Alpha," Irene said, cupping her hand under his chin and lifting his gaze toward her. "I'm Miss Irene. Don't worry. You'll be just fine here."

Irene stopped at the bookcase and selected a collection of Grimms' Fairy Tales. She sat on the edge of the old Adirondack chair, and smoothed her skirt down over her knees until it draped to the floor. As she looked out across the vast room of cots, she saw Richard's head pop up and his hand wave excitedly. O'Brien swung one leg out over the side of his bed to get a head start whenever Irene gave the word. Q, with his bed right next to the chair, knew he would just have to roll off his bed to get the best spot. Waldemar, a few rows back, was already getting stressed knowing that he was too far back and would have to struggle for a clear seat on the floor as usual. But this wasn't usual. This was Miss Irene. This would be even more fun than Mr. Solomon. He wanted a prime location.

Irene drew a deep breath, looked over at Pennington and winked. Then, scanning the rows of cots she said, "O.K. Who would like to hear a story?"

AFTERWORD

Twenty-five years after treating the office boys to a night out for pizza, I stood next to Desmond Plunkett at a deli on West 43rd Street in Manhattan. He glanced quickly at the menu board and then confidently placed his order. Far from the uncertain boy he had been so long ago in Kingston, he had developed his tastes and become a man comfortable making decisions. We sat in Bryant Park and Desmond told me stories of his life and with his wife and two children. I learned of his work as an associate pastor at an evangelical mission church in a tough Kingston neighborhood. Now it was his turn to tell me stories of his outreach ministry to troubled teens who live on the streets on Kingston. When he and his family joined mine in Pleasantville, New York for a backyard barbecue, our paths as sons of Alpha were again on parallel courses.

I returned to Alpha on spring break each year during law school and for a few years afterward, always with a project in mind, hoping to contribute some value, but really just happy to reconnect. By the third year I returned, Marie Therese had retired and moved to a retreat home in the hills outside of Kingston.

Ignatius funeral in 2003 was held at the National Cathedral and was presided over by the Archbishop himself. She had become the public face of Alpha and was well known on the island.

Betty Check visited Alpha with Dr. Check every year until she passed away in 2010. Dr. Check continues his ministry in her honor.

Q is a proud father. He teaches computer science at a school in St. Mary's Parish, and has his own website design firm.

Richard, O'Brien, Wilbert and Worldhead left Alpha for jobs, the military, jail, or the streets, their fates as diverse as those of any other poor young men.

Morris Mathers never came back.

Irene and I stayed in touch over the years, meeting each other's spouses and watching each other's kids grow up in a string of holiday cards.

I saw Magdalen for the last time in 1990, when I brought my fiancée, Mary, to meet her. In 1996, Mary and I named our second daughter in her honor. Two years later, Magdalen was driving an old boy to the beach in Port Antonio when a truck veered out of its lane and collided with her Volvo head on. She never fully recovered from the injuries. She died in 2001.

I consider myself blessed to have crossed paths with the sisters, the boys, the Checks and all of the other people who passed through Alpha Boys School. I think of them every morning when I say the Prayer of St. Francis.

Alpha is still operated by the Sisters of Mercy and continues to provide loving support and care for Kingston's most vulnerable boys.

To learn more about the wonderful work of the Sisters of Mercy, visit www.mercysc.org.

To learn more about Alpha Boys School, visit:
www.alphaboysschool.org

TOPICS FOR DISCUSSION

1. What does it mean to be "culturally
   sensitive?" In what ways were
   the BC teachers in tune with their
   surroundings?

2. The author limited his experience in
   Jamaica to two institutions, Alpha and
   St. George's. Was this self-restriction a
   matter of necessity, of practicality, or of
   avoidance?

3. Unlike the characters in many stories, the boys and teachers in this
   book are presented in small doses. Some of the boys are introduced
   in one chapter, only to disappear in the next. In what ways does this
   reinforce the nature of the relationships at Alpha? In what ways does
   it limit your ability to understand the boys fully?

4. Do you agree with the author's assessment that those helping the boys
   could never fully appreciate their world, and that the boys could
   never fully escape their past as children raised in an institution
   rather than in a family?

5. Alpha was created by Roman Catholic nuns in a desire to live the
   ideals of their faith, and yet the institution did not push Catholicism
   on the boys. The author attempted to do the same with the book
   – stay true to a sense of mission, without making the book overtly

religious. To what extent did the author succeed?

6. Should Irene have taken some of the boys home for the Christmas holidays?

7. The author, the Checks, the staff at Alpha, and the sisters all committed parts of their life to the boys at Alpha. Do the commitments differ just in duration or in quality, or are they the same thing?

8. What are Sister Magdalen's main personality traits that you glean strictly from her letters? Is the Sister Magdalen reflected in the letters in line with the author's portrayal of her?

9. Sisters Magdalen, Marie Therese and Ignatius lived together for roughly two decades. How would you describe the community they created for themselves?

10. The book begins and ends with Morris Mathers. Why is he a central character?

11. The author searched to define an identity for himself and to ensure that identity added value. To what extent are those same goals reflected in the lives of the other characters?

12. The boys, the nuns and the American teachers all created communities. How important are those communities in helping their members to survive and to thrive? To what extent is the same true for all of us?

ABOUT THE AUTHOR

Jay Sullivan, is the Managing Partner of Exec|Comm, LLC, a communications consulting firm. In between graduating from Boston College and attending Fordham Law School, he taught English in Kingston, Jamaica. He was a featured columnist in the *New York Law Journal*, where his Art of Communication column appeared regularly. His articles and poetry, both humorous and serious, have appeared in *The Golfer, Boston College Magazine, Catholic Digest, Parents Magazine*, and other publications. He lives in Pleasantville, New York, with his wife and four children.

Apprentice House is the country's only campus-based, student-staffed book publishing company. Directed by professors and industry professionals, it is a nonprofit activity of the Communication Department at Loyola University Maryland.

Using state-of-the-art technology and an experiential learning model of education, Apprentice House publishes books in untraditional ways. This dual responsibility as publishers and educators creates an unprecedented collaborative environment among faculty and students, while teaching tomorrow's editors, designers, and marketers.

Outside of class, progress on book projects is carried forth by the AH Book Publishing Club, a co-curricular campus organization supported by Loyola University Maryland's Office of Student Activities.

Eclectic and provocative, Apprentice House titles intend to entertain as well as spark dialogue on a variety of topics. Financial contributions to sustain the press's work are welcomed. Contributions are tax deductible to the fullest extent allowed by the IRS.

To learn more about Apprentice House books or to obtain submission guidelines, please visit www.apprenticehouse.com.

Apprentice House
Communication Department
Loyola University Maryland
4501 N. Charles Street
Baltimore, MD 21210
Ph: 410-617-5265 • Fax: 410-617-2198
info@apprenticehouse.com
www.apprenticehouse.com

CPSIA information can be obtained at www.ICGtesting.com
Printed in the USA
BVOW05s0317020514

352104BV00004B/8/P